Important Amazon Review

If you feel this book has provided value, please visit www.amazon.com and write a review.

It will help others to improve their players, teams and demystify the art of youth soccer coaching. Something that will take you only a few moments will help me out today and for years to come. Thank you.

Copyright © 2015 by Christoph Friedrich.

All rights reserved worldwide. No part of this publication may be replicated, redistributed, or given away in any form without the prior written consent of the Christoph Friedrich or the terms relayed to you herein.

Christoph Friedrich,
Top Soccer Drills
Bronx, NY, 10468
U.S.

Website: http://www.top-soccer-drills.com/
Facebook: www.facebook.com/topsoccerdrills
Twitter: https://twitter.com/TopSoccerDrill
Youtube: http://www.youtube.com/topsoccerdrill
Pinterest: http://pinterest.com/topsoccerdrills

―――► Run without Ball   - - - ► Passing/Shooting   ~~~► Dribbling

1-2 Combination

Click Here To View The Drill Animation!
Age Group: (5-7yrs) (8-11yrs) (12-15yrs)
Emphasis: Passing - Finishing
Description:
- first player passes and receives the ball from at least three different wall players before he passes into the mini goal with one touch
- next player starts as soon as the previous player makes his second pass

Variation:
- starting players must pass to all wall players
- play with only two wall players on each side
- wall players must play one touch
- adjust spacing depending on the age and ability of the group

Coaching Points:
weight of pass, accuracy, vision, first touch

1-2 Passes

Click Here To View The Drill Animation!
Age Group: (5-7yrs) (8-11yrs) (12-15yrs)
Emphasis: passing - dribbling
Description:
- players dribble around grid and play 1-2 wall passes with players at corners
- next player starts as soon previous player gets to second corner
- pass must be made at red cones as shown

Variation:
- specify how players must pass/ receive (left or right foot, inside or outside foot etc.)
- adjust spacing depending on the age and ability of the group

Coaching Points: weight of pass, accuracy, first touch, communication

1v1 Attacking Zone

Click Here To View The Drill Animation!
Age Group: (8-11yrs) (12-15yrs) (16-Adult)
Emphasis: finishing - passing - attacking - defending
Description:
- each team defends and attacks a goal with goalie
- play 4v4 in the middle zone
- one defender and one attacker in each end zone
- all players must stay in their zone
- players inside the middle zone attempt to pass to their striker who plays 1v1 versus a defender from the opposing team inside the attacking zone
- switch forward/defender

Variation:
- player who makes the pass to striker can move into attacking zone to create 2v1 situation
- play always starts in middle zone
- forward has to finish on first/second touch
- play 5v5, 6v6, 7v7 in the middle zone etc.
- limit number of touches
- adjust spacing depending on the age and ability of the group

Coaching Points:
weight of pass, accuracy, disguise, quality of preparation touch, aggressive and positive mentality, vision and anticipation, placement versus power, positioning to gain an advantage

1v1 Battle

Click Here To View The Drill Animation!
Age Group: (5-7yrs) (8-11yrs) (12-15yrs) (16-Adult)
Emphasis: dribbling - passing
Description:
- coach plays in the game ball
- the first player from each team enters the grid chases after the ball and plays a 1v1 versus his opponent
- first player to pass to coach is awarded a point for his team
- next game starts if the ball goes out of bounce or a pass is completed to coach
- coach must be able to control the ball for it to count
- team with most points wins

Variation:
- set a time limit for each game (i.e. 30 seconds)
- the player with the ball must beat his opponent before he can pass to coach
- the player must play a lofted pass to coach
- adjust spacing depending on the age and ability of the group if necessary

Coaching Points:
Dribbling: deception, set up defender, change of speed & direction, protect the ball, close control, soft touch
Passing: weight of pass, accuracy, disguise
Defending: angle and speed of approach, body shape, balance, and foot positioning, control and restraint, delay and channel, deny turn

1v1 Goal Line Targets

Click Here To View The Drill Animation!
Age Group: (5-7yrs) (8-11yrs) (12-15yrs) (16-Adult)
Emphasis: dribbling - passing
Description:
- play 1v1
- the player with the ball attempts to pass the ball to a target on the opposite end line
- if the target receives a pass he switches roles with the passer and then tries to connect a pass to the target on the opposite end line
- if the defender wins the ball he tries to make a pass to player on the opposite side

Variation:
- passes can only be made past the middle line
- attacker can use player on his own end line for support
- adjust size of field if necessary

Coaching Points:
angle of support, decision making, verbal and visual communication, change of direction and speed, deception - set up defender - protect the ball - vision - close control - weight of pass - accuracy

1v1 Goal Target Player # 1

Click Here To View The Drill Animation!
Age Group: (5-7yrs) (8-11yrs) (12-15yrs) (16-Adult)
Emphasis: dribbling - passing
Description:
- players try to dribble around the opponent and score by passing it through the cone goal to the target player
- players cannot pass to target player from inside the end zone
- direction of play changes if a goal is scored, ball goes out of bounds or the defender wins the ball
- players cannot score on same target twice in a row
- switch roles after 2-3 minutes

Variation:
- play 2v2, 3v3 etc.
- players lose possession automatically if they stand still or dribble backwards
- receiving player switches role with pass giver
- adjust spacing depending on the age and ability of the group

Coaching Points:
deception - set up defender - protect the ball - vision - close control - agility and balance - change of direction and speed = weight of pass - accuracy - disguise

1v1 Goal Target Player # 2

Click Here To View The Drill Animation!
Age Group: (5-7yrs) (8-11yrs) (12-15yrs) (16-Adult)
Emphasis: dribbling - passing
Description:
- players try to dribble around the opponent and score by passing it through the cone goal to the target player
- direction of play changes if a goal is scored, ball goes out of bounds or the defender wins the ball
- players cannot score on same target twice in a row
- switch roles after 2-3 minutes

Variation:
- play 2v2, 3v3 etc.
- players lose possession automatically if they stand still or dribble backwards
- receiving player switches role with pass giver
- adjust spacing depending on the age and ability of the group

Coaching Points:
deception - set up defender - protect the ball - vision - close control - agility and balance - change of direction and speed - weight of pass - accuracy - disguise

1v1 Receiving Square

Click Here To View The Drill Animation!
Age Group: (5-7yrs) (8-11yrs) (12-15yrs) (16-Adult)
Emphasis: dribbling - passing
Description:
- players inside squares move towards ball, receive it and dribble to next corner
- 2-3 defenders try to win possession once the attacker leaves the square (defender cannot intercept the pass)
- play is over once a player (attacker or defender) dribbles out of the grid and high fives the next player in line at the next corner
- defenders switch roles with the attacker that they took the ball from
- player at the corner follows his pass into square

Variation:
- vary number of defenders
- play with passive defenders
- adjust spacing depending on the age and ability of the group if necessary

Coaching Points: close control - change of speed & direction - communication - protect your ball - deception - set up defender - weight of pass - accuracy - good first touch

2v2 Each Half # 2

Click Here To View The Drill Animation!
Age Group: (5-7yrs) (8-11yrs) (12-15yrs) (16-Adult)
Emphasis: finishing - passing
Description:
- play 2v2 in each half
- players must stay in their half

Variations:
- vary numbers in each half
- the player who makes a pass into the attacking half may follow it to support the other attackers
- one attacking player is allowed into the defending half to advance the ball into the attacking half
- limit number of touches
- adjust spacing depending on the age and ability of the group

Coaching Points:
Attacking: quality of preparation touch - aggressive and positive mentality - vision and anticipation - placement versus power - quick transition - quick finish
Defending: control and restraint - delay and channel - angle and distance of cover - intercept pass - changing role of pressure and cover - visual and verbal communication

2v2 Finishing Activity

Click Here To View The Drill Animation!
Age Group: (8-11yrs) (12-15yrs) (16-Adult)
Emphasis: finishing - passing
Description:
- attackers vs. defenders
- play 2v2 inside the grid
- players from both teams around the grid as shown
- on coach's command a wall player from the attacking team plays the ball in to his teammates who attempt to score a goal
- switch roles only if the defending team clears the ball outside the grid
- if the shot is on target or a goal is scored the attacking team continues to attack

Variation:
- play 3v3 inside the grid
- players on the outside must make a lofted pass to their teammates
- allow the attacking players to combine with their teammates on the outside
- allow the passer to enter grid to create a 3v2 situation
- allow the attacking player on the outside to enter the grid by dribbling to make it a 3v2 situation
- limit number of touches
- adjust spacing depending on the age and ability of the group

Coaching Points:
Attacking: accurate passes - quick finish - aggressive and positive mentality - placement versus power - supporting angle and distance to ball - unbalancing the defense - create space for others - attack space behind defense
Defending: angle and speed of approach - delay and channel - intercept pass - deny turn - deny penetration - changing role of pressure and cover - visual and verbal communication

3 Zone Passing

Click Here To View The Drill Animation!
Age Group: (5-7yrs) (8-11yrs) (12-15yrs) (16-Adult)
Emphasis: passing
Description:
- each pair has a player start in opposite zones
- one pair starts in the middle zone
- players must stay in their designated zones
- partners try to pass to each other through the middle zone
- if a player in the middle zone intercepts a pass they switch roles with the pair that made the pass
- players in the outer zones must try to keep the ball in bounce

Variation:
- vary number players/pairs in middle zone
- limit number of touches for players in the outer zones
- specify how players must pass (left or right foot, inside or outside foot etc.)
- adjust spacing depending on the age and ability of the group
-

Coaching Points: angle, distance and timing of support - vision - decision making - verbal and visual communication - accuracy - weight of pass - first touch

3v1 Plus 4

Click Here To View The Drill Animation!
Age Group: (5-7yrs) (8-11yrs) (12-15yrs) (16-Adult)
Emphasis: passing - possession
Description:
- 3 attackers versus 1 defender play inside the grid
- 4 target players are positioned around the grid
- one outside player starts the game by passing to one of the attacking players
- attacking players try to connect three passes before they attempt to score by passing and receiving a pass from a different outside player from which the first pass came
- outside players must play one-touch
- switch roles after 3-4 minutes or if defender intercepts the ball 5 times

Variation:
- limit number of touches for attacking team
- play 3v2, 4v2 etc.
- adjust spacing depending on the age and ability of the group

Coaching Points: first touch away from pressure - create supporting angles - vision - body position – open to field - decision making - verbal and visual communication

3v2 Each Half

Click Here To View The Drill Animation!
Age Group: (8-11yrs) (12-15yrs) (16-Adult)
Emphasis: finishing, passing
Description:
- play 3v2 in each half
- players must stay in their designated half
- defending players can only defend with two men
- third defender drops back next to his goal until possession is won back or the attacking team scores

Variations:
- vary numbers in each half
- the player who makes a pass into the attacking half may follow it to support the other attackers
- one attacking player is allowed into the defending half to advance the ball into the attacking half
- limit number of touches
- adjust size of field if necessary

Coaching Points: quality of preparation touch - aggressive and positive mentality - vision and anticipation - placement versus power - quick transition - quick finish - close down the shooter quickly - pressure the ball first and cut down the shooters angle

3v2 Plus Target Players

Click Here To View The Drill Animation!
Age Group: (8-11yrs) (12-15yrs) (16-Adult)
Emphasis: finishing - passing
Description:
- play 3v2 in the middle
- 4 target players around the grid as shown
- target players start the game by passing a ball in to one of the attacking (red) players
- attacking team scores by passing to a target player through a different cone goal from which the first pass came
- defending team tries to keep possession for as long as possible
- play then restarts from the goal into which a goal was scored
- players switch roles after 5-10 minutes

Variation:
- play 3v1, 4v2, 2v2, 3v3 etc.
- defending team switches roles with the attackers if they keep the ball for 7 seconds
- limit number of touches for attackers
- goal must be scored with the first touch
- adjust spacing depending on the age and ability of the group

Coaching Points:
quality of preparation touch - contact surface - aggressive and positive mentality - vision and anticipation - placement versus power - positioning to gain an advantage - angle, distance and timing of support - vision - body position – open to field - decision making - verbal and visual communication

3v3 Plus 2

Click Here To View The Drill Animation!
Age Group: (5-7yrs) (8-11yrs) (12-15yrs) (16-Adult)
Emphasis: dribbling - passing - attacking - defending
Description:
- teams have to pass to one of the target players before dribbling through one of the two cone goals
- wall players can move from side to side along end line to receive the ball

Variation:
- both wall players have to touch the ball before a team can score
- minimum of 2-3 touches for field players
- maximum of 2-3 touches for wall players
- adjust spacing depending on the age and ability of the group if necessary

Coaching Points:
angle, distance and timing of support - vision - decision making - verbal and visual communication - set up defender - change of speed & direction - protect the ball

3v3 Breakaway

Click Here To View The Drill Animation!
Age Group: (8-11yrs) (12-15yrs) (16-Adult)
Emphasis: dribbling - finishing - attacking - defending
Description:
- teams play 3v3 in designated area
- defending team scores by passing it to a teammate inside end zone (receiving player has to time his run into zone - he cannot wait for the ball inside the zone)
- attacking player who dribbles across defender's end line into the box can only be followed by one defender (or after attacker's first touch inside box)
- if the ball goes out of bounce it is dribbled back in
- switch roles after 5-10 minutes

Variation:
- play 4v3, 5v4 etc.
- attacking player inside the box is free for a 1v1 with the goalie (no additional defender allowed inside the box)
- limit number of touches for attacker inside the box
- adjust size of field if necessary

Coaching Points:
Attacking: set up defender - change of speed & direction - protect the ball - vision - close control - supporting angle and distance to ball - create space for others - quality of preparation touch - aggressive and positive mentality - vision and anticipation - placement versus power - quick finish
Defending: angle and distance of cover - change role of pressure and cover - visual and verbal communication - control and restraint - delay and channel

3v3 Plus 3 Possession

Click Here To View The Drill Animation!
Age Group: (5-7yrs) (8-11yrs) (12-15yrs) (16-Adult)
Emphasis: passing - possession
Description:
- 3v3 plus 3
- 2 teams (6v3) are responsible for keeping possession
- all players of the defending team must pick-up and hold a cone before they can start to defend
- if defending team (blue) wins the ball they drop the cones and the new defending team (the team that lost possession) picks up the cones and starts defending
- if a ball goes out of bounce the team that lost possession now becomes the defending team

Variation:
- play 4v2 etc.
- limit number of touches for teams in possession
- adjust spacing depending on the age and ability of the group

Coaching Points: quick transitions - angle, distance and timing of support - vision - body position — open to field - decision making - verbal and visual communication

3v3 Plus Target Player

Click Here To View The Drill Animation!
Age Group: (5-7yrs) (8-11yrs) (12-15yrs) (16-Adult)
Emphasis: finishing - passing - attacking - defending
Description:
- play 3v3 with a ball feeder at the opposite side of the goal
- one team is attacking the goal while the other team is defending it
- if the ball goes out of bounce or a goal is scored the ball feeder always plays the ball back in to the attacking team
- teams switch roles if the defending wins the ball and completes a pass to the ball feeder

Variation:
- on coach's command the feeder can enter the grid and help the attacking team for 10-20 seconds
- vary how the ball is played in (high/low throw, high/low pass)
- limit number of touches (only for attackers)
- adjust spacing depending on the age and ability of the group

Coaching Points:
Attacking: unbalance the defense - create space for others - attack space behind defense - positioning to provide cover and balance
Defending: intercept pass - defend vital space (squeeze toward center) - defend space behind

3v3 Plus Wall Players

Click Here To View The Drill Animation!

Age Group: (8-11yrs) (12-15yrs) (16-Adult)
Emphasis: passing - finishing - attacking - defending
Description:
- each team has target players positioned around grid as shown
- teams have to pass to a target player before they can score

Variation:
- target player is allowed to enter the grid for 10 seconds after connecting a pass to a teammate
- target players are limited to two touches
- target players on goal line are limited to one touch
- adjust spacing depending on the age and ability of the group

Coaching Points:
accurate passes - quick decision making - quick finish - good angle of support - communication - vision

3v3 Plus Wall Players In Attacking Half

Click Here To View The Drill Animation!

Age Group: (8-11yrs) (12-15yrs) (16-Adult)
Emphasis: passing - finishing - attacking - defending
Description:
- each team has target players positioned around grid as shown
- teams have to pass to a target player before they can score

Variation:
- target player is allowed to enter the grid for 10 seconds after connecting a pass to a teammate
- target players are limited to two touches
- target players on goal line are limited to one touch
- adjust spacing depending on the age and ability of the group

Coaching Points:
accurate passes - quick decision making - quick finish - good angle of support - communication - vision

3v3 Through Pass

Click Here To View The Drill Animation!

Age Group: (8-11yrs) (12-15yrs) (16-Adult)
Emphasis: passing - attacking - defending
Description:
- play 3v3 plus 2
- teams score by connecting at least two passes before making a pass outside the small grid which is received by a teammate or neutral player
- pass must be controlled before the ball leaves the large grid
- players cannot wait in target area to receive the pass

Variation:
- one player from the defending team can follow to prevent the pass from being controlled
- the receiver cannot make the run through the same gate as the pass
- limit number of touches
- adjust spacing depending on the age and ability of the group

Coaching Points:
angle, distance and timing of support - vision - body position — open to field - decision making - verbal and visual communication - shape of team to maintain possession - switch point of attack - create space for others - support position lateral to ball

3v3 w Cone Goals

Click Here To View The Drill Animation!
Age Group: (5-7yrs) (8-11yrs) (12-15yrs)
Emphasis: dribbling - attacking - defending
Description:
- teams score by dribbling through cone goals
- team cannot score on same cone goal twice in a row

Variation:
- play 4v4, 5v5 etc.
- teams score by stopping the ball between any cone goal
- if a team manages to dribble through all the cone goals it is awarded an extra point
- vary number and size of cone goals
- adjust spacing depending on the age and ability of the group if necessary

Coaching Points:
Attacking: deception - set up defender - change of speed & direction - protect the ball - close control - angle, distance and timing of support - vision - body position – open to field - decision making - verbal and visual communication
Defending: angle and speed of approach - body shape, balance, and foot positioning - control and restraint - delay and channel - timing and decision to tackle - angle and distance of cover - intercept pass - changing role of pressure and cover - visual and verbal communication

3v3 w Moving Targets

Click Here To View The Drill Animation!
Age Group: (5-7yrs) (8-11yrs) (12-15yrs)
Emphasis: dribbling - attacking - defending
Description:
- teams score by laying off the ball to one of the target players (players must dribble the ball directly to target player's feet)
- target players can move from side to side along end line to receive the ball
- target player then switches with field player

Variation:
- minimum of 2-3 touches
- one target player on each of the four sidelines (each team has two designated targets)
- adjust spacing depending on the age and ability of the group if necessary

Coaching Points:
angle, distance and timing of support - body position – open to field - decision making - verbal and visual communication - agility and balance - contact surface of foot - change of direction and speed - deception - set up defender - protect the ball - vision - close control

3v3 Sweeper

Click Here To View The Drill Animation!
Age Group: (5-7yrs) (8-11yrs) (12-15yrs) (16-Adult)
Emphasis: dribbling - passing - finishing - attacking - defending
Description:
- each team defends and attacks 2 cone goals
- sweeper acts as a defender/goalie who cannot leave the end zone

Variation:
- allow sweeper to use his hands
- limit number of touches for field players and/or sweepers
- adjust spacing depending on the age and ability of the group

Coaching Points:
switch point of attack - awareness of goalkeeper's position - quick finish - attack open space - spread out attack - set up defender - protect the ball - vision

3v3 w Target Goals

Click Here To View The Drill Animation!
Age Group: (8-11yrs) (12-15yrs) (16-Adult)
Emphasis: passing - attacking - defending
Description:
- teams score by passing from outside the end zone to team's target player through either cone goal as shown
- target player switches with passer

Variation:
- limit number of touches
- play without end zones
- both target players are neutral
- add a third cone goal on each side
- adjust size of field if necessary

Coaching Points:
communication - constant movement - accuracy over power - timing of passes - good first touch

3v3 w Target Players

Click Here To View The Drill Animation!
Age Group: (5-7yrs) (8-11yrs) (12-15yrs) (16-Adult)
Emphasis: dribbling - passing - finishing - attacking - defending
Description:
- play 3v3
- teams score by passing to the team's designated target player who receives the ball inside the target area
- target player cannot leave his area
- target player switches with pass giver

Variation:
- if the target player's team is not in possession he is allowed to support the opposing team from inside the target area
- limit number of touches
- adjust spacing depending on the age and ability of the group

Coaching Points:
create space for others - spread out attack - supporting angle and distance to ball - combination play (1-2, double pass, overlap, take over) - weight of pass - accuracy - vision - first touch

4 Color Game

Click Here To View The Drill Animation!
Age Group: (5-7yrs) (8-11yrs) (12-15yrs) (16-Adult)
Emphasis: passing
Description:
- play with two or three balls to start
- 4 different groups of colors
- each group must pass to another color and receive from a third color

Variation:
- vary number of balls
- play with three groups
- limit number of touches
- specify how players must pass/receive (left or right foot, inside or outside foot, high or low etc.)
- adjust spacing depending on the age and ability of the group

Coaching Points:
angle, distance and timing of support - verbal and visual communication - weight of pass - accuracy - vision - first touch

4 Goal Game

Click Here To View The Drill Animation!
Age Group: (5-7yrs) (8-11yrs) (12-15yrs) (16-Adult)
Emphasis: finishing - passing
Description:
- teams must connect 4 (5) passes before they can score on any of the four goals

Variation:
- each team defends and attacks 2 goals
- add a neutral player
- a goal must come off a first touch shot
- limit number of touches
- adjust spacing depending on the age and ability of the group

Coaching Points:
angle, distance and timing of support - decision making - verbal and visual communication - quality of preparation touch - aggressive and positive mentality - vision and anticipation - placement versus power

4 Plus 1

Click Here To View The Drill Animation!
Age Group: (5-7yrs) (8-11yrs) (12-15yrs) (16-Adult)
Emphasis: passing - defending
Description:
- supporting players (gray) on the outside attempt to combine with a target player (red) in the middle
- defending player (white & blue) in the middle tries to intercept the ball
- switch target player in the middle if he completes 6 passes to players on the outside
- switch defender if he intercepts 3 passes

Variation:
- vary number of supporting players
- one touch passing for supporting players
- limit number of touches for player in the middle
- limit number of touches for supporting players
- adjust spacing depending on the age and ability of the group

Coaching Points: constant movement - angle, distance and timing of support - vision - decision making - verbal and visual communication - weight of pass - accuracy - first touch

4 Team Game

Click Here To View The Drill Animation!
Age Group: (5-7yrs) (8-11yrs) (12-15yrs) (16-Adult)
Emphasis: finishing - dribbling - attacking - defending
Description:
- two games of 3v3
- one game plays with goal number 1 + 2 and the other game with goal number 3 + 4

Variation:
- play 1v1, 2v2 etc.
- tournament style
- add neutral players
- adjust spacing depending on the age and ability of the group

Coaching Points:
angle, distance and timing of support - decision making - verbal and visual communication - aggressive and positive mentality - vision and anticipation

4v1 Keep Away

Click Here To View The Drill Animation!
Age Group: (5-7yrs) (8-11yrs) (12-15yrs) (16-Adult)
Emphasis: passing - possession - defending
Description:
- players on the outside of grid try to keep possession by passing the ball around
- defending player switches with the attacking player who makes an error
- players can move up and down their lines but cannot come inside the grid
- first pass is free

Variation:
- outside players cannot pass back to pass giver
- add a second defender
- regular 4v1 keep away with all players inside the grid
- switch defender if he intercepts 3 passes
- limit number of touches for players on the outside
- adjust spacing depending on the age and ability of the group

Coaching Points:
angle, distance and timing of support - vision - body position - open to field - decision making - verbal and visual communication - good first touch takes ball away from pressure - weight of pass - accuracy - disguise

4v1 Passing Game w Target

Click Here To View The Drill Animation!
Age Group: (5-7yrs) (8-11yrs) (12-15yrs) (16-Adult)
Emphasis: passing - finishing - possession
Description:
- outside players pass the ball around from outside the grid trying to find an opening to knock the ball off the cone in the center box
- the defender moves around the center box to block all shots
- the defender cannot leave the grid to pressure the ball

Variation:
- add a second defender
- add another target (ball placed on cone)
- add a second ball for the attackers to pass around
- limit number of touches
- adjust spacing depending on the age and ability of the group

Coaching Points:
weight of pass - accuracy - disguise - quality of preparation touch - contact surface - aggressive and positive mentality - vision and anticipation

4v2

Click Here To View The Drill Animation!
Age Group: (5-7yrs) (8-11yrs) (12-15yrs)
Emphasis: dribbling - attacking - defending - possession
Description:
- 4 attackers versus 2 defenders
- attackers start with the ball at their end line and attempt to dribble across the defender's end line
- if a defender wins the ball he switches roles with the attacker who touched the ball last

Variation:
- play 3v1 in multiple grids
- no forward passes allowed
- players must take a maximum of 3 touches
- attackers must stop the ball dead on defender's end line
- attackers and defenders switch roles every 2-3 minutes
- adjust spacing depending on the age and ability of the group if necessary

Coaching Points:
Attacking: decision making - change of direction and speed - deception - setting up defender - protecting the ball - vision
Defending: delay and channel - timing and decision to tackle - angle and distance of cover - intercept pass - changing role of pressure and cover - visual and verbal communication

4v2 Each Half

Click Here To View The Drill Animation!
Age Group: (8-11yrs) (12-15yrs) (16-Adult)
Emphasis: possession - passing - finishing - attacking - defending
Description:
- 4 attackers vs. 2 defenders in each half
- each team defends and attacks a goal
- players must stay in their designated zone

Variation:
- two (three) attackers drop back next to the opponent's goal until possession is won back or the opposing team scores
- limit number of touches for attackers
- attackers must connect three passes before they can score
- adjust spacing depending on the age and ability of the group

Coaching Points:
accurate passes - quick decision making - protect the ball - good angle of support - movement on and off the ball - aggressive and positive mentality - vision and anticipation - placement versus power - positioning to gain an advantage

4v2 Forward Pass

Click Here To View The Drill Animation!
Age Group: (5-7yrs) (8-11yrs) (12-15yrs) (16-Adult)
Emphasis: finishing - passing - possession
Description:
- play 4v2 in bottom half
- the attackers must connect 6 passes before they can pass to the forward in the end zone
- the forward has two touches before he can finish on goal
- one defender can enter the end zone once the pass was made to prevent the forward from scoring
- if a defender wins the ball he may finish on goal

Variation:
- play 4v2, 5v2 with a defender already marking the forward
- the player who passes to the forward can enter the end zone to create a 2v1 situation
- limit number of touches
- adjust spacing depending on the age and ability of the group

Coaching Points:
angle, distance and timing of support - vision - body position – open to field - decision making - verbal and visual communication - quality of preparation touch - aggressive and positive mentality - vision and anticipation - placement versus power - positioning to gain an advantage

4v2 Keep Away

Click Here To View The Drill Animation!
Age Group: (5-7yrs) (8-11yrs) (12-15yrs) (16-Adult)
Emphasis: passing - possession
Description:
- play 4v2 keep away with one defender in each half
- 4 outside attacking players move around the grid
- attacking players must play pass across at least one half of the grid
- defenders must stay in their designated half
- defending player switches with the attacking player who makes an error

Variation:
- outside players earn an extra life by passing in between the two defenders
- limit number of touches
- adjust spacing depending on the age and ability of the group

Coaching Points:
angle, distance and timing of support - vision - body position – open to field - decision making - verbal and visual communication - good first touch takes ball away from pressure

4v2 Keep Away # 2

Click Here To View The Drill Animation!
Age Group: (8-11yrs) (12-15yrs) (16-Adult)
Emphasis: passing - possession
Description:
- play 6v4 keep away with one defender in each grid
- 4 outside attacking players move around the grid
- defenders must stay in their designated grid
- attacking team scores by combining with the two players in the middle

Variation:
- attacking team scores by passing to the player in the middle who passes the ball to a third player
- defending player switches with the attacking player who makes an error
- limit number of touches for outside players
- adjust spacing depending on the age and ability of the group

Coaching Points:
angle, distance and timing of support - vision - body position – open to field - decision making - verbal and visual communication - good first touch takes ball away from pressure - weight of pass - accuracy - disguise - first touch

4v2 Keep Away # 3

Click Here To View The Drill Animation!

Age Group: (5-7yrs) (8-11yrs) (12-15yrs) (16-Adult)
Emphasis: passing - possession
Description:
- play 4v2 keep away with one defender (blue) in each half
- attackers can go anywhere in the grid
- defenders must stay in their designated half
- defenders switch roles with the attackers if they intercept 6 passes

Variation:
- attackers must connect a minimum of 3 passes in each half
- defender switches with the attacker who makes an error
- limit number of touches
- adjust spacing depending on the age and ability of the group

Coaching Points:
angle, distance and timing of support - vision - body position – open to field - decision making - verbal and visual communication - good first touch takes ball away from pressure

4v2 Keep Away # 4

Click Here To View The Drill Animation!
Age Group: (5-7yrs) (8-11yrs) (12-15yrs) (16-Adult)
Emphasis: passing - possession
Description:
- play 4v2 keep away with one defender in each half
- defenders must stay in their designated half
- attackers can go anywhere in the grid
- defender switches with the attacker who makes an error

Variation:
- attackers must connect a minimum of 3 passes in each half
- defenders switch roles with if they intercept 6 passes
- limit number of touches
- adjust spacing depending on the age and ability of the group

Coaching Points:
angle, distance and timing of support - vision - body position - open to field - decision making - verbal and visual communication - good first touch takes ball away from pressure

4v2 Keep Away w Outer Grids

Click Here To View The Drill Animation!
Age Group: (5-7yrs) (8-11yrs) (12-15yrs) (16-Adult)
Emphasis: possession - passing
Description:
- play keep away
- attackers cannot leave their designated area
- only one defender is allowed in the outer grid at one time
- if a player in the outer grid loses the ball or makes a mistake he then switches role with a defender
- first pass is free

Variation:
- play with only one defender to start
- allow both defenders to enter an outer grid
- limit number of touches
- adjust spacing depending on the age and ability of the group

Coaching Points:
angle, distance and timing of support - vision - body position – open to field - decision making - verbal and visual communication - weight of pass - accuracy - disguise - first touch

4v2 w Mini Goal

Click Here To View The Drill Animation!
Age Group: (5-7yrs) (8-11yrs) (12-15yrs) (16-Adult)
Emphasis: possession - passing - attacking - defending
Description:
- attackers can score on both mini goals
- if defenders win the ball they give it right back to the attackers
- attackers cannot score on the same goal twice in a row
- defenders switch roles with attackers if they intercept 10 passes

Variation:
- defenders switch roles with attackers if they dribble the ball out of the grid 3-4 times
- vary number of attackers and/or defenders
- adjust spacing depending on the age and ability of the group

Coaching Points:
angle, distance and timing of support - vision - body position - open to field - decision making - verbal and visual communication - weight of pass - accuracy - disguise - first touch

4v2 w End Zone

Click Here To View The Drill Animation!
Age Group: (5-7yrs) (8-11yrs) (12-15yrs) (16-Adult)
Emphasis: dribbling - passing - attacking - defending
Description:
- play 4v4
- each team defends an end zone
- teams score by dribbling into end zone or if a player receives a pass inside the end zone
- if a team loses possession two players from that team must immediately drop back into to their designated end zone (4v2)

Variation:
- play 3v3, 5v5 etc.
- if a team loses possession one player from that team must immediately drop back into to his designated end zone (4v3)
- limit number of touches
- adjust spacing depending on the age and ability of the group

Coaching Points:
create space for others - spread out attack - angle, distance and timing of support - vision - decision making - verbal and visual communication - combination play (1-2, double pass, overlap, take over). - set up defender - protect the ball - first touch

4v3 Keep Away

Click Here To View The Drill Animation!
Age Group: (5-7yrs) (8-11yrs) (12-15yrs) (16-Adult)
Emphasis: passing - possession
Description:
- play 4v3 keep away with one defender in each half
- 4 outside attacking players move around the grid
- attacking players must play pass across at least one half of the grid
- one defender must stay in each half, the third defender is allowed to enter both halves
- defending player switches with the attacking player who makes an error

Variation:
- attacking players score by passing in between two defenders
- limit number of touches
- adjust spacing depending on the age and ability of the group

Coaching Points:
angle, distance and timing of support - vision - body position – open to field - decision making - verbal and visual communication - good first touch takes ball away from pressure - weight of pass - accuracy - disguise

4v3 w 5 Cone Goals

Click Here To View The Drill Animation!
Age Group: (5-7yrs) (8-11yrs) (12-15yrs) (16-Adult)
Emphasis: dribbling - attacking - defending
Description:
- 4 attackers versus 3 defenders
- 4 attackers defend three cone goals and 3 defenders two cone goals
- switch roles every 5 minutes

Variation:
- play 3v2, 6v5 etc.
- teams score by dribbling through cone goals
- minimum of 3 touches for attackers

Coaching Points:
Attacking: support teammates from good angle - quick transitions - switch point of attack - set up defender - change of speed & direction - protect the ball - vision - close control - create space for others - attack space behind defense
Defending: position to provide cover and balance - intercept pass - squeeze toward center - defending space behind - track players

4v3 w Designated Attacker

Click Here To View The Drill Animation!
Age Group: (5-7yrs) (8-11yrs) (12-15yrs) (16-Adult)
Emphasis: dribbling - passing - attacking - defending
Description:
- each team defends and attacks 2 cone goals
- each team has one designated player who must stay in the attacking half
- designated player has to pass to at least one other teammate before he or another teammate can score

Variation:
- vary number and positions of cone goals
- play with mini goals instead of cone goals
- teams can only score by dribbling through cone goal
- designated player has to take at least 2-3 touches before he can score
- if a defender wins the ball he must dribble across the halfway line before he attempts to pass to the designated player
- adjust spacing depending on the age and ability of the group if necessary

Coaching Points:
Attacking: weight of pass - accuracy - first touch - angle, distance and timing of support - vision - decision making - verbal and visual communication - quick transitions - switch point of attack - set up defender - change of speed & direction - protect the ball - close control
Defending: angle and speed of approach - control and restraint - delay and channel - angle and distance of cover - intercept pass - change role of pressure and cover - visual and verbal communication

4v4 Cone Knock Down

Click Here To View The Drill Animation!
Age Group: (5-7yrs) (8-11yrs) (12-15yrs) (16-Adult)
Emphasis: passing - finishing - attacking - defending
Description:
- team in possession passes the ball to knock over the opposing team's cones from outside the end zone
- each time a team scores the cone is put back up again

Variation:
- once a cone has been knocked over it stays down
- once a cone has been knocked over it is added to the scoring teams side (6 cones on one side versus 4 cones on the other)
- limit number of touches
- add a neutral player
- play 5v5, 6v6 etc.
- adjust size of field if necessary

Coaching Points:
switch point of attack - quick finish - quality of preparation touch - aggressive and positive mentality - vision and anticipation - placement versus power

4v4 End Zone

Click Here To View The Drill Animation!
Age Group: (8-11yrs) (12-15yrs) (16-Adult)
Emphasis: passing - possession - attacking - defending
Description:
- teams score if a player receives a pass inside the end zone
- the player must make a run into the end zone to receive the pass (he cannot wait inside the end zone)

Variation:
- teams must connect two (three) passes before they can make a pass into the end zone
- limit number of touches
- add a neutral player
- play 5v5, 6v6 etc.
- adjust spacing depending on the age and ability of the group

Coaching Points:
weight of pass - accuracy - timing of passes - good first touch into space - angle, distance and timing of support - vision - body position — open to field - decision making - verbal and visual communication - constant movement

4v4 Finishing

Click Here To View The Drill Animation!
Age Group: (5-7yrs) (8-11yrs) (12-15yrs) (16-Adult)
Emphasis: passing - finishing - attacking - defending
Description:
- play 4v4
- balls placed on cones are positioned 5-6yrds in from the end lines
- teams score by knocking the ball off the cone with the game ball
- if ball goes out of bounds the ball is kicked back in (kick-ins)

Variation:
- vary number of targets
- one target in each corner
- tall cones as targets instead of balls
- limit number of touches
- adjust spacing depending on the age and ability of the group

Coaching Points:
communication - create supporting angles - quick transitions - quick finish - switch point of attack - quality of preparation touch - aggressive and positive mentality - vision and anticipation - placement versus power

4v4 Finishing # 2

Click Here To View The Drill Animation!
Age Group: (5-7yrs) (8-11yrs) (12-15yrs) (16-Adult)
Emphasis: passing - finishing - attacking - defending
Description:
- play 4v4
- tall cones are positioned 5-6yrds in from the end lines
- teams score by knocking down a cone with the game ball
- teams can attack all targets
- if ball goes out of bounds the ball is kicked back in (kick-ins)

Variation:
- vary number and position of targets
- limit number of touches
- adjust spacing depending on the age and ability of the group

Coaching Points:
communication - create supporting angles - quick transitions - quick finishing - eye on ball - quality of preparation touch - aggressive and positive mentality - placement versus power - positioning to gain an advantage

4v4 Passing Game

Click Here To View The Drill Animation!
Age Group: (5-7yrs) (8-11yrs) (12-15yrs) (16-Adult)
Emphasis: attacking - defending - passing - possession
Description:
- play 4v4
- each team defends and attacks a goal with goalie
- if a team has possession two (three) different players of that team must touch the ball before they can score
- kick-ins only

Variation:
- limit number of touches
- teams gets as many points as passes were completed before a goal
- adjust spacing depending on the age and ability of the group

Coaching Points:
angle, distance and timing of support - vision - body position – open to field - decision making - verbal and visual communication - first touch - communication - quick decision making - accuracy - speed of play

4v4 Plus 2

Click Here To View The Drill Animation!
Age Group: (5-7yrs) (8-11yrs) (12-15yrs) (16-Adult)
Emphasis: possession - passing
Description:
- play 4v4 plus 2 neutrals
- teams score by making 5 or 10 consecutive passes

Variation:
- players must run and toe tap an outside cone after completing a pass
- maximum of two touches
- minimum of two touches
- adjust spacing depending on the age and ability of the group

Coaching Points:
angle, distance and timing of support - vision - body position – open to field - decision making - verbal and visual communication - constant movement

4v4 Plus 2 Into 6v4

Click Here To View The Drill Animation!
Age Group: (8-11yrs) (12-15yrs) (16-Adult)
Emphasis: possession - passing
Description:
- play 4v4
- attacking team attempts to pass to one of the two neutral players who run around the grid freely
- once a neutral player receives the ball both neutral players come on the field (now a 6v4) trying to make 6 passes in a row with the team in possession
- if the ball is lost during the 6v4 both neutral players return to the outside of the grid

Variation:
- teams score by keeping the ball for 15, 30 or 60 seconds
- vary number of consecutive passes
- add a third (fourth) neutral player
- adjust spacing depending on the age and ability of the group

Coaching Points:
communication - create supporting angles - play the way you face and away from pressure - keep the ball moving with quick accurate passing - constant movement

4v4 Plus 2 Target Players

Click Here To View The Drill Animation!
Age Group: (8-11yrs) (12-15yrs) (16-Adult)
Emphasis: defending - attacking - passing - possession
Description:
- each team has two target players positioned outside the grid by the middle line as shown
- if a team wins possession the two target players can enter the grid to create a numbers up situation on the attack
- once the ball is lost both players must leave the grid again and the target players of the other team can enter the grid
- offside rules apply

Variation:
- play without offside
- target players start from opponent's goal line
- teams must connect 4 (5) passes before they can score
- adjust spacing depending on the age and ability of the group

Coaching Points:
accurate passes - quick decision making - quick finish - good angle of support - movement on and off the ball - quick transitions - find the open space

4v4 Plus 2 Targets

Click Here To View The Drill Animation!
Age Group: (8-11yrs) (12-15yrs) (16-Adult)
Emphasis: possession - passing
Description:
- 2 teams play 4v4 inside the playing area
- each team has one target player on opposite sides as shown
- teams score by passing to one target player and then to the other one without losing possession

Variation:
- target players must play one (two) touch
- limit number of touches
- teams score by making 5 consecutive passes
- adjust spacing depending on the age and ability of the group

Coaching Points:
first touch away from pressure - angle, distance and timing of support - vision - body position – open to field - decision making - verbal and visual communication

4v4 plus 2+2

Click Here To View The Drill Animation!
Age Group: (5-7yrs) (8-11yrs) (12-15yrs) (16-Adult)
Emphasis: possession - passing
Description:
- play 4v4
- each team has 2 target players on adjacent end lines
- teams score by passing to one of their two target players who passes it back to a third player on the field

Variation:
- limit number of touches for field players
- passer switches with target player after pass
- target players must play one touch
- teams score by making 5 consecutive passes
- adjust spacing depending on the age and ability of the group

Coaching Points:
angle, distance and timing of support - vision - body position – open to field - decision making - verbal and visual communication - first touch - constant movement

4v4 plus 4

Click Here To View The Drill Animation!
Age Group: (8-11yrs) (12-15yrs) (16-Adult)
Emphasis: passing - possession
Description:
- 2 teams play 4v4 inside the playing area
- another team is positioned around the grid
- teams score a point by passing to a target player who passes it back to a third player

Variation:
- target players must play one or two touch
- teams score by making 7 consecutive passes
- players on the outside are allowed to pass to each other

Coaching Points:
angle, distance and timing of support - vision - decision making - verbal and visual communication

4v4 plus 4 Combination

Click Here To View The Drill Animation!
Age Group: (8-11yrs) (12-15yrs) (16-Adult)
Emphasis: possession - passing
Description:
- 2 teams play 4v4 inside the playing area
- another team (neutral players) is positioned around the grid
- teams in the middle score a point by passing to a neutral player who passes it to any other neutral player around the grid who connects it back to the team that had possession of the ball last

Variation:
- neutral player must pass it to neutral on the opposite end line who then tries to a player of the team that had possession last to complete the sequence
- neutral players must play one (two) touch
- teams score by making 5 consecutive passes
- players on the outside are allowed to pass to each other

Coaching Points:
angle, distance and timing of support - vision - body position – open to field - decision making - verbal and visual communication - first touch

4v4 Plus 4 Multiple Balls

Click Here To View The Drill Animation!
Age Group: (8-11yrs) (12-15yrs) (16-Adult)
Emphasis: possession - passing
Description:
- play 4v4 inside the grid
- 4 neutral players around the grid
- two of the four neutral players have soccer balls
- players inside the grid score by passing to a neutral player who doesn't have a ball
- once a goal is scored the passer runs to receive a new ball from another neutral player as shown
- team with most "goals" after 5 minutes stays and other team switches roles with neutral players

Variation:
- vary number of pairs inside the grid
- vary number of neutral players with a ball
- adjust spacing depending on the age and ability of the group

Coaching Points:
disguise - vision - first touch - communication - quick decision making - accuracy over power

4v4 Plus 4 Possession

Click Here To View The Drill Animation!
Age Group: (8-11yrs) (12-15yrs) (16-Adult)
Emphasis: passing - possession
Description:
- 4v4v4
- 2 teams (8v4) are responsible for keeping possession
- if defending team (blue) wins the ball, the team who made the mistake automatically becomes the defending team
- if a ball goes out of bounce it is considered loss of possession by that team and that team then becomes the defending team

Variation:
- limit number of touches
- play with a designated defending team who must win the ball and then pass it to coach (who moves around the grid) 5 times to switch roles with an attacking team
- players must toe tap an outside cone after completing a pass
- group of 8 must pass to each team alternately - for example, a red player must pass to a gray player who must then pass to a red player etc.
- rotate defenders every 4-5 minutes rather than automatically switching after loss of possession
- adjust spacing depending on the age and ability of the group

Coaching Points:
angle, distance and timing of support - vision - body position - open to field - decision making - verbal and visual communication - first touch

4v4 plus 4 w Long Pass

Click Here To View The Drill Animation!
Age Group: (8-11yrs) (12-15yrs) (16-Adult)
Emphasis: possession - passing
Description:
- 2 teams play 4v4 inside the playing area
- neutral players on the outside of the field support the team in possession
- teams score by maintaining possession before playing to one of the neutral players who then plays a one-touch pass to the target player opposite of him
- if the receiving player successfully controls the long pass the team is awarded a point
- switch roles after 4-5 minutes

Variation:
- players on the outside are allowed to pass to each other
- adjust spacing depending on the age and ability of the group

Coaching Points:
angle, distance and timing of support - vision - body position - open to field - decision making - verbal and visual communication - first touch

4v4 plus 4 with Mini Goals

Click Here To View The Drill Animation!
Age Group: (8-11yrs) (12-15yrs) (16-Adult)
Emphasis: possession - passing - finishing - attacking - defending
Description:
- 2 teams play 4v4 inside the playing area
- each team defends and attacks two mini goals
- neutral players are positioned at the sideline and goal line
- teams attempt to score by utilizing neutral players
- teams switch roles every 6-8 minutes

Variation:
- team in possession has to include neutral players before they can score
- limit number of touches
- adjust spacing depending on the age and ability of the group

Coaching Points:
angle, distance and timing of support - vision - body position - open to field - decision making - verbal and visual communication - first touch

4v4 Plus 4+4

Click Here To View The Drill Animation!
Age Group: (8-11yrs) (12-15yrs) (16-Adult)
Emphasis: possession - passing
Description:
- 2 teams play 4v4 inside the playing area
- rest of the players are on the outside
- players can only pass to their (same color) target players
- teams score by passing to a target player who passes it back to a third player
- switch roles every 5-10 minutes
- players on the outside cannot challenge each other

Variation:
- play 3v3 etc.
- limit number of touches
- players on the outside are allowed to pass to each other
- adjust size of field if necessary

Coaching Points:
angle, distance and timing of support - vision - body position - open to field - decision making - verbal and visual communication - first touch

4v4 Plus 4+4 Switch

Click Here To View The Drill Animation!
Age Group: (8-11yrs) (12-15yrs) (16-Adult)
Emphasis: passing - possession
Description:
- 2 teams play 4v4 inside the playing area
- rest of the players are on the outside
- players can only pass to their own color
- teams score by passing to the outside to on of their teammates who then comes in the middle and connects for one more pass to a teammate
- player who passes the ball outside immediately takes the receiver's position
- players on the outside cannot challenge each other

Variation:
- play 3v3 etc.
- players on the outside must play one touch
- adjust spacing depending on the age and ability of the group

Coaching Points:
angle, distance and timing of support - vision - body position - open to field - decision making - verbal and visual communication - first touch - constant movement

4v4 Plus Neutral

Click Here To View The Drill Animation!
Age Group: (5-7yrs) (8-11yrs) (12-15yrs) (16-Adult)
Emphasis: dribbling - attacking - defending
Description:
- one team defends the goal with goalie and the other team defends 2 mini goals
- neutral player always supports the losing team
- if the score is tied the neutral player supports the team that has possession switch roles after 5-10 minutes

Variation:
- neutral player is not allowed to score
- direction of play changes if the team which defends the goal with goalie scores on one of the two mini goals
- players of the winning team have to take 3 touches minimum
- adjust spacing depending on the age and ability of the group if necessary

Coaching Points:
Attacking: quick transition - switch point of attack - deception - set up defender - change of speed & direction - protect the ball - close control - angle, distance and timing of support - vision - body position - open to field - decision making - verbal and visual communication
Defending: angle and speed of approach - control and restraint - delay and channel - angle and distance of cover - intercept pass - change role of pressure and cover - visual and verbal communication

4v4 Shooting Game

Click Here To View The Drill Animation!
Age Group: (8-11yrs) (12-15yrs) (16-Adult)
Emphasis: finishing - attacking - defending
Description:
- play 2v2 in each half
- players must stay in their half

Variation:
- allow the defender who makes a pass to his forward to move into the attacking half to create 3v2 situation
- goals can only be scored off a first touch
- limit number of touches
- adjust spacing depending on the age and ability of the group

Coaching Points:
Attacking: accurate passes - quick finish - aggressive and positive mentality - placement versus power - supporting angle and distance to ball - unbalancing the defense - create space for others - attack space behind defense
Defending: angle and speed of approach - delay and channel - deny turn - tracking - recovery runs - changing role of pressure and cover - visual and verbal communication

4v4 Sweeper Keeper Counter Goals

Click Here To View The Drill Animation!
Age Group: (5-7yrs) (8-11yrs) (12-15yrs) (16-Adult)
Emphasis: dribbling - finishing - attacking - defending
Description:
- defending team defends the large goal with goalie
- attacking team defends 2 cone goals with sweeper keeper (keeper covers both goals)
- sweeper keeper must stay in his zone but can be used as a negative target (two touch max.) for support

Variation:
- no players allowed in end zone except for sweeper keeper
- if ball goes out of bounce corner kicks are to be taken from goal line with large goal
- if the defending team scores it switches roles with the attacking team
- play 5v5, 6v6, 7v7, 8v8 etc.
- adjust size of field if necessary

Coaching Points:
change of speed & direction - vision - quick finish - quick transitions - switch point of attack

4v4 Two Neutrals

Click Here To View The Drill Animation!
Age Group: (8-11yrs) (12-15yrs) (16-Adult)
Emphasis: passing - possession
Description:
- play 4v4
- teams score if they complete a pass to a neutral player who then dribbles onto the grid and helps the team in possession to connect 6 passes (other neutral player enters the grid as well = 6v4)

Variation:
- only one neutral player enters the grid
- limited number of touches
- adjust spacing depending on the age and ability of the group

Coaching Points:
first touch away from pressure - create supporting angles - vision - body position – open to field - decision making - verbal and visual communication

4v4 w Cone Goals

Click Here To View The Drill Animation!
Age Group: (5-7yrs) (8-11yrs) (12-15yrs) (16-Adult)
Emphasis: finishing - passing - possession - attacking - defending
Description:
- play 4v4
- each team defends and attacks two goals
- goals count if the shot is taken with a first touch

Variation:
- add a neutral player
- use mini goals instead of cone goals
- limit number of touches
- adjust spacing depending on the age and ability of the group

Coaching Points:
quality of preparation touch - aggressive and positive mentality - vision and anticipation - placement versus power - positioning to gain an advantage - angle, distance and timing of support - body position – open to field - decision making - verbal and visual communication

4v4 w Target Player

Click Here To View The Drill Animation!
Age Group: (8-11yrs) (12-15yrs) (16-Adult)
Emphasis: passing - possession
Description:
- teams score by connecting 6 passes in a row or by passing to the neutral player who passes to a third player

Variation:
- players must toe tap an outside cone after completing a pass
- limit number of touches
- adjust spacing depending on the age and ability of the group

Coaching Points:
angle, distance and timing of support - vision - decision making - verbal and visual communication - weight of pass - accuracy - first touch

4v4 w Wall Players and End Zones

Click Here To View The Drill Animation!
Age Group: (8-11yrs) (12-15yrs) (16-Adult)
Emphasis: attacking - defending - dribbling - possession - passing
Description:
- play 4v4 with 2 wall players on each side line
- teams score by dribbling into any end zone
- teams must pass to a wall player before they can score
- wall players cannot be challenged
- switch wall players after 5 goals

Variation:
- wall players must play one-touch
- wall player switches with pass giver
- teams must pass to both wall players before they can score
- teams can only score by dribbling into a designated end zone
- adjust spacing depending on the age and ability of the group

Coaching Points:
constant movement - angle, distance and timing of support - vision - body position — open to field - decision making - verbal and visual communication - good first touch into space

4v4 Two Neutrals

Click Here To View The Drill Animation!
Age Group: (5-7yrs) (8-11yrs) (12-15yrs) (16-Adult)
Emphasis: finishing - passing - attacking - defending
Description:
- play 4v4 plus 2
- two neutral players play for the team that has possession

Variation:
- each neutral player must stay in designated half
- play with only one neutral player
- neutral players only have one touch
- neutral players cannot score goals
- limit number of touches for attackers
- goals can only be scored on a first touch
- adjust spacing depending on the age and ability of the group

Coaching Points:
quality of preparation touch - aggressive and positive mentality - vision and anticipation - placement versus power - positioning to gain an advantage - angle, distance and timing of support - body position – open to field - decision making - verbal and visual communication - shape of team to maintain possession - quick finish - quick transitions

4v4 with Wall Players

Click Here To View The Drill Animation!

Age Group: (8-11yrs) (12-15yrs) (16-Adult)
Emphasis: finishing - passing - possession - attacking - defending
Description:
- play 4v4
- each team has two wall players on the opponent's goal line
- a goal is awarded three points if a player scores off a pass by one of the wall players otherwise only one point
- wall player switches roles after goal is scored

Variation:
- wall player can come on the field to support his team after completing a pass (he must return after team's loss of possession)
- wall players must play one touch
- goals can only be scored on a first touch
- adjust spacing depending on the age and ability of the group

Coaching Points:
quality of preparation touch - aggressive and positive mentality - vision and anticipation - placement versus power - positioning to gain an advantage - angle, distance and timing of support - body position – open to field - decision making - verbal and visual communication - shape of team to maintain possession - quick finish

5v2 Finishing Practice

Click Here To View The Drill Animation!
Age Group: (8-11yrs) (12-15yrs) (16-Adult)
Emphasis: passing - attacking - defending - finishing
Description:
- play 3v2 inside the grid plus two attackers on the flanks
- the server passes to the two defenders who keep possession until the three attackers win the ball
- next the attackers must play wide (wingers) then forward before they can score

Variation:
- add a defender
- limit number of touches
- attackers can only score off a cross by a winger
- adjust spacing depending on the age and ability of the group

Coaching Points:
Attacking: quality of preparation touch - quick finish - unbalancing the defense - create space for others - attack space behind defense - aggressive and positive mentality - vision and anticipation - placement versus power - positioning to gain an advantage
Defending: angle and distance of cover - intercept pass (deny turn, deny penetration) - tracking (recovery runs etc.) - changing role of pressure and cover - visual and verbal communication

5v2 Keep Away

Click Here To View The Drill Animation!
Age Group: (5-7yrs) (8-11yrs) (12-15yrs) (16-Adult)
Emphasis: passing - possession
Description:
- 5 attackers attempt to keep the ball away from 2 defenders
- defenders dribble a ball and switch roles if they manage to pass their ball against the ball that is being passed around among the 5 attackers

Variation:
- play 6v2 etc.
- defenders have only one ball which they can pass to each other
- limit number of touches for group of 5
- adjust size of field if necessary

Coaching Points:
constant movement - communication is vital - good angle and distance of support to receive ball - play the way you face and away from pressure - first touch away from pressure - players should accelerate towards the ball

5v2 Keep Away # 2

Click Here To View The Drill Animation!
Age Group: (8-11yrs) (12-15yrs) (16-Adult)
Emphasis: passing - possession
Description:
- play 5v2 keep away with one defender in each half
- 4 outside attacking players move around the grid
- the attacking player inside the grid can move all over the grid
- attacking team scores if the target player inside the grid receives and passes the ball to an outside player
- defenders must stay in their designated half
- outside players may pass to each other

Variation:
- limit number of touches for outside players
- target player cannot pass to the outside player from which he received the pass
- adjust spacing depending on the age and ability of the group

Coaching Points:
angle, distance and timing of support - vision - body position – open to field - decision making - verbal and visual communication - good first touch takes ball away from pressure

5v2 Keep Away # 3

Click Here To View The Drill Animation!
Age Group: (5-7yrs) (8-11yrs) (12-15yrs) (16-Adult)
Emphasis: passing - possession
Description:
- 5 attackers attempt to keep ball away from 2 defenders
- one defender starts with a ball in his hands
- defenders attempt to throw their ball against the ball that is being passed around among the 5 attackers
- defenders pass the ball to each other by throwing
- if the ball is hit, the defender who made the throw switches roles with the player who touched the ball last

Variation:
- both defenders have a ball in their hands
- limit number of touches for attackers
- adjust size of field and/or number of touches allowed if necessary

Coaching Points:
constant movement - angle, distance and timing of support - vision - body position – open to field - decision making - verbal and visual communication - first touch

5v3 Multiple Targets

Click Here To View The Drill Animation!
Age Group: (5-7yrs) (8-11yrs) (12-15yrs) (16-Adult)
Emphasis: passing - possession - finishing
Description:
- play 5v3
- attackers (5 players) score by knocking over the cones with the ball
- defenders score by completing a pass to a teammate who receives it outside the grid
- if ball goes out of bounds the ball is kicked back in (kick-ins)
- players switch roles after 7 goals by the attackers and 4 goals by the defenders

Variation:
- play 6v3, 5v2 etc.
- vary number of defenders and attackers but make sure to have one target per defender on the griddefenders score by passing to coach who moves around the grid
- attackers must knock down a cone with a first touch
- limit number of touches for attackers
- adjust spacing depending on the age and ability of the group

Coaching Points:
decision making - communication - create supporting angles - quick transitions - quick finishing - quality of preparation touch - aggressive and positive mentality - placement versus power

5v3 Possession & Finishing

Click Here To View The Drill Animation!
Age Group: (5-7yrs) (8-11yrs) (12-15yrs) (16-Adult)
Emphasis: passing - possession - finishing
Description:
- play 5v3
- tall cones are positioned 5-6yds in from the end lines
- teams score by knocking over the cones with the game ball
- defenders can block shots and maintain possession themselves
- if ball goes out of bounds the ball is kicked back in (kick-ins)
- switch roles every 2-3 minutes

Variation:
- vary number of defenders and attackers but make sure to have one target per defender on the grid
- limit number of touches
- adjust spacing depending on the age and ability of the group

Coaching Points:
communication - create supporting angles - quick transitions - quick finishing - eye on ball - quality of preparation touch - aggressive and positive mentality - placement versus power - positioning to gain an advantage (behind targets?)

5v3 Shooting Game

Age Group: (8-11yrs) (12-15yrs) (16-Adult)
Emphasis: finishing - passing - attacking - defending
Description:
- play 5v5 (5v3)
- each team defends a goal with a goalie
- one of the two teams always has two players run around the grid
- once the players have completed their lap two players from the other team leave the game and run around the grid

Variation:
- goals must be scored with the first touch
- players must run two laps before they can return
- limit number of touches for attackers
- adjust spacing depending on the age and ability of the group

Coaching Points:
body mechanics and control of body - body position and balance - eye on ball - quality of preparation touch - contact surface - aggressive and positive mentality - vision and anticipation - placement versus power - positioning to gain an advantage - angle, distance and timing of support - vision - body position – open to field - decision making - verbal and visual communication

5v4 Attacking

Click Here To View The Drill Animation!
Age Group: (8-11yrs) (12-15yrs) (16-Adult)
Emphasis: attacking - defending - dribbling - passing
Description:
- the defending team (4 field players) scores by passing through one of the two cone goals to their target player (2points)
- the attacking team (5 players) can score on the goal with goalie (2 points) or by dribbling through one of the two cone goals (1 points)
- all restarts due to out of bounds, fouls, goals, are started by the goalies
- switch roles after 5-10 minutes

Variation:
- play 4v3, 6v5 etc.
- add neutral player
- minimum of 2-3 touches
- if a team scores it keeps possession and direction of play changes
- adjust size of field and/or cone goals if necessary

Coaching Points:
angle, distance and timing of support - vision - decision making - verbal and visual communication - combination play - create space for others - quick transitions - quick finish

5v4 Ball Feeders

Click Here To View The Drill Animation!
Age Group: (8-11yrs) (12-15yrs) (16-Adult)
Emphasis: dribbling - attacking - defending
Description:
- 4 defenders defend the goal with goalie and score by dribbling through cone goals or by keeping possession for 10 seconds
- 5 attackers defend 2 cone goals and can score on goal with goalie
- 2 players from the attacking team always feed the ball to attacking team (throw-ins, high or low pass etc.)
- if ball goes out of bounce or goal is scored, ball is always distributed by ball feeders
- switch roles after 5-10 minutes

Variation:
- add a neutral player
- minimum of 2-3 touches for attackers
- adjust spacing depending on the age and ability of the group if necessary

Coaching Points:
Attacking: weight of pass - accuracy - first touch - angle, distance and timing of support - vision - decision making - verbal and visual communication - quick transitions - switch point of attack - set up defender - change of speed & direction - protect the ball - close control
Defending: angle and speed of approach - control and restraint - delay and channel - angle and distance of cover - intercept pass - change role of pressure and cover - visual and verbal communication

5v4 Two Adjacent Goals

Click Here To View The Drill Animation!
Age Group: (8-11yrs) (12-15yrs) (16-Adult)
Emphasis: dribbling - finishing - attacking - defending
Description:
- play 5v4
- defending team (4 players) scores by keeping possession for 7-10 seconds
- attacking team (5 players) can score on both goals with goalies
- switch roles after 5-10 minutes

Variation:
- minimum of 2-3 touches (for attackers)
- play 5v5, 6v4, 7v6, 8v6 etc.
- attackers can only score off headers / volleys
- defenders switch roles with attackers if they score
- defenders score by dribbling across attacker's end line
- adjust spacing depending on the age and ability of the group if necessary

Coaching Points:
Attacking: quick transitions - quick finish - supporting angle and distance to ball - create space for others - attack space behind defense - quality of preparation touch - aggressive and positive mentality - vision and anticipation - placement versus power
Defending: angle and distance of cover - change role of pressure and cover - visual and verbal communication - control and restraint - delay and channel

5v5 Chip Pass

Click Here To View The Drill Animation!
Age Group: (8-11yrs) (12-15yrs) (16-Adult)
Emphasis: passing - attacking
Description:
- play 5v5 with goalies
- teams score by making a lofted pass over the marked lines into the goalie's hands without a bounce
- goalkeepers must stay their zone
- goalkeeper feeds the ball back to the team that was scored upon
- teams can score on either goalkeeper
- teams cannot score on the same goalie twice in a row

Variation:
- pass must come from own half
- pass must come from attacking half
- teams can only score on one designated goalkeeper
- limit number of touches
- adjust size of field if necessary

Coaching Points:
accuracy - vision - decision making - verbal and visual communication

5v5 Four Mini Goals

Click Here To View The Drill Animation!
Age Group: (8-11yrs) (12-15yrs) (16-Adult)
Emphasis: passing - dribbling - attacking - defending
Description:
- each team defends and attacks two mini goals
- each team selects one player that has unlimited touches
- all other players must play 1 (2) touch
- goals by player with unlimited touches count 3 points
- switch roles after 3-5 minutes

Variation:
- each team selects two players that have unlimited touches
- cone goals instead of mini goals
- adjust spacing depending on the age and ability of the group if necessary

Coaching Points:
Attacking: quick transition - switch point of attack - deception - set up defender - change of speed & direction - protect the ball - close control - angle, distance and timing of support - vision - body position - open to field - decision making - verbal and visual communication
Defending: angle and speed of approach - control and restraint - delay and channel - angle and distance of cover - intercept pass - change role of pressure and cover - visual and verbal communication

5v5 Goalie Target

Click Here To View The Drill Animation!
Age Group: (8-11yrs) (12-15yrs) (16-Adult)
Emphasis: passing - possession - goalkeeping
Description:
- each team attempts to keep possession and complete 5 passes before a player can chip the ball into the goalkeepers hands to be awarded a point for his team
- goalie feeds the ball back to the team that scored

Variation:
- play 4v4, 6v6, 7v7 etc.
- team must connect 3 passes before the chip
- limit number of touches
- adjust size of field if necessary

Coaching Points:
constant movement - angle, distance and timing of support - vision - body position – open to field - decision making - verbal and visual communication

5v5 Man To Man

Click Here To View The Drill Animation!
Age Group: (5-7yrs) (8-11yrs) (12-15yrs) (16-Adult)
Emphasis: possession - passing - dribbling
Description:
- each player is assigned a player from the opposing team
- players can only defend their assigned player
- teams score by making 5 consecutive passes

Variation:
- limited number of touches
- adjust spacing depending on the age and ability of the group

Coaching Points:
angle, distance and timing of support - vision - body position – open to field - decision making - verbal and visual communication

5v5 One-Touch Passing

Click Here To View The Drill Animation!
Age Group: (5-7yrs) (8-11yrs) (12-15yrs) (16-Adult)
Emphasis: passing - possession
Description:
- teams play keep away
- team is awarded a point for every completed one-touch pass
- first team with 15 points wins
- play multiple rounds

Variation:
- play 4v4, 6v6, 6v5, 6v4, 5v3 etc.
- add a neutral player
- adjust spacing depending on the age and ability of the group

Coaching Points:
accuracy - constant movement - angle, distance and timing of support - vision - body position – open to field - decision making - verbal and visual communication - speed of play

5v5 Open Up Play

Click Here To View The Drill Animation!
Age Group: (5-7yrs) (8-11yrs) (12-15yrs)
Emphasis: passing - possession
Description:
- each team defends and attacks two mini goals
- players must run around the nearest cone after completing a pass

Variation:
- play a possession game without goals (same rules as above)
- adjust spacing depending on the age and ability of the group

Coaching Points:
accuracy - weight of pass - quick decision making - protect the ball - angle, distance and timing of support - vision - body position – open to field - decision making - verbal and visual communication

5v5 Six Cone Goals w Wall Players

Click Here To View The Drill Animation!
Age Group: (8-11yrs) (12-15yrs) (16-Adult)
Emphasis: passing - attacking - defending
Description:
- each team defends and attacks three cone goals
- teams must pass to a wall player before they can score
- wall players must play one-touch

Variation:
- vary number of touches allowed for wall players and/or field players
- vary number of goals on each goal line
- adjust spacing depending on the age and ability of the group

Coaching Points:
constant movement - angle, distance and timing of support - vision - body position — open to field - decision making - verbal and visual communication - switch point of attack

5v5 Through Hot Corners

Click Here To View The Drill Animation!

Age Group: (8-11yrs) (12-15yrs) (16-Adult)
Emphasis: passing - dribbling - attacking - defending
Description:
- teams score by moving the ball through one of the corner areas in the attacking half
- attackers cannot be challenged within corner area
- goal after a cross counts 2 points

Variation:
- teams must pass and receive a ball in a corner area before they can score
- players must dribble into corner area and then play a cross
- ·2 touches maximum for all players
- 2 touches maximum only for player inside corner area
- attacker inside corner area can be challenged
- adjust size of corner areas if necessary

Coaching Points:
switch point of attack - angle, distance and timing of support - vision - decision making - verbal and visual communication

5v5 Through Pass

Click Here To View The Drill Animation!

Age Group: (8-11yrs) (12-15yrs) (16-Adult)
Emphasis: passing - attacking - defending
Description:
- each team defends three mini goals
- players can score by passing through any cone goal with a teammate receiving the ball inside the end zone
- players may not be waiting behind the goals
- defenders cannot follow attackers into end zone

Variation:
- direction of play changes after each goal
- players can wait behind the goals
- adjust spacing depending on the age and ability of the group

Coaching Points:
vision - attack open space - time your run - communication - good supporting angle - movement on and off the ball

5v5 w Goalies

Click Here To View The Drill Animation!

Age Group: (8-11yrs) (12-15yrs) (16-Adult)
Emphasis: passing - possession
Description:
- 5v5 with goalies positioned on opposite goal lines
- each team attempts to keep possession and complete 5 passes before a player can chip the ball into the goalies hands to be awarded a point for his team
- goalie feeds the ball back to the team that scored

Variation:
- play with one target player on each end line who must control a chipped pass with their feet for a team to be awarded a point
- each team can only score on one designated goalie
- goalies move around inside the grid
- goalies move around the outside of the grid
- limit number of touches
- adjust spacing depending on the age and ability of the group

Coaching Points:
constant movement - angle, distance and timing of support - vision - body position – open to field - decision making - verbal and visual communication

5v5 King Player

Click Here To View The Drill Animation!

Age Group: (5-7yrs) (8-11yrs) (12-15yrs) (16-Adult)
Emphasis: finishing - passing - possession
Description:
- play 5v5
- each team selects a player whose goals counts for 3 points; all other goals just one point
- switch roles after 4-5 minutes

Variation:
- 2-3 selected players for each team
- limit number of touches
- adjust spacing depending on the age and ability of the group

Coaching Points:
quality of preparation touch - aggressive and positive mentality - vision and anticipation - placement versus power - positioning to gain an advantage - angle, distance and timing of support - body position – open to field - decision making - verbal and visual communication - shape of team to maintain possession - quick finish

6v2 Possession Game

Click Here To View The Drill Animation!
Age Group: (5-7yrs) (8-11yrs) (12-15yrs) (16-Adult)
Emphasis: passing - possession - defending
Description:
- 6 attacking players play keep away from two defenders
- attacking team scores a point with every pass
- defending team scores 2 points if they intercept the ball or force it out of bounce

Variation:
- play 6v3, 6v4, 5v2 etc.
- limit number of touches
- adjust spacing depending on the age and ability of the group

Coaching Points:
communication - create supporting angles - play the way you face and away from pressure - vision - body position – open to field - decision making

6v3 Keep Away

Click Here To View The Drill Animation!

Age Group: (8-11yrs) (12-15yrs) (16-Adult)
Emphasis: passing - possession
Description:
- attackers attempt to keep ball away from defenders
- attackers have 2 touches
- defenders have unlimited number of touches
- switch roles every 3-5 minutes

Variation:
- play 5v2, 4v2, 6v5, 7v5, 7v4 etc.
- attackers must play one-touch
- adjust spacing depending on the age and ability of the group

Coaching Points:
constant movement - communication is vital - good angle and distance of support to receive ball - play the way you face and away from pressure - vision

6v3 Possession

Click Here To View The Drill Animation!

Age Group: (8-11yrs) (12-15yrs) (16-Adult)
Emphasis: passing - possession - defending
Description:
- 6 attackers versus 3 defenders
- attacking team attempts to keep possession and complete 10 passes to be awarded a point
- defending team scores by winning possession and passing it into one of the mini goals
- switch roles every 3-4 minutes

Variation:
- cone goals instead of mini goals
- limit number of touches for attackers
- adjust spacing depending on the age and ability of the group

Coaching Points:
constant movement - angle, distance and timing of support - vision - body position – open to field - decision making - verbal and visual communication - first touch

7v2 Possession Game

Click Here To View The Drill Animation!
Age Group: (5-7yrs) (8-11yrs) (12-15yrs) (16-Adult)
Emphasis: passing - possession
Description:
- 7 attacking players play keep away from two defenders
- defender switches role with the attacker if he manages to tag the player that is in possession of the ball

Variation:
- play 8v3, 8v4, 7v3, 6v2, 6v3 etc.
- limit number of touches
- adjust spacing depending on the age and ability of the group

Coaching Points:
communication - create supporting angles - play the way you face and away from pressure - vision - body position – open to field - decision making

7v5 Numbers Up

Click Here To View The Drill Animation!

Age Group: (5-7yrs) (8-11yrs) (12-15yrs) (16-Adult)
Emphasis: passing - possession - finishing - attacking - defending
Description:
- each team defends and attacks one goal without goalie
- if a team loses possession two designated players from the defending team drop back to be temporary goalies
- goalies must remain on goal line until possession is won back (goalies may use their hands to block shots)

Variations:
- limit number of touches
- all players must be in the attacking before a team can score
- teams must connect 5 passes before they can score
- adjust spacing depending on the age and ability of the group

Coaching Points:
angle, distance and timing of support - vision - body position – open to field - decision making - verbal and visual communication - aggressive and positive mentality - placement versus power

7v5 Wall Players

Click Here To View The Drill Animation!

Age Group: (8-11yrs) (12-15yrs) (16-Adult)
Emphasis: dribbling - passing - possession - attacking - defending
Description:
- one team (4 players plus goalie) defends goal with goalie and other team (5 field players plus 2 wall players) defends cone goals
- attacking team has two wall players on the side line who can dribble the ball onto the field and support their team until they lose possession or take a shot on goal (then they must go back to the side line)
- defending team can score by dribbling through cone goals
- switch roles after 8-10 minutes

Variation:
- play 6v4, 8v6 etc.
- wall players are neutral
- minimum of 2-3 touches for attackers
- vary position of wall players (next to goal with goalie or next to cone goals)
- if one wall player dribbles onto the field the other wall player is allowed to enter it as well until team loses possession or takes a shot on goal
- adjust spacing depending on the age and ability of the group if necessary

Coaching Points:
Attacking: weight of pass - accuracy - first touch - angle, distance and timing of support - vision - decision making - verbal and visual communication - quick transitions - switch point of attack - set up defender - change of speed & direction - protect the ball - close control
Defending: angle and speed of approach - control and restraint - delay and channel - angle and distance of cover - intercept pass - change role of pressure and cover - visual and verbal communication

8v4 Keep Away # 1

Click Here To View The Drill Animation!

Age Group: (5-7yrs) (8-11yrs) (12-15yrs) (16-Adult)
Emphasis: passing - possession
Description:
- 8 attackers attempt to keep ball away from 4 defenders
- attackers have 2 touches
- defenders have unlimited number of touches
- attackers score by making 6 consecutive passes
- defenders score by dribbling out of the grid
- switch roles every 3-5 minutes

Variation:
- play 6v3, 4v2 etc.
- once a player has made a play on the ball they must immediately turn and run around the nearest cone before getting back onto the field again
- attackers must play one-touch
- adjust spacing depending on the age and ability of the group

Coaching Points:
constant movement - angle, distance and timing of support - vision - body position — open to field - decision making - verbal and visual communication - speed of play

8v6 Possess to Finish

Click Here To View The Drill Animation!

Age Group: (8-11yrs) (12-15yrs) (16-Adult)
Emphasis: attacking - defending - possession - finishing - passing
Description:
- play 8v6
- each team defends a goal
- the attacking team with 8 players can only take three touches in their defending half and two (one) touches in the attacking half
- the defending team has no restrictions
- the defending can also score by connecting five passes in a row
- switch roles after 7-10 minutes

Variations:
- vary number of players and/or touch restriction
- attacking team has to score a goal with a first touch
- adjust spacing depending on the age and ability of the group

Coaching Points:
quick transitions - switch point of attack - aggressive and positive mentality - vision and anticipation - placement versus power - positioning to gain an advantage - angle, distance and timing of support - body position — open to field - decision making - verbal and visual communication - shape of team to maintain possession

Attack On Two Goals

Click Here To View The Drill Animation!

Age Group: (8-11yrs) (12-15yrs) (16-Adult)
Emphasis: finishing - possession - passing - attacking - defending
Description:
- play 4v4, 5v5, 6v6, 7v7, 8v8 etc.
- the attacking team can score on both goals
- the defending team scores by connecting 5-7 passes
- the defending team can pass to the goalkeepers making it a numbers up situation
- switch roles after 5-8 minutes

Variation:
- limit number of touches
- adjust spacing depending on the age and ability of the group

Coaching Points:
Attacking: unbalancing the defense - create space for others - attack space behind defense - aggressive and positive mentality - vision and anticipation - placement versus power - positioning to gain an advantage
Defending: positioning to provide cover and balance - intercepting pass - defending vital space (compactness-concentration) - defending space behind - tracking players - angle, distance and timing of support - decision making - verbal and visual communication

Attackers vs. Defenders # 4

Click Here To View The Drill Animation!

Age Group: (5-7yrs) (8-11yrs) (12-15yrs) (16-Adult)
Emphasis: dribbling - finishing - attacking - defending
Description:
- play 4v4
- the attacking team can score as many goals as possible on both goals within 5 minutes
- once the attackers score they have to dribble across middle line before they can score again
- if defenders win the ball they try to keep possession as long as possible
- attackers always start with the ball on a dead ball
- switch roles after 5 minutes
- team with most goals after two rounds wins

Variation:
- minimum of 2-3 touches
- defenders can score by connecting 5 passes
- add a neutral player
- adjust spacing depending on the age and ability of the group if necessary

Coaching Points:
quick transitions - angle, distance and timing of support - decision making - verbal and visual communication - quick finish - good first touch - aggressive and positive mentality - vision and anticipation - placement versus power

Attacking Game w Touch Restriction

Click Here To View The Drill Animation!

Age Group: (8-11yrs) (12-15yrs) (16-Adult)
Emphasis: dribbling - attacking - defending
Description:
- defending team plays with one player less on the field than the attacking team
- defending team defends the goal with goalie
- attacking team defends the goal line opposite to the goal with goalie
- attackers have maximum of 2-3 touches in defending half and unlimited touches in the attacking half
- defending team scores by dribbling across the attacker's goal line
- switch roles after 5-10 minutes

Variation:
- defending team scores by keeping possession for more than 7 seconds
- defending team scores by passing to a target player behind the attacker's end line
- if an attacker beats a defender with a move his team is awarded 1 point
- if an attacker beats the goalie with a move he is awarded 2 points
- adjust spacing depending on the age and ability of the group if necessary

Coaching Points:
Attacking: set up defender - change of speed & direction - close control - angle, distance and timing of support - vision - decision making - verbal and visual communication - quality of preparation touch - aggressive and positive mentality - vision and anticipation - placement versus power
Defending: angle and speed of approach - control and restraint - delay and channel - angle and distance of cover - intercept pass - change role of pressure and cover - visual and verbal communication

Attacking Play w Neutrals

Click Here To View The Drill Animation!

Age Group: (8-11yrs) (12-15yrs) (16-Adult)
Emphasis: attacking - finishing - passing
Description:
- each team defends and attacks one goal
- teams must pass to a neutral wall player before they can score
- wall players can only participate from the outside the middle zone

Variation:
- allow neutral player to work from inside the middle zone only
- limit number of touches for neutral wall players
- adjust spacing depending on the age and ability of the group

Coaching Points:
angle, distance and timing of support - body position – open to field - decision making - verbal and visual communication - quick finish - support position lateral to ball - switch point of attack - spread out the attack

Attacking versus Possession

Click Here To View The Drill Animation!
Age Group: (8-11yrs) (12-15yrs) (16-Adult)
Emphasis: finishing - passing - possession
Description:
- play 4v4
- one team scores by connecting 7 passes with the help of the two goalkeepers
- the other team scores by winning the ball in one half and scoring on the goal in the other half with the help of the wing players
- switch roles after 5-10 minutes

Variation:
- switch roles after each score
- limit number of touches
- adjust spacing depending on the age and ability of the group

Coaching Points:
angle, distance and timing of support - decision making - verbal and visual communication - shape of team to maintain possession - quality of preparation touch - aggressive and positive mentality - vision and anticipation - placement versus power - positioning to gain an advantage

Awareness Game # 1

Click Here To View The Drill Animation!

Age Group: (5-7yrs) (8-11yrs) (12-15yrs) (16-Adult)
Emphasis: passing - possession
Description:
- two groups play 3v1 in the same grid
- target players in each zone
- attackers score by passing the ball to a target player who controls the ball
- defender scores by dribbling out of the grid
- attackers cannot score on same target player twice in a row

Variation:
- add another target player for each end zone
- play 3v2, 4v2 etc. with two groups
- adjust spacing depending on the age and ability of the group

Coaching Points:
spread out attack - angle, distance and timing of support - vision - body position — open to field - decision making - verbal and visual communication

Awareness Game # 2

Click Here To View The Drill Animation!

Age Group: (5-7yrs) (8-11yrs) (12-15yrs) (16-Adult)
Emphasis: passing - possession
Description:
- two groups play 4v1 keep away in the same grid
- attackers score by connecting 7 passes
- defenders score by dribbling out of the grid
- switch roles often

Variation:
- limit number of touches for attackers
- play 3v1, 4v2 or 5v2 etc. with two groups
- adjust spacing depending on the age and ability of the group

Coaching Points:
spread out attack - angle, distance and timing of support - vision - body position — open to field - decision making - verbal and visual communication

Balanced Attack

Click Here To View The Drill Animation!

Age Group: (5-7yrs) (8-11yrs) (12-15yrs) (16-Adult)
Emphasis: attacking - defending - finishing
Description:
- regular scrimmage
- first team to have three (four, five or six) different players score a goal wins

Variation:
- limit number of touches
- adjust spacing depending on the age and ability of the group

Coaching Points:
quality of preparation touch - aggressive and positive mentality - vision and anticipation - placement versus power - positioning to gain an advantage

Box Passing with Neutrals

Click Here To View The Drill Animation!

Age Group: (8-11yrs) (12-15yrs) (16-Adult)
Emphasis: passing - finishing - attacking - defending
Description:
- 4 attackers vs. 4 defenders
- attacking team must pass the ball to a wall player before it can score on goal with goalie
- defending team scores by connecting 6 passes

Variation:
- vary number and position of wall players
- both teams can score on goal with goalie
- wall players can only make one-touch passes
- goals for attackers only count off headers or volleys
- adjust spacing depending on the age and ability of the group

Coaching Points:
angle, distance and timing of support - vision - body position — open to field - decision making - verbal and visual communication - quick finish - aggressive and positive mentality - vision and anticipation - placement versus power - positioning to gain an advantage

Building From The Back

Click Here To View The Drill Animation!

Age Group: (8-11yrs) (12-15yrs) (16-Adult)
Emphasis: passing - dribbling - attacking - defending
Description:
- each team defends and attacks one goal
- defenders cannot be challenged in defending third
- defenders have maximum of 3 touches in defending third
- middle third cannot be bypassed
- if rule is broken automatic free kick for the other team

Variation:
- maximum of 2 touches in attacking third
- players must dribble the ball from the middle third into the attacking third
- adjust spacing depending on the age and ability of the group if necessary

Coaching Points:
Attacking: protect the ball - close control - angle, distance and timing of support - vision - decision making - verbal and visual communication - weight of pass - accuracy- first touch - aggressive and positive mentality in front of goal - placement versus power in front of goal
Defending: angle and speed of approach - control and restraint - delay and channel - angle and distance of cover - intercept pass - change role of pressure and cover - visual and verbal communication

Bumper Ball

Click Here To View The Drill Animation!
Age Group: (5-7yrs) (8-11yrs)
Emphasis: dribbling - passing
Description:
- players dribble inside playing area with reg. size ball
- one or two players dribble a beach ball
- objective of the game is to have possession of the beach ball at the end of the game
- players switch balls if a player kicks his reg. size ball against one of the beach balls

Variation:
- specify how players must pass/shoot (left or right foot, inside or outside foot etc.)
- vary number of players with a target ball
- adjust spacing depending on the age and ability of the group if necessary

Coaching Points:
keep ball rolling - accuracy - weight of pass - vision - protect the ball with your body

Cannon Ball

Click Here To View The Drill Animation!
Age Group: (5-7yrs) (8-11yrs) (12-15yrs)
Emphasis: passing - dribbling
Description:
- in pairs
- players pass to their partner on opposite side
- 2 players at one time attempt to dribble across grid without being hit
- pass giver with most hits wins
- switch roles after 4-5 minutes

Variation:
- one touch only for passing players
- specify how players must pass/receive (left or right foot, inside or outside foot)
- adjust spacing depending on the age and ability of the group

Coaching Points:
low passes only - body mechanics - balance - first touch

Change Of Games

Click Here To View The Drill Animation!

Age Group: (5-7yrs) (8-11yrs) (12-15yrs) (16-Adult)
Emphasis: finishing - passing - possession - attacking - defending
Description:
- play starts in grid 1
- each team defends two mini goals in grid 1
- on coach's command direction of play changes and the team in possession at that moment attempts to finish on the goal with the goalie in grid 2
- if the defending team wins the ball they pass to the coach at the goal line in grid 2 to end the sequence

Variation:
- play with cone goals instead of mini goals
- coach calls out one player from each team to play a 1v1
- towards the goal with the goalie if the defending team wins the ball they can score on goal with goalie as well

Coaching Points:
quick transition - switch point of attack - angle, distance and timing of support - vision - body position – open to field - decision making - verbal and visual communication - aggressive and positive mentality - anticipation - placement versus power - positioning to gain an advantage

Channel Game # 1

Click Here To View The Drill Animation!

Age Group: (8-11yrs) (12-15yrs) (16-Adult)
Emphasis: dribbling - attacking - defending
Description:
- each team defends and attacks one goal
- if the attacking team has the ball inside a channel the defending team must have all its players move out of the opposite channel before they can challenge the ball
- goals on mini goals only count if all attackers are out of opposite channel

Variation:
- play with one neutral player in each channel
- limit number of touches for players inside the channel
- ball has to go through both channels before a team can score
- adjust spacing depending on the age and ability of the group if necessary

Coaching Points:
Attacking: quick transition - shift as a unit - protect the ball - close control - angle, distance and timing of support - vision - decision making - verbal and visual communication - weight of pass - accuracy - first touch
Defending: delay and channel - angle and distance of cover - intercept pass - change role of pressure and cover - visual and verbal communication - track recovery runs

Channel Players # 1

Click Here To View The Drill Animation!
Age Group: (8-11yrs) (12-15yrs) (16-Adult)
Emphasis: passing - finishing - attacking - defending
Description:
- all restarts due to out of bounds, fouls, goals, are started by the goalies
- if the goalie has the ball at least one of his teammates must move into the channel area to receive the ball
- goals off a cross from inside the channel area count 2 points

Variation:
- defenders can enter channel once an attacker receives a pass inside that channel
- teams can only score if at least one player of the team receives a pass inside the channel area
- limit number of touches (for channel players)
- adjust spacing depending on the age and ability of the group

Coaching Points:
shift as a unit - constant movement - communication is vital - create supporting angles - combination play

Channel Players # 3

Click Here To View The Drill Animation!

Age Group: (8-11yrs) (12-15yrs) (16-Adult)
Emphasis: passing - attacking - defending
Description:
- one neutral player in each channel
- if a neutral channel receives the ball and dribbles into the middle area the other neutral channel player enters the field as well to help out as a defender
- both neutral players return to their channel if possession changes

Variation:
- teams must pass to a channel player before they can score
- limit number of touches
- adjust spacing depending on the age and ability of the group

Coaching Points:
constant movement - communication is vital - vision - create supporting angles - speed of play - quick transitions - quick finish

Channel Players # 4

Click Here To View The Drill Animation!
Age Group: (8-11yrs) (12-15yrs) (16-Adult)
Emphasis: possession - passing - attacking - defending
Description:
- all players must stay in their zone
- goalies and defenders must pass the ball to their channel player who crosses it in to the attackers
- channel players cannot be challenged

Variation:
- vary numbers in middle zones (play 3v2, 2v3 etc.)
- limit number of touches for channel players
- if a channel player has the ball allow the channel player in the opposite zone to enter the grid up to the far post
- channel players can be challenged in their zone as soon as they have possession
- adjust spacing depending on the age and ability of the group

Coaching Points:
body mechanics and control of body - body position and balance - eye on ball - quality of preparation touch - contact surface - aggressive and positive mentality - vision and anticipation - placement versus power - positioning to gain an advantage - accurate passing - constant movement - communication is vital - good angle and distance of support to receive ball

Channel Players # 5

Click Here To View The Drill Animation!
Age Group: (8-11yrs) (12-15yrs) (16-Adult)
Emphasis: possession - passing - attacking - defending
Description:
- play 4v4
- players have a maximum of three touches in the middle zone
- unlimited touches in the channel areas
- goals count only if the final pass comes from inside the channel

Variation:
- limited number of touches for players inside channel area
- player inside a channel cannot be challenged
- adjust spacing depending on the age and ability of the group

Coaching Points:
quality of preparation touch - aggressive and positive mentality - vision and anticipation - placement versus power - positioning to gain an advantage - accurate passing - constant movement - communication is vital - good angle and distance of support to receive ball

Channel-Possession # 4

Click Here To View The Drill Animation!
Age Group: (8-11yrs) (12-15yrs) (16-Adult)
Emphasis: possession - passing - attacking - defending
Description:
- teams score by keeping possession and moving through all three zones
- players must pass to switch into the next zone

Variation:
- limit number of touches
- players must play a lofted pass to switch the zone
- adjust spacing depending on the age and ability of the group

Coaching Points:
constant movement - communication is vital - vision - angle, distance and timing of support - speed of play - quick transitions - quick finish

Channel Possession Game # 5

Click Here To View The Drill Animation!
Age Group: (8-11yrs) (12-15yrs) (16-Adult)
Emphasis: possession - passing - defending - attacking
Description:
- grid is divided into six smaller grids as shown
- teams score by keeping possession and moving through four different grids
- players must pass to switch into the next channel

Variation:
- limit number of touches
- players must play a lofted pass to switch the grid
- adjust spacing depending on the age and ability of the group

Coaching Points:
constant movement - angle, distance and timing of support - vision - body position – open to field - decision making - verbal and visual communication - speed of play - accuracy - switch point of attack

Channel Possession Game # 6

Click Here To View The Drill Animation!
Age Group: (8-11yrs) (12-15yrs) (16-Adult)
Emphasis: possession - passing - attacking - defending
Description:
- play 4v4
- each team defends and attacks two mini goals
- players can move around between zones
- ball cannot bounce or be received inside the middle zone
- if the ball bounces or is received by a player inside the middle zone the defending team automatically gets possession
- if a ball is won in one zone and switched into another and a player ends up scoring the goal is awarded three points; all other goals just one point

Variation:
- teams can only score on one of the two mini goals in designated outer channel
- play 5v5, 6v6 etc.
- limit number of touches
- adjust spacing depending on the age and ability of the group

Coaching Points:
angle, distance and timing of support - vision - body position — open to field - decision making - verbal and visual communication - angle, distance and timing of support

Channel Possession Game # 7

Click Here To View The Drill Animation!
Age Group: (8-11yrs) (12-15yrs) (16-Adult)
Emphasis: attacking - defending - possession - passing
Description:
- play 4v4
- each team defends two mini goals and a regular size goal
- players can move around between zones but cannot play the ball from inside the middle zone
- ball cannot bounce or be received inside the middle zone
- if the ball bounces or is received by a player inside the middle zone the defending team automatically gets possession
- if a ball is won in one zone and switched into another and a player ends up scoring the goal is awarded three points; all other goals just one point
- teams can score on the big goals on one-touch from the outer channels

Variation:
- play 5v5, 6v6 etc.
- limit number of touches
- adjust size of field/channel if necessary

Coaching Points:
quick decision making - accurate passing - vision - angle, distance and timing of support - aggressive and positive mentality - vision and anticipation - placement versus power - positioning to gain an advantage

Circle Passing # 1

Click Here To View The Drill Animation!
Age Group: (5-7yrs) (8-11yrs) (12-15yrs) (16-Adult)
Emphasis: passing
Description:
- players pass to teammate across circle as shown
- team that completes most passes within 90 sec. wins

Variation:
- pass giver has to call receiver's name before making a pass
- one team passes in clockwise direction; other team in counterclockwise direction
- each group with two balls
- one touch passing between teammates
- specify how players must pass/receive (left or right foot, inside or
-   outside foot, high or low etc.)
- adjust spacing depending on the age and ability of the group

Coaching Points:
accuracy over power - communication - make eye contact - players should try to develop a rhythm with their passing - good first touch

Circle Passing # 2

Click Here To View The Drill Animation!
Age Group: (8-11yrs) (12-15yrs) (16-Adult)
Emphasis: passing
Description:
- play 8v1 keep away
- one group of 4 in red pinnies and another group of 4 in blue pinnies
- outside players must pass to player from the other team (e.g. red passes to blue and blue passes to red)
- if defender touches the ball he then switches roles with the outside player who touched it last

Variation:
- vary numbers of attackers and defenders
- two touch passing
- one touch passing
- add a second defender
- adjust size of grid if necessary

Coaching Points:
outside players must stay between cones - accuracy over power - communication - make eye contact - good first touch - vision

Circle Passing # 3

Click Here To View The Drill Animation!
Age Group: (8-11yrs) (12-15yrs) (16-Adult)
Emphasis: passing
Description:
- play two 4v1 keep away
- white team plays keep away from one red defender
- red team plays keep away from one blue defender
- unlimited touches to begin
- if defender wins the ball he switches roles with player who touched it last

Variation:
- two touch passing
- one touch passing
- adjust spacing depending on the age and ability of the group

Coaching Points:
outside players must stay between cones - accuracy over power - communication - make eye contact - good first touch - vision

Circle-Passing # 4

Click Here To View The Drill Animation!
Age Group: (8-11yrs) (12-15yrs) (16-Adult)
Emphasis: passing
Description:
- players on the outside play two-touch keep away from a single defender

Variation:
- one-touch passing after 2 minutes
- back to two-touch but now add a defender
- one-touch keep away from 2 defenders
- adjust spacing depending on the age and ability of the group

Coaching Points:
accuracy over power - communication - make eye contact - good first touch

Collective Attack

Click Here To View The Drill Animation!
Age Group: (8-11yrs) (12-15yrs) (16-Adult)
Emphasis: passing - possession - attacking - defending
Description:
- play 5v5
- each team defends and attacks a goal with goalie
- every player on the team in possession must have touched the ball at least once during that possession for that team to be allowed to score

Variation:
- vary number of players that must touch the ball before a team can score (4,3,2 etc.)
- limit number of touches
- adjust spacing depending on the age and ability of the group

Coaching Points:
angle, distance and timing of support - vision - body position – open to field - decision making - verbal and visual communication - speed of play

Combination Play w Cross

Click Here To View The Drill Animation!
Age Group: (8-11yrs) (12-15yrs) (16-Adult)
Emphasis: finishing - passing
Description:
- players pass and shoot on goal in the sequence as shown

Variation:
- specify how players must shoot (left or right foot, inside or laces, high or low etc.)
- add a defender
- limit number of touches
- adjust spacing depending on the age and ability of the group

Coaching Points:
quality of preparation touch - contact surface - aggressive and positive mentality - placement versus power - weight of pass - accuracy of pass

Comeback Game

Click Here To View The Drill Animation!
Age Group: (8-11yrs) (12-15yrs) (16-Adult)
Emphasis: finishing - attacking defending
Description:
- each team defends a goal
- the team which is up by one goal has a maximum of three touches
- if a team is up by two or more goals it can only score off headers and volley shots (first touch goals in general)

Variation:
- limited number of touches only in attacking or defending half
- adjust spacing depending on the age and ability of the group

Coaching Points:
quality of preparation touch - aggressive and positive mentality - vision and anticipation - placement versus power - positioning to gain an advantage

Communication Passing # 1

Click Here To View The Drill Animation!
Age Group: (5-7yrs) (8-11yrs) (12-15yrs) (16-Adult)
Emphasis: passing
Description:
- players dribble inside the grid and pass the ball to another player whose name they call out before the pass is made
- player who receives the ball accelerates into space and then makes a pass

Variation:
- players must turn and run around the nearest cone after completing a pass
- players throw the ball to each other for a warm-up
- players with the ball only make lead passes into space
- specify how players must pass (left foot, right foot, high or low passes etc.)
- adjust spacing depending on the age and ability of the group

Coaching Points:
accuracy - weight of pass - get into line of flight of the ball - communication

Communication Passing # 2

Click Here To View The Drill Animation!
Age Group: (5-7yrs) (8-11yrs) (12-15yrs) (16-Adult)
Emphasis: passing
Description:
- players without a ball call for a lead pass into space as shown

Variation:
- designated group of players with the ball play a 1-2 wall pass with other players to regain the ball - switch roles after 2-3 minutes
- specify how players must pass (left or right foot, inside or outside foot, high or low etc.)
- adjust spacing depending on the age and ability of the group

Coaching Points:
weight of pass - accuracy - vision - first touch - communication

Cone Knock Down # 1

Click Here To View The Drill Animation!
Age Group: (5-7yrs) (8-11yrs) (12-15yrs) (16-Adult)
Emphasis: passing
Description:
- play 4v1
- players on the outside of the grid pass the ball around the defender in the grid in attempt to knock down the cone with a pass
- defender attempts to prevent the cone from being knocked down
- switch defenders often

Variation:
- specify how players must pass (left or right foot, inside or outside foot)
- place a ball on a flat cone as a target instead of using a tall cone
- adjust spacing depending on the age and ability of the group

Coaching Points:
weight of pass - accuracy - disguise - vision - constant movement - communication is vital - good angle of support

Cone Knock Down # 2

Click Here To View The Drill Animation!
Age Group: (5-7yrs) (8-11yrs) (12-15yrs)
Emphasis: finishing - passing
Description:
- each player on one side of the grid has a partner directly opposite
- one player passes the ball towards his partner and tries to knock over a cone in the center grid
- the pass must be made from outside the grid
- players put cones back up once all cones get knocked over
- pair with most points after 4 minutes wins

Variation:
- specify how players must pass (left or right foot, inside or outside foot, high or low etc.)
- adjust spacing depending on the age and ability of the group

Coaching Points:
body mechanics - balance - weight of pass - accuracy

Cone Knock Down 3

Click Here To View The Drill Animation!
Age Group: (5-7yrs) (8-11yrs) (12-15yrs) (16-Adult)
Emphasis: passing - possession - finishing
Description:
- teams try to keep possession and knock down the cones
- team that knocks over the most cones wins the game
- kick-ins only

Variation:
- limit number of touches
- goal scorer must finish on one touch
- add a neutral player
- play 5v5, 6v6 etc.
- adjust spacing depending on the age and ability of the group

Coaching Points:
communication - constant movement - accurate passes - good first touch into space - quick decision making

Cone Knock Down 4

Click Here To View The Drill Animation!
Age Group: (5-7yrs) (8-11yrs) (12-15yrs) (16-Adult)
Emphasis: passing - possession - finishing
Description:
- each team defends the cones at their end of the grid
- teams can score by knocking down one of the cones
- if a cone is knock down it must stay down
- players can shoot only from outside the end zone

Variation:
- play with 2 balls
- limit number of touches
- if a cone is knocked down the scoring team must take that cone and add it to their own line of cones
- goal scorer must finish on one-touch
- teams can knock down cones at both ends of the grid
- adjust size of field and number of tall cones if necessary

Coaching Points:
quick decision making - quick finish - good angle of support - movement on and off the ball - quality of preparation touch - aggressive and positive mentality - vision and anticipation - placement versus power

Cone Knock Down 5

Click Here To View The Drill Animation!
Age Group: (5-7yrs) (8-11yrs) (12-15yrs) (16-Adult)
Emphasis: passing - possession - finishing
Description:
- limit number of touches
- each team defends the cones at their end of the grid
- teams can score by knocking down one of the cones
- if a cone is knock down it must stay down
- players can shoot only from outside the end zone

Variation:
- if a cone is knocked down the scoring team must take that cone and add it to their own line of cones
- goal scorer must finish on one-touch
- teams can knock down cones at both ends of the grid
- adjust size of field and number of tall cones if necessary

Coaching Points:
accurate passes - quick decision making - protect the ball - good angle of support - movement on and off the ball

Cone Knock Down 9

Click Here To View The Drill Animation!
Age Group: (5-7yrs)
Emphasis: dribbling - passing
Description:
- tall cones are randomly placed in playing area
- players dribble and knock down tall cones to get a point
- coaches stand cones back up right away
- player with most points at the end of the game wins

Variation:
- specify how players must pass (left or right foot, inside or outside foot etc.)
- players must perform a specific move and then try to knock down a cone (with their next touch)
- players must shoot/pass the ball with their second touch
- adjust spacing depending on the age and ability of the group

Coaching Points:
vision - close control - soft touch - weight of pass - accuracy - aggressive and positive mentality - placement versus power

Cone Knock Down 10

Click Here To View The Drill Animation!
Age Group: (5-7yrs) (8-11yrs)
Emphasis: passing
Description:
- player passes to knock down cone on opposite side to be awarded a point
- player with most points after 3-4 minutes wins

Variation:
- specify how players must pass (left or right foot, inside or outside foot)
- adjust spacing depending on the age and ability of the group

Coaching Points:
accuracy - weight of pass - body mechanics

Cone Knock Down 11

Click Here To View The Drill Animation!
Age Group: (5-7yrs) (8-11yrs) (12-15yrs)
Emphasis: passing - possession - finishing
Description:
- each team is assigned a specific color cone that they have to try to knock down to score a point (red team - yellow cones & blue team - orange cones)
- each time a cone is knocked down put it back up
- kick-ins only

Variation:
- limit number of touches
- if a cones is knocked down it stays down
- goal scorer must finish on one touch
- add a neutral player who cannot score
- play 5v5, 6v6 etc.
- adjust spacing depending on the age and ability of the group

Coaching Points:
communication - constant movement - accurate passes - good first touch into space - quick decision making

Cone Knock Down Contest

Click Here To View The Drill Animation!
Age Group: (5-7yrs) (8-11yrs)
Emphasis: passing
Description:
- players try to knock down cones to score a point
- passes must be made from outside the grid
- team with the most points wins the game

Variation:
- specify how players must pass (left or right foot, inside or outside foot etc.)
- adjust spacing depending on the age and ability of the group

Coaching Points:
weight of pass - accuracy

Consecutive Passes

Click Here To View The Drill Animation!
Age Group: (5-7yrs) (8-11yrs) (12-15yrs) (16-Adult)
Emphasis: possession - passing
Description:
- play 3v3
- players attempt to keep possession and complete as many passes to their teammates as possible (3 passes = 1 goal)

Variation:
- play 4v4, 5v5 etc.
- 5 passes = 1 goal
- first team to connect 10 passes wins
- specify how players must pass (left or right foot, inside or outside foot, high or low etc.)
- adjust size of grid if necessary

Coaching Points:
angle, distance and timing of support - vision - body position – open to field - decision making - verbal and visual communication - shape of team to maintain possession

Control High Pass 1

Click Here To View The Drill Animation!
Age Group: (12-15yrs) (16-Adult)
Emphasis: finishing - passing - defending
Description:
- one group is attacking and the other defending
- the server of the attacking team makes a lofted pass to the goalie who catches it and throw/punts the ball to the first player of the attacking team
- the attacker then controls the ball and attempts to dribble through the cone goal to finish on goal
- once the attacker receives the ball the defender behind him can start to put pressure on until the attacker dribbles through the cone goal
- after each sequence the attacking and defending roles switch
- keep team score

Variation:
- the server passes directly to the first player of his team
- adjust spacing depending on the age and ability of the group

Coaching Points:
Attacking: seal off defender - quality of preparation touch - contact surface - aggressive and positive mentality - placement versus power
Defending: angle and speed of approach - timing and decision to tackle - control and restraint

Control High Pass 2

Click Here To View The Drill Animation!
Age Group: (8-11yrs) (12-15yrs) (16-Adult)
Emphasis: finishing - passing
Description:
- server makes a lofted pass to the goalie who catches it and throw/punts the ball to the other server who makes a throw-in to the first player in line who dribbles through the cone goal and finishes on goal

Variation:
- add a defender at the cone goal who can only defend the goal line (he can only move sideways)
- adjust spacing depending on the age and ability of the group

Coaching Points:
Attacking: seal off defender - quality of preparation touch - contact surface - aggressive and positive mentality - placement versus power
Defending: angle and speed of approach - timing and decision to tackle - control and restraint

Corridor Game

Click Here To View The Drill Animation!
Age Group: (5-7yrs) (8-11yrs)
Emphasis: dribbling - passing
Description:
- dribblers attempt to get from side to side without getting hit by the passers ball
- 1 or 2 dribblers go simultaneously across the grid to the other side
- next dribbler(s) repeat sequence
- passers focus on making accurate passes to their partner on the opposite side (passers don't try hit dribbler's ball!)

Variation:
- passers aim for the dribbler's ball (one point for each hit - switch roles and compare score to determine winner)
- specify how players must pass/receive (left or right foot, inside or outside foot, high or low etc.)
- specify how players must dribble (left or right foot, inside or outside foot etc.)
- vary number of dribblers/passer
- limit number of touches for passers
- adjust spacing depending on the age and ability of the group if necessary

Coaching Points:
accuracy - weight of pass - head up - protect ball - close control - contact surface of foot - change of speed &direction - protect the ball - vision

Counter Attack 1

Click Here To View The Drill Animation!
Age Group: (8-11yrs) (12-15yrs) (16-Adult)
Emphasis: attacking - defending - finishing - passing
Description:
- each team defends and attacks one goal
- teams play 2v2 in one half and 4v4 in the other half
- one neutral player in each center square
- players must stay in their designated zone
- a defending player must try to pass to a neutral player inside the middle square
- the neutral player then passes to a player from the team in possession into the attacking half
- the neutral player may advance into the attacking half to support the attacking players
- one neutral player always must be in the neutral zone as a supporting player
- neutral players return to their square as soon as the attacking team loses the ball
- switch roles after appr. 10 minutes

Variation:
- allow only the team with four defenders in one half to pass directly to their two attackers (without support by the neutral players)
- allow only the team with two defenders in one half to pass directly to their four attackers (without support by the neutral players)
- limit number of touches
- adjust spacing depending on the age and ability of the group

Coaching Points:
Attacking: angle, distance and timing of support - body position – open to field - decision making - verbal and visual communication - quick finish - quick transitions - support position lateral to ball
Defending: angle and distance of cover - changing role of pressure and cover - visual and verbal communication - positioning to provide cover and balance - intercepting pass - defending vital space (squeeze toward center) - defending space behind - tracking players - quick transitions

Crashing The Box Finishing Activity

Click Here To View The Drill Animation!
Age Group: (8-11yrs) (12-15yrs) (16-Adult)
Emphasis: finishing - passing
Description:
- player A passes to player B who lays it off to player C who then crosses the ball in for player D + E
- repeat sequence from the other side
- players must try to finish on first touch
- players switch position after 3-4 minutes

Variation:
- players F + B can play to either player E or C
- allow player F (B) to enter the grid as a defender
- players must try to finish off headers or volley shots
- adjust spacing depending on the age and ability of the group

Coaching Points:
Attacking: accurate passes - quick finish - aggressive and positive mentality - placement versus power - angle of approach - preparation touch before crossing - quality of cross (weight of cross, speed of cross)
Defending: angle and speed of approach - intercept pass - deny turn - timing and decision to tackle - control and restraint

Crossing # 1

Click Here To View The Drill Animation! **Age Group:** (5-7yrs) (8-11yrs) (12-15yrs) (16-Adult)
Emphasis: passing - attacking - defending
Description:
- play 6v6
- goals are set up diagonally from one another
- goals after a cross count double

Variations:
- goals must come off headers or volleys
- limit number of touches
- adjust size of field if necessary

Coaching Points:
vision and awareness - communication - quick transition - keep balance

Crossing # 2

Click Here To View The Drill Animation!
Age Group: (5-7yrs) (8-11yrs) (12-15yrs) (16-Adult)
Emphasis: passing - finishing
Description:
- play 4v4
- target areas are set up diagonally from one another
- teams score by passing into the square to a target player who must be able to control the pass
- target player switches with pass giver

Variation:
- play 5v5, 6v6 etc.
- teams score if the target player connects to a third teammate with a 1 or 2 touch pass
- players must play a lofted pass to target player
- limit number of touches for field players
- adjust spacing depending on the age and ability of the group

Coaching Points:
first touch - quick transition - aggressive and positive mentality - vision and anticipation - quick decision making - accurate passes

Crossing # 3

Click Here To View The Drill Animation!
Age Group: (12-15yrs) (16-Adult)
Emphasis: passing - possession
Description:
- play 4v4
- target areas are set up diagonally from one another
- each team defends one designated area
- teams score by making a lofted pass over the marked lines into the goalkeeper's hands without a bounce
- goalkeepers must stay in their zone
- goalkeeper feeds the ball back to the team that was scored upon
- teams attempt to prevent the chip by closing and pressing

Variation:
- play 5v5, 6v6 etc.
- teams must connect 4 passes before they can chip the ball to the goalkeeper
- limit number of touches
- adjust spacing depending on the age and ability of the group

Coaching Points:
first touch - quick transition - aggressive and positive mentality - vision and anticipation - quick decision making - accurate passes

Diamond Dribble Pass 1

Click Here To View The Drill Animation!
Age Group: (5-7yrs) (8-11yrs) (12-15yrs)
Emphasis: dribbling - passing
Description:
- players dribble and pass in the sequence as shown
- first player at blue cones start dribbling simultaneously
- next player repeats sequence

Variation:
- specify how players must dribble (inside or outside of foot, left or right foot only etc.)
- change direction
- players perform a move (scissor, step over etc.) in front of the red cone
- adjust spacing depending on the age and ability of the group if necessary

Coaching Points:
timing - agility and balance - change of speed & direction - close control - soft touches - weight of pass - accuracy

Diamond Dribble Pass 2

Click Here To View The Drill Animation!
Age Group: (5-7yrs) (8-11yrs) (12-15yrs)
Emphasis: dribbling - passing
Description:
- players dribble and pass in the sequence as shown
- first player at blue cones start dribbling simultaneously
- next player repeats sequence

Variation:
- specify how players must dribble (inside or outside of foot, left or right foot only etc.)
- change direction
- players perform a move (scissor, step over etc.) in front of the red cone
- adjust spacing depending on the age and ability of the group if necessary

Coaching Points:
timing - agility and balance - change of speed & direction - close control - soft touches - weight of pass - accuracy

Diamond Dribble Pass 3

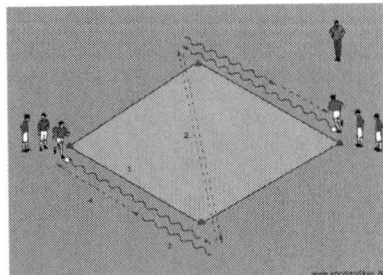

Click Here To View The Drill Animation!
Age Group: (5-7yrs) (8-11yrs) (12-15yrs)
Emphasis: dribbling - passing
Description:
- players dribble and pass in the sequence as shown
- first player at blue cones start dribbling simultaneously
- next player repeats sequence

Variation:
- specify how players must dribble (inside or outside of foot, left or right foot only etc.)
- change direction
- players perform a move (scissor, step over etc.) in front of the red cone
- adjust spacing depending on the age and ability of the group if necessary

Coaching Points:
timing - agility and balance - change of speed & direction - close control - soft touches - weight of pass - accuracy

Diamond Passing Sequence w Shot

Click Here To View The Drill Animation!
Age Group: (8-11yrs) (12-15yrs) (16-Adult)
Emphasis: finishing - passing
Description:
- players pass to each other in the sequence as shown and then take position of the receiver of their pass
- last player to receive a pass has only one touch before he can shoot

Variation:
- same as before just vary sequence of passing
- last player to receive a pass must seek a 1v1 with goalie
- one touch passing
- specify how players must shoot (left or right foot, inside or laces etc.)
- adjust spacing depending on the age and ability of the group

Coaching Points:
accurate passes - first touch - get the shot off as quickly as possible - positive mentality - eye on ball - accuracy before power - try to be deceptive with the shot

1v1 with goalkeeper: if the goalkeeper charges out – slot the ball under him or dribble around him - if the goalkeeper's feet are moving, shoot quickly - identify the goalkeepers starting position

Different Objectives

Click Here To View The Drill Animation!
Age Group: (5-7yrs) (8-11yrs) (12-15yrs) (16-Adult)
Emphasis: dribbling - attacking - defending
Description:
- one team scores by keeping possession for 10 seconds
- if the other team wins possession it can only score by dribbling through the goal farthest away
- switch roles after 5-10 minutes

Variation:
- if the other team wins possession it can only score by dribbling through the goal which is the closest
- one team scores by connecting 5 passes without losing possession
- adjust size of field and/or cone goals if necessary

Coaching Points:
set up defender - change of speed & direction - protect the ball - vision - close control - quality of preparation touch - switch point of attack - angle, distance and timing of support - verbal and visual communication - attack open space - decision making - quick transitions - first touch

Different Objectives 2

Click Here To View The Drill Animation!
Age Group: (8-11yrs) (12-15yrs) (16-Adult)
Emphasis: dribbling - passing - attacking - defending
Description:
- one team scores by keeping possession for 10 seconds
- if the other team wins possession it can only score by dribbling through the goal farthest away
- 2 wall players on side line
- switch roles after 5-10 minutes

Variation:
- if the other team wins possession it can only score by dribbling through the goal which is the closest
- one team scores by connecting 5-7 passes without losing possession
- adjust size of field and/or cone goals if necessary

Coaching Points:
set up defender - change of speed & direction - protect the ball - vision - close control - quality of preparation touch - switch point of attack - angle, distance and timing of support - verbal and visual communication - attack open space - decision making - quick transitions - first touch

Directional Game 4 goals

Click Here To View The Drill Animation!
Age Group: (5-7yrs) (8-11yrs) (12-15yrs) (16-Adult)
Emphasis: dribbling - passing - attacking - defending
Description:
- each team defends and attacks two cone goals
- play 4v4 with one or two subs on each side
- 3 points to dribble through and 1 point to pass it through

Variation:
- play a tournament with three or four teams
- each team defends and attacks two goals on opposite sides
- minimum of two (three) touches
- adjust spacing depending on the age and ability of the group

Coaching Points:
change of direction and speed - deception - set up defender - protect the ball - vision - close control - angle, distance and timing of support - decision making - verbal and visual communication

Dodge Ball

Click Here To View The Drill Animation!
Age Group: (5-7yrs) (8-11yrs) (12-15yrs)
Emphasis: passing - dribbling
Description:
- dribblers dribble inside playing area
- taggers freeze others by throwing and hitting their ball
- player whose ball is hit, picks it up and waits until a teammate unfreezes him by passing the ball through his legs
- switch taggers every 2-4 minutes

Variation:
- vary number of taggers
- player whose ball is hit becomes a tagger as well
- player whose ball is hit switches role with the tagger
- adjust spacing depending on the age and ability of the group

Coaching Points:
accuracy - weight of pass - quick decision making - change of direction and speed - deception - set up defender - protect the ball - vision - close control

Double Gate Passing

Click Here To View The Drill Animation!
Age Group: (5-7yrs) (8-11yrs) (12-15yrs)
Emphasis: passing
Description:
- players pass through one opening and receive the ball through another (as shown)
- 2 touch passing
- pairs move to a different gate after each 1-2 combination

Variation:
- one touch passing
- specify how players must pass (left foot, right foot, receive with one foot and pass with another)
- adjust spacing depending on the age and ability of the group

Coaching Points:
accuracy - weight of pass - close control - first touch

Double Shot

Click Here To View The Drill Animation!
Age Group: (8-11yrs) (12-15yrs) (16-Adult)
Emphasis: finishing - passing
Description:
- players pass and shoot on goal in the sequence as shown
- on the first shooting attempt the player can take a preparatory touch and on the second attempt he must finish one-touch
- switch pass-givers after appr. 5 minutes
- switch sides after appr. 10 minutes

Variation:
- first shot has to be taken with the the inside and the second with the laces
- specify how players must shoot (left or right foot, inside or laces, high or low etc.)
- adjust spacing depending on the age and ability of the group

Coaching Points:
body mechanics and control of body - body position and balance - eye on ball - quality of preparation touch - contact surface - aggressive and positive mentality - placement versus power - first touch - good ball speed

Double Shot 2

Click Here To View The Drill Animation!
Age Group: (5-7yrs) (8-11yrs) (12-15yrs) (16-Adult)
Emphasis: finishing - passing
Description:
- players pass and shoot on goal in the sequence as shown
- the second shot attempt must be one-touch
- switch pass-givers after appr. 5 minutes
- switch sides after appr. 10 minutes

Variation:
- first shot has to be taken with the inside and the second with the laces
- both shots cannot touch the ground
- specify how players must shoot (left or right foot, inside or laces, high or low etc.)
- adjust spacing depending on the age and ability of the group

Coaching Points:
body mechanics and control of body - body position and balance - eye on ball - quality of preparation touch - contact surface - aggressive and positive mentality - placement versus power - first touch - good ball speed

Dribble and Pass

Click Here To View The Drill Animation!
Age Group: (5-7yrs) (8-11yrs)
Emphasis: dribbling - passing
Description:
- players dribble around cone and pass back to next player as shown
- players go to the next corner after their pass

Variation:
- players perform a move in front of middle cone and then make a pass
- players make a self pass towards the middle cone, catch up with it and dribble around the cone and then pass back and move to the next corner
- adjust spacing depending on the age and ability of the group if necessary

Coaching Points:
quick turn - close control - accurate pass to feet - move towards ball when receiving - good first touch - eye contact - weight of pass - accuracy

Dribble and Pass 2

Click Here To View The Drill Animation!
Age Group: (5-7yrs) (8-11yrs)
Emphasis: dribbling - passing
Description:
- players dribble around cones as shown
- players follow their pass

Variation:
- specify how players must dribble (inside or outside of foot, sole, left or right foot only etc.)
- players perform a move in front of middle cone and then make a pass
- players make a self pass towards the middle cone, catch up with it and dribble around the cone and then pass and follow to the next player/cone
- adjust spacing depending on the age and ability of the group if necessary

Coaching Points:
quick turn - close control - accurate pass to feet - move towards ball when receiving - good first touch - eye contact - weight of pass - accuracy

Dribble and Pass 3

Click Here To View The Drill Animation!
Age Group: (5-7yrs) (8-11yrs)
Emphasis: dribbling - passing
Description:
- players dribble to cone and then pass to player of other group whose first touch should take them in the direction he goes
- next player repeats sequence

Variation:
- specify how players must pass/receive (left or right foot, inside or outside foot, high or low etc.)
- zig zag around cones on dribbling side
- adjust spacing depending on the age and ability of the group

Coaching Points:
awareness - communication - close control - weight of pass - accuracy - first touch

Dribble Pass 1

Click Here To View The Drill Animation!
Age Group: (5-7yrs) (8-11yrs)
Emphasis: dribbling - passing
Description:
- players dribble and pass in the sequence as shown
- next player repeats sequence
- run activity for 5-7 rounds

Variation:
- make it competitive (e.g. first group back to its original position wins)
- players must touch the ball a certain number of times (e.g. 40x) before they can pass the ball to the next player
- players must perform a certain number of moves before they can pass the ball to the next player
- specify how players must dribble (left or right foot, inside or outside foot etc.)
- adjust spacing depending on the age and ability of the group

Coaching Points: awareness - close control - accuracy - communication

Dribble Pass 2

Click Here To View The Drill Animation!
Age Group: (5-7yrs) (8-11yrs)
Emphasis: dribbling - passing
Description:
- players dribble zig zag around cones and pass in the sequence as shown
- players follow their pass
- next player repeats sequence
- run activity for 5-7 rounds

Variation:
- make it competitive (e.g. first group back to its original position wins)
- players must touch the ball a certain number of times (e.g. 40x) before they can pass the ball to the next player
- players must perform a certain number of moves before they can pass the ball to the next player
- specify how players must dribble (left or right foot, inside or outside foot etc.)
- adjust spacing depending on the age and ability of the group

Coaching Points: awareness - close control - accuracy - communication

Dribble Triangles

Click Here To View The Drill Animation!
Age Group: (5-7yrs) (8-11yrs) (12-15yrs)
Emphasis: dribbling - passing
Description:
- players dribble inside playing area
- players make a pass to another player inside a triangle who receives the pass and dribbles out of the triangle with speed as shown
- the player inside the triangle cannot dribble the ball out the same side that the pass came through (see graphic)

Variation:
- players inside triangle play a 1-2 pass with the dribbler
- specify how players must pass/receive (left or right foot, inside or outside foot, high or low etc.)
- adjust spacing depending on the age and ability of the group if necessary

Coaching Points: communication - good first touch into space - close control - accuracy - weight of pass

Dribblers and Shooters

Click Here To View The Drill Animation!
Age Group: (5-7yrs) (8-11yrs)
Emphasis: dribbling - passing - finishing
Description:
- one team is the "dribblers" who try to dribble around and prevent their balls from being hit by the "shooters"
- other team, "shooters", try to kick their balls into the "dribblers" balls for a point
- switch roles after 2-3 minutes
- team with most points after two rounds wins

Variation:
- specify how players must dribble (inside or outside of foot, left or right foot only etc.)
- specify how players must pass/shoot (left or right foot, inside or outside foot etc.)
- shooters pass around 1-3 balls and try to hit the dribbler's ball
- shooters can also hit dribblers' legs to score a point (easier)
- adjust spacing depending on the age and ability of the group if necessary

Coaching Points:
no passes/shots above knee level
Dribbling: deception - set up defender - change of speed & direction - protect the ball - vision - close control - soft touch
Passing: weight of pass - accuracy - disguise
Shooting: quality of preparation touch - contact surface - aggressive and positive mentality - vision and anticipation - placement versus power

Dribbling Square 1

Click Here To View The Drill Animation!
Age Group: (5-7yrs) (8-11yrs) (12-15yrs)
Emphasis: dribbling - passing
Description:
- players perform a move before dribbling in and out of middle square
- players then pass to next player on their left
- players must make a pass off their first touch out of the middle square
- all players follow their pass in a clockwise direction

Variation:
- specify how players must pass/receive (left or right foot, inside or outside foot, high or low etc.)
- reverse direction
- players perform a move inside the middle square and then make a pass to next player
- players dribble around 2 cones before making a pass
- play with only three balls and let players choose freely which player to pass it to
- adjust spacing depending on the age and ability of the group if necessary

Coaching Points: close control - good turn - vision - accurate passing - eye contact

Dribbling Warm Up with Final Pass

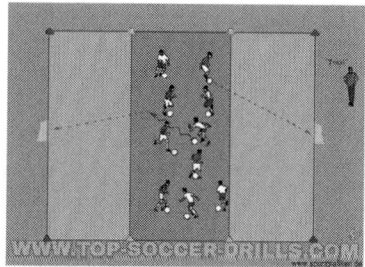

Click Here To View The Drill Animation!
Age Group: (5-7yrs) (8-11yrs) (12-15yrs)
Emphasis: dribbling - passing - finishing
Description:
- each player one both teams is given a number from 1-5
- players dribble inside middle zone
- when coach calls out a number the respective player from each team attempts to pass the ball into either mini goal from within the middle zone
- players can score on the same goal
- first player to score is awarded a point

Variation:
- specify how players must dribble (left or right foot, inside or outside foot etc.)
- specify how players must shoot (left or right foot, inside or laces, high or low etc.)
- players must perform a move before they shoot on target
- players cannot score on the same goal
- players must dribble through cone goals which are positioned on touchline between middle and end zone before they shoot on target off their first touch within end zone
- adjust spacing depending on the age and ability of the group if necessary

Coaching Points: decision making - change of speed & direction - vision - change of direction and speed - close control - eye on ball - quality of preparation touch - aggressive and positive mentality

Dynamic Passing 1

Click Here To View The Drill Animation!
Age Group: (8-11yrs) (12-15yrs) (16-Adult)
Emphasis: passing
Description:
- player at center cone starts with the ball
- players pass to each other in the sequence as shown

Variation:
- reverse direction
- specify how players must pass (left or right foot, inside or outside foot, high or low etc.)
- adjust spacing depending on the age and ability of the group

Coaching Points: weight of pass - accuracy - vision - first touch

Dynamic Passing 2

Click Here To View The Drill Animation!
Age Group: (5-7yrs) (8-11yrs) (12-15yrs) (16-Adult)
Emphasis: passing
Description:
- players pass to each other in the sequence as shown

Variation:
- reverse direction
- specify how players must pass/receive (left or right foot, inside or outside foot, high or low etc.)
- adjust spacing depending on the age and ability of the group

Coaching Points: body mechanics - balance - weight of pass - accuracy - first touch

Dynamic Passing 3

Click Here To View The Drill Animation!
Age Group: (8-11yrs) (12-15yrs) (16-Adult)
Emphasis: passing
Description:
- players make a square
- players start off passing to each other while standing
- next step: players pass to each other while moving as a group and maintaining a square shape

Variation:
- add a second ball
- vary number of players
- adjust spacing depending on the age and ability of the group

Coaching Points: make sure players go in all directions (sideways, backwards etc.) - players must keep same distance to each other when moving - vision - first touch - communication - accuracy

Dynamic Passing 4

Click Here To View The Drill Animation!
Age Group: (5-7yrs) (8-11yrs) (12-15yrs) (16-Adult)
Emphasis: passing
Description:
- players pass two balls around into same direction as shown

Variation:
- one touch passing
- vary number of players
- reverse direction
- specify how players must pass (left or right foot, inside or outside foot, high or low etc.)
- adjust spacing depending on the age and ability of the group

Coaching Points: awareness - first touch into space - make eye contact - accuracy over power - players should try to develop a rhythm with their passing

Dynamic Passing 5

Click Here To View The Drill Animation!
Age Group: (5-7yrs) (8-11yrs) (12-15yrs)
Emphasis: passing
Description:
- players pass diagonally to their partner as shown
- pair to complete most passes within 90 seconds wins

Variation:
- one touch passing
- specify how players must pass (left or right foot, inside or outside foot, high or low etc.)
- adjust spacing depending on the age and ability of the group

Coaching Points: awareness - make eye contact - accuracy over power - players should try to develop a rhythm with their passing

Everybody Is It

Click Here To View The Drill Animation!
Age Group: (5-7yrs) (8-11yrs) (12-15yrs)
Emphasis: dribbling - passing
Description:
- players attempt to pass their ball against another player's ball to be awarded a point
- if a player's ball is hit then this player must dribble around grid before he can come back to rejoin the game
- players must keep score

Variation:
- players try to pass their ball against another player's legs (below the knee) to be awarded a point
- specify how players must pass (left or right foot, inside or outside foot etc.)
- adjust spacing depending on the age and ability of the group

Coaching Points: keep ball on the ground - stay within bounds - keep ball rolling - change direction and speed - keep ball close to feet - fake passes - shielding

Everybody Is It 2

Click Here To View The Drill Animation!
Age Group: (5-7yrs) (8-11yrs) (12-15yrs)
Emphasis: dribbling - passing
Description:
- players attempt to shoot their ball against another player's ball
- if a player's ball is hit then this player must leave the grid and practice juggling until the end of the game
- last player inside the grid wins

Variation:
- players try to shoot their ball against another player's legs (below the knee)
- specify how players must pass (left or right foot, inside or outside foot etc.)
- adjust spacing depending on the age and ability of the group

Coaching Points: keep ball on the ground - stay within bounds - keep ball rolling - change direction and speed - keep ball close to feet - fake passes - shielding

Everybody Is It 3

Click Here To View The Drill Animation!
Age Group: (5-7yrs) (8-11yrs) (12-15yrs)
Emphasis: dribbling - passing
Description:
- players attempt to pass their ball against another player's ball to be awarded a point
- if a player's ball is hit then this player must dribble around grid before he can come back to rejoin the game
- players must keep score

Variation:
- players try to pass their ball against another player's legs (below the knee) to be awarded a point
- specify how players must pass (left or right foot, inside or outside foot etc.)
- adjust spacing depending on the age and ability of the group if necessary

Coaching Points: keep ball on the ground - stay within bounds - keep ball rolling - change direction and speed - keep ball close to feet - fake passes - shielding

Fast Transitions

Click Here To View The Drill Animation!
Age Group: (8-11yrs) (12-15yrs) (16-Adult)
Emphasis: passing - attacking - defending
Description:
- team stays on that passed into end zone they attack
- team then defends against the team (white-blue) which received the pass
- team (white) is off and goes into end zone they were defending

Variation:
- limit number of touches
- play 4v4 or 5v5 etc.
- adjust spacing depending on the age and ability of the group

Coaching Points: communication - constant movement - keep possession - fast transition from offense to defense - quick decision making

Final Pass

Click Here To View The Drill Animation!
Age Group: (8-11yrs) (12-15yrs) (16-Adult)
Emphasis: attacking - defending - passing
Description:
- each team defends and attacks a goal with goalie
- a goal is awarded three points if the last pass before a goal splits the defenders
- kick-ins only

Variation:
- limit number of touches
- adjust spacing depending on the age and ability of the group

Coaching Points: angle, distance and timing of support - vision - body position – open to field - decision making - verbal and visual communication - first touch - communication - quick decision making

Finishing Combination Play 1

Click Here To View The Drill Animation!
Age Group: (8-11yrs) (12-15yrs) (16-Adult)
Emphasis: finishing - passing
Description:
players pass and finish on goal in the sequence as shown
repeat sequence from the other side
Variation:
- shooter replaces one player in the center
- specify how players must shoot (left or right foot, inside or laces, high or low etc.)
- players must finish by dribbling around the goalie
- adjust spacing depending on the age and ability of the group

Coaching Points: accurate passes - quality of preparation touch - contact surface - aggressive and positive mentality - placement versus power

Finishing Combination Play 2

Click Here To View The Drill Animation!
Age Group: (8-11yrs) (12-15yrs) (16-Adult)
Emphasis: finishing - passing
Description:
- players pass and finish on goal in the sequence as shown
- repeat sequence from the other side

Variation:
- player who crosses the ball in replaces the player who finishes on goal
- players must finish on goal off headers or volley shots
- adjust spacing depending on the age and ability of the group

Coaching Points: accurate passes - aggressive and positive mentality - placement versus power - angle of approach - preparation touch before crossing - quality of cross (weight of cross, speed of cross)

Finishing Game 1

Click Here To View The Drill Animation!
Age Group: (8-11yrs) (12-15yrs) (16-Adult)
Emphasis: finishing - passing
Description:
- play 7v5 plus goalie
- attacking team defends a goal without a goalie and the defending team one with a goalie
- defending team can score only with first touch shots from inside the attacking half

Variation:
- play 6v4, 9v7 etc.
- limit number of touches for attackers
- adjust spacing depending on the age and ability of the group

Coaching Points:
Attacking: aggressive and positive mentality - vision and anticipation - placement versus power - positioning to gain an advantage - unbalancing the defense - create space for others - attack space behind defense
Defending: angle and distance of cover - tracking – recovery runs - changing role of pressure and cover - visual and verbal communication - positioning to provide cover and balance - intercepting pass - defending vital space – squeeze toward center (compactness-concentration) - defending space behind - tracking players

Finishing Game 5

Click Here To View The Drill Animation!
Age Group: (8-11yrs) (12-15yrs) (16-Adult)
Emphasis: finishing - attacking - defending
Description:
- play 4v4
- players must attempt to make a pass into the end zone to a teammate who is making a run to receive and finish on goal
- defenders and attackers can only enter the zone once the pass was made into the end zone

Variation:
- play 5v5, 6v6, 7v7 etc.
- defender can follow into end zone after attacker's first touch
- adjust spacing depending on the age and ability of the group

Coaching Points:
body mechanics and control of body - body position and balance - eye on ball - quality of preparation touch - contact surface - aggressive and positive mentality - vision and anticipation - placement versus power - positioning to gain an advantage

Finishing Game w Neutral Wall Players

Click Here To View The Drill Animation!
Age Group: (8-11yrs) (12-15yrs) (16-Adult)
Emphasis: finishing - passing
Description:
- play 4v4 with three neutral wall players around the grid
- 2 points awarded for a goal if the final pass came from a wall player
- wall players must play two touch

Variation:
- wall players must play one touch
- goals only count if they come off headers or volley shots
- adjust spacing depending on the age and ability of the group

Coaching Points:
body mechanics and control of body - body position and balance - eye on ball - quality of preparation touch - contact surface - aggressive and positive mentality - vision and anticipation - placement versus power - positioning to gain an advantage

Finishing w Time Limit

Click Here To View The Drill Animation!
Age Group: (5-7yrs) (8-11yrs) (12-15yrs) (16-Adult)
Emphasis: finishing - possession - passing - attacking - defending
Description:
- play 5v5
- one attacking team and one defending team
- attacking team can score on both goals
- defending team attempts to keep possession for as long as possible
- after each goal the attacking team must cross the middle line before it can score again
- teams switch roles after 6-8 minutes
- team with most goals after 2 rounds wins

Variation:
- play with mini goals
- play 6v4, 7v5, 8v6 etc. (attacking team with numbers up)
- the defending team scores by connecting 6 passes
- adjust spacing depending on the age and ability of the group

Coaching Points:
quality of preparation touch - aggressive and positive mentality - vision and anticipation - placement versus power - positioning to gain an advantage - angle, distance and timing of support - body position – open to field - decision making - verbal and visual communication - shape of team to maintain possession - quick finish

Flank Players In Zone

Click Here To View The Drill Animation!
Age Group: (8-11yrs) (12-15yrs) (16-Adult)
Emphasis: possession - passing - attacking - defending
Description:
- each team defends a goal
- each team has two attacking players in designated areas
- defenders cannot enter designated area until flank player receives the ball
- flank players can leave area only with the ball and must return if team loses possession
- teams must utilize flank players in designated area before they can score

Variation:
- limit number of touches for flank players
- goals off a cross by a flank player count double
- adjust spacing depending on the age and ability of the group

Coaching Points:
accurate passes - quick decision making - protect the ball - good angle of support - movement on and off the ball

Forward Passes 1

Click Here To View The Drill Animation!
Age Group: (8-11yrs) (12-15yrs) (16-Adult)
Emphasis: passing - finishing - attacking - defending
Description:
- teams play 3v3 in each end zone
- each teams defends an end zone with 2 mini goals
- teams score by passing the ball to a teammate in the attacking zone who then attempts by utilizing his teammates to score on either mini goal
- switch roles every 4-5 minutes

Variation:
- defenders must make a lofted pass to teammates in attacking zone
- limit number of touches for attackers and/or defenders
- adjust spacing depending on the age and ability of the group

Coaching Points:
angle, distance and timing of support - vision - decision making - verbal and visual communication - spread out attack - quick finish - first touch takes ball away from pressure

Forward Passes 2

Click Here To View The Drill Animation!
Age Group: (8-11yrs) (12-15yrs) (16-Adult)
Emphasis: passing - finishing - attacking - defending
Description:
- teams play 3v3 in each end zone
- each teams defends an end zone with 2 mini goals
- teams score by passing the ball to a teammate in the attacking zone who then attempts to score by utilizing his teammates
- switch roles every 4-5 minutes

Variation:
- defenders must make a lofted pass to teammates in attacking zone
- limit number of touches for attackers and/or defenders
- adjust spacing depending on the age and ability of the group

Coaching Points:
angle, distance and timing of support - vision - body position - decision making - verbal and visual communication - spread out attack - quick finish - first touch takes ball away from pressure - support position lateral to ball

Forward Passes 3

Click Here To View The Drill Animation!
Age Group: (8-11yrs) (12-15yrs) (16-Adult)
Emphasis: passing - finishing - attacking - defending
Description:
- teams play 3v2 in each end zone
- teams score by passing the ball to a teammate in the attacking zone who then attempts to score by utilizing his teammates
- switch roles every 4-5 minutes

Variation:
- defenders must make a lofted pass to teammates in attacking zone
- limit number of touches for attackers and/or defenders
- adjust spacing depending on the age and ability of the group

Coaching Points:
angle, distance and timing of support - vision - body position - decision making - verbal and visual communication - spread out attack - quick finish - first touch takes ball away from pressure
 - support position lateral to ball

Four Grid Keep Away

Click Here To View The Drill Animation!
Age Group: (8-11yrs) (12-15yrs) (16-Adult)
Emphasis: possession - passing
Description:
- play 3v2
- grid is divided into four smaller grids as shown
- attackers score by splitting the defenders (passing between the defenders)
- defenders become attackers if they win the ball 7 times

Variation:
- defenders become attackers if they win the ball and then connect one pass 7 times
- play 4v2, 5v2, 3v1 etc.
- limit number of touches
- adjust spacing depending on the age and ability of the group

Coaching Points:
communication - create supporting angles - play the way you face and away from pressure - vision - body position – open to field - decision making

Four Grid Keep Away 2

Click Here To View The Drill Animation!
Age Group: (8-11yrs) (12-15yrs) (16-Adult)
Emphasis: possession - passing
Description:
- play 3v2
- grid is divided into four smaller grids as shown
- attackers score by making one-touch passes
- players switch roles after 4-5 minutes

Variation:
- play 4v2, 5v2 etc.
- limit number of touches
- attackers score if they all touch the ball one after the other
- attackers score a point for each 1-2 combination
- adjust spacing depending on the age and ability of the group

Coaching Points:
communication - create supporting angles - play the way you face and away from pressure - vision - body position – open to field - decision making

Game Changer

Click Here To View The Drill Animation!
Age Group: (5-7yrs) (8-11yrs) (12-15yrs) (16-Adult)
Emphasis: dribbling - attacking - defending
Description:
- each team is assigned one side line (with cone goals) and one reg. goal to defend
- teams start by playing on goals with goalies only
- on coach's command teams continue game on cone goals only
- coach changes direction of play every 3-4 min.
- switch goalkeepers if necessary

Variation:
- teams defend reg. goal and cone goals simultaneously
- adjust size and/or number of cone goals
- add a neutral player who cannot score
- adjust spacing depending on the age and ability of the group if necessary

Coaching Points:
quick finish on goal - quick transition - angle, distance and timing of support - decision making - verbal and visual communication - deception - set up defender - change of speed & direction - protect the ball - vision - close control

Game Mix

Click Here To View The Drill Animation!
Age Group: (5-7yrs) (8-11yrs) (12-15yrs) (16-Adult)
Emphasis: finishing - passing - attacking - defending
Description:
- play 5v5, 6v6, 7v7 etc.
- coach calls out which game to play
- for game no.1 and no.2 players pass to each other by throwing the ball with their hands
- Game1: teams score if a player heads the ball back to the pass-giver (to a third player)
- possession changes if the ball is dropped or the other team intercepts the pass
- player with the ball can only take two steps
- younger age groups are not allowed to wrestle for the ball
- Game2:
- teams score by heading/volleying the ball into the goal
- each team defends a goal
- possession changes if the ball is dropped or the other team intercepts the pass
- player with the ball can only take two steps
- no self passes allowed
- younger age groups are not allowed to wrestle for the ball
- Game3:
- teams play one touch soccer with each team defending a goal (no more handball!)
- Game4: goals only count if the goalscorer touched the ball with his heel

Variation:
- adjust spacing depending on the age and ability of the group

Coaching Points:
quick adjustment to new rules - body mechanics and control of body - body position and balance - contact surface - aggressive and positive mentality - vision and anticipation - placement versus power - positioning to gain an advantage - angle, distance and timing of support - decision making - verbal and visual communication

Game Of Silence

Click Here To View The Drill Animation!
Age Group: (5-7yrs) (8-11yrs) (12-15yrs) (16-Adult)
Emphasis: passing - attacking - defending - possession
Description:
- play 6v6
- teams must connect 2-3 passes before they can score
- players cannot make a sound nor clap with their hands etc. (absolute silence!)
- visual signs are allowed
- if the rule is broken the opposing team is automatically awarded a free-kick

Variations:
- play 4v4, 5v5 etc.
- limit number of touches
- adjust spacing depending on the age and ability of the group

Coaching Points:
vision and awareness - communication - concentration

Game Of Volleys

Click Here To View The Drill Animation!
Age Group: (8-11yrs) (12-15yrs) (16-Adult)
Emphasis: finishing - possession - passing
Description:
- each team defends and attacks one goal
- players can only take two steps with the ball in their hands
- players pass the ball by volleying to their teammates
- players cannot wrestle for the ball
- team is awarded 2 points if a goal is scored without catching the ball first

Variation:
- teams lose possession if the ball hits the ground, goes out of bounce or is intercepted
- adjust spacing depending on the age and ability of the group

Coaching Points:
weight of pass - accuracy - angle, distance and timing of support - vision - body position (open to field) - decision making - verbal and visual communication - quality of preparation touch - contact surface - aggressive and positive mentality - vision and anticipation - placement versus power - positioning to gain an advantage

Game Speed 1

Click Here To View The Drill Animation!
Age Group: (5-7yrs) (8-11yrs) (12-15yrs) (16-Adult)
Emphasis: possession - passing
Description:
- play 5v5
- teams score only on one-touch passes
- kick-ins only

Variation:
- play 6v6, 7v7 etc.
- each 1-2 combination is awarded one point
- first team to connect 8 passes wins
- adjust spacing depending on the age and ability of the group

Coaching Points:
angle, distance and timing of support - vision - body position – open to field - decision making - verbal and visual communication - shape of team to maintain possession

Gate Passing

Age Group: (5-7yrs) (8-11yrs) (12-15yrs) (16-Adult)
Emphasis: passing
Description:
- players attempt to pass through gates to their partner
- two defenders (red) try to intercept passes
- if ball is won by a defender he gives it right back
- players can't score on same gate twice in a row
- pair to make 15 passes first wins

Variation:
- add defender(s)
- players must make 2 (3) passes through a gate to score before moving on to another gate
- pair to make most passes within 90 sec. wins
- adjust spacing depending on the age and ability of the group

Coaching Points:
weight of pass - accuracy - vision - constant movement

Gate Passing SSG 2

Click Here To View The Drill Animation!
Age Group: (5-7yrs) (8-11yrs) (12-15yrs) (16-Adult)
Emphasis: passing - possession
Description:
- 6 attackers versus 3 defenders
- attackers score by passing through goal to a teammate
- attackers cannot score on same goal twice in a row
- defenders score my connecting two passes
- switch roles if attackers have 8 points or defender 4 points

Variation:
- attackers score by making two passes through the same goal
- limit number of touches for attackers
- play 5v3, 5v2, 4v2, 6v4 etc.
- adjust spacing depending on the age and ability of the group

Coaching Points:
weight of pass - accuracy - vision - constant movement - players should accelerate towards the ball - good angle and distance of support to receive ball

Gate Race

Click Here To View The Drill Animation!
Age Group: (5-7yrs) (8-11yrs) (12-15yrs)
Emphasis: dribbling - ball control
Description:
- each group is assigned to a grid
- one player from each group dribbles through all the cone goals
- last group to have all players dribble through all cone goals does 20 push ups

Variation:
- specify how players must dribble (inside or outside of foot, sole, left or right foot only etc.)
- 2-3 players from each group dribble through cone at the same time
- players perform a specific move on each goal line
- players make self pass through each gate
- adjust spacing depending on the age and ability of the group

Coaching Points:
close control of ball - head up - good turns - agility and balance - change of speed & direction

Gate Race 2

Click Here To View The Drill Animation!
Age Group: (5-7yrs) (8-11yrs) (12-15yrs)
Emphasis: dribbling
Description:
- players count the number of goals that they dribble through in 45 sec.
- players attempt to increase that number on future attempts

Variation:
specify how players must dribble (inside or outside of foot, left or
 right foot only etc.)
players with most points after 3-4 rounds wins
players dribble through and around goals in a figure eight to be
 awarded a point
players dribble around both cones of a goal to be awarded a point
players perform a specific move in front of each goal to be awarded
 a point
adjust spacing depending on the age and ability of the group if necessary
Coaching Points:
awareness - change of speed & direction - explosiveness - close control

Get Coach

Click Here To View The Drill Animation!
Age Group: (5-7yrs) (8-11yrs)
Emphasis: dribbling - passing
Description:
- coach/assistant/parent/player moves around the area with his legs open
- players dribble towards the coach and try to shoot through his legs
- players must receive their own pass to earn a point

Variation:
- 2 players/coaches holding on to a pinnie and present a goal through which players have to pass
- in pairs, players pass through the coach's legs to their partner
- specify how players must pass (left or right foot, inside or outside foot etc.)
- parents or assistant coaches present additional targets
- adjust spacing depending on the age and ability of the group

Coaching Points:
head up - weight of pass - accuracy - change of speed & direction - vision - close control

Get past the defender 1

Click Here To View The Drill Animation!
Age Group: (5-7yrs) (8-11yrs) (12-15yrs)
Emphasis: dribbling
Description:
- the defender in the middle is restricted to move from side to side only on the middle line trying to stop the dribbling attacker
- once the attacker is past the defender the next player from the opposite side repeats the sequence
- the attacker is awarded a point if he gets past the defender without having the defender touch the ball
- the attacker with the most points wins
- switch defenders every 2-3 minutes

Variation:
- add another line on which a second defender can only move from side to side also
- the attacker has to dribble through a zone with a defender which is 3-6 yds deep
- adjust spacing depending on the age and ability of the group

Coaching Points:
close control - deception - set up defender - change of speed & direction - protect the ball

Get past the defender 2

Click Here To View The Drill Animation!
Age Group: (5-7yrs) (8-11yrs) (12-15yrs) (16-Adult)
Emphasis: dribbling - defending
Description:
- players dribble from the starting point with the ball to first area and try to get past the defender into the save zone
- next the player must now take on the second defender
- switch defenders after 2-3 minutes

Variation:
- start activity with passive defenders as a warm up
- the defender is restricted to move from side to side only trying to stop the dribbling attacker
- adjust spacing depending on the age and ability of the group

Coaching Points:
Attacking: deception - set up defender - change of speed & direction - protect the ball
Defending: close down - angle and speed of approach - body shape, balance, and foot positioning - control and restraint - delay and channel

Goal Kick Game

Click Here To View The Drill Animation!
Age Group: (8-11yrs) (12-15yrs) (16-Adult)
Emphasis: finishing - passing - possession
Description:
- players pass by shooting the ball from their hands (goal kick style) to their teammates
- the teammate then receives the ball in the air and catches it without allowing it to bounce or possession changes automatically
- teams can score by shooting on goal without allowing it to bounce
- the player with the ball can make two steps only

Variation:
- players can only score off headers or volley shots
- adjust spacing depending on the age and ability of the group

Coaching Points:
angle, distance and timing of support - vision - decision making - verbal and visual communication quality of preparation touch - aggressive and positive mentality - anticipation - placement versus power - positioning to gain an advantage

Goal Numbers

Click Here To View The Drill Animation!
Age Group: (5-7yrs) (8-11yrs) (12-15yrs) (16-Adult)
Emphasis: finishing - passing - possession
Description:
- play 4v4
- each goal is assigned a number
- coach calls out a number and players can only score on the goal with the respective number

Variation:
- play 3v3, 5v5, 6v6 etc.
- use mini goals instead of cone goals
- limit number of touches
- coach calls out two (three) numbers
- adjust spacing depending on the age and ability of the group

Coaching Points:
quality of preparation touch - contact surface - aggressive and positive mentality - vision and anticipation - placement versus power - positioning to gain an advantage - angle, distance and timing of support - vision - body position – open to field - decision making - verbal and visual communication

Goal Numbers 2

Click Here To View The Drill Animation!
Age Group: (5-7yrs) (8-11yrs) (12-15yrs)
Emphasis: finishing
Description:
- each goal is assigned a number
- coach calls out two goals to which the first player has to dribble through and then finish on goal

Variation:
- specify how players must shoot (left or right foot, inside or laces, high or low etc.)
- players have to perform a move at each goal
- coach (or another player) calls out three numbers
- adjust spacing depending on the age and ability of the group

Coaching Points:
body mechanics and control of body - body position and balance - eye on ball - quality of preparation touch - contact surface - aggressive and positive mentality - placement versus power - close control

Goalie Center Square

Click Here To View The Drill Animation!
Age Group: (8-11yrs) (12-15yrs) (16-Adult)
Emphasis: possession - passing
Description:
- teams score by making a lofted pass to the goalkeeper who must catch the ball out of the air for the point to count
- goalkeeper must stay inside target zone
- players cannot run through target zone

Variation:
- limit number of touches
- adjust spacing depending on the age and ability of the group

Coaching Points:
angle, distance and timing of support - vision - decision making - verbal and visual communication - accuracy - weight of pass

Goalkeeper Passing

Click Here To View The Drill Animation!
Age Group: (8-11yrs) (12-15yrs) (16-Adult)
Emphasis: possession - passing - goalkeeping
Description:
- teams score by making a pass to the goalie who picks the ball up
- goalie gives it back to the team that scored last

Variation:
- vary number of goalies
- teams score only by making a high pass that is caught out of the air by the goalie
- adjust spacing depending on the age and ability of the group

Coaching Points:
angle, distance and timing of support - vision - body position – open to field - decision making - verbal and visual communication

Grid Possession Game

Click Here To View The Drill Animation!
Age Group: (8-11yrs) (12-15yrs) (16-Adult)
Emphasis: passing - possession
Description:
- teams try to keep possession
- teams score by connecting 7 passes in a row
- players must stay in their designated grid

Variation:
- each player has five seconds to play the ball
- no verbal communication allowed
- limit number of touches
- adjust spacing depending on the age and ability of the group

Coaching Points:
angle, distance and timing of support - vision - body position – open to field - decision making - verbal and visual communication - good first touch takes ball away from pressure

Grid Possession Game 2

Click Here To View The Drill Animation!
Age Group: (8-11yrs) (12-15yrs) (16-Adult)
Emphasis: passing - possession
Description:
- each team passes two balls around the entire grid
- teams have to make sure that both balls don't end up in the same grid
- players must stay in their designated grid
- team to keep it going the longest without making an error wins

Variation:
- each player has three seconds to play the ball
- add a third ball for each team
- limit number of touches
- adjust spacing depending on the age and ability of the group

Coaching Points:
angle, distance and timing of support - vision - body position – open to field - decision making - verbal and visual communication - good first touch takes ball away from pressure

Grid Possession Game 3

Click Here To View The Drill Animation!
Age Group: (8-11yrs) (12-15yrs) (16-Adult)
Emphasis: passing - possession
Description:
- one neutral target player on each side of the grid
- teams score by passing to one target player and then to the other without losing possession
- players must stay in their designated grid

Variation:
- each player has five seconds to play the ball
- no verbal communication allowed
- limit number of touches
- adjust spacing depending on the age and ability of the group

Coaching Points:
angle, distance and timing of support - vision - body position – open to field - decision making - verbal and visual communication - good first touch takes ball away from pressure

Group Tag

Click Here To View The Drill Animation!
Age Group: (5-7yrs) (8-11yrs) (12-15yrs) (16-Adult)
Emphasis: dribbling - passing
Description:
- one player from each team carries a ball trying tag a player from the other team
- once a player is tagged the tagger passes (throws, volleys etc.) the ball to a teammate who then becomes the tagger
- team that has all players apply a tag first wins

Variation:
- specify how players must run (backwards, sideways, hop on one leg etc.)
- adjust size of grid depending on the age and ability of the group

Coaching Points:
deception - setting up defender - change of speed & direction - close control - vision

Handball 1

Click Here To View The Drill Animation!
Age Group: (5-7yrs) (8-11yrs) (12-15yrs) (16-Adult)
Emphasis: passing - attacking - defending
Description:
- each team defends and attacks one end zone
- players pass by throwing
- teams score by passing the ball to a teammate who makes a run the opponent's end zone (he cannot wait inside the end zone)
- players cannot take more than two steps with the ball
- possessions switches when the ball is dropped, a pass intercepted, a player takes too many steps or goal is scored
- players may not wrestle the ball from an opponent

Variation:
- set time limit for player with the ball to get rid of it (i.e. 3 seconds)
- players by volleying / drop kicking
- adjust spacing depending on the age and ability of the group if necessary

Coaching Points:
angle, distance and timing of support - vision - body position — open to field - decision making - verbal and visual communication - accuracy

Handball 2

Click Here To View The Drill Animation!
Age Group: (5-7yrs) (8-11yrs) (12-15yrs) (16-Adult)
Emphasis: passing - attacking - defending
Description:
- players throw the ball to their teammates and attempt make three consecutive passes to be awarded a point
- players cannot take more than two steps with the ball
- possessions switches when the ball is dropped, a pass intercepted, a player takes too many steps or goal is scored
- players cannot take more than two steps with the ball
- players may not wrestle the ball from an opponent

Variation:
- vary number of passes to be awarded a point
- players can only catch and throw the ball with one hand
- adjust spacing depending on the age and ability of the group

Coaching Points:
angle, distance and timing of support - vision - body position - open to field - decision making - verbal and visual communication - accuracy

Handball 3

Click Here To View The Drill Animation!
Age Group: (5-7yrs) (8-11yrs) (12-15yrs) (16-Adult)
Emphasis: passing - attacking - defending
Description:
- each team defends and attacks one goal
- players pass by throwing
- players cannot take more than two steps with the ball
- possession changes if the ball is dropped, the other team intercepts the pass, a player takes more than two steps or a goal is scored
- players may not wrestle the ball from an opponent
- goal is scored by throwing it into opponent's goal

Variation:
- goal can be only scored by volleying or heading it into the goal (self pass is allowed)
- players can only catch and throw the ball with one hand
- play with goalies
- adjust spacing depending on the age and ability of the group

Coaching Points:
angle, distance and timing of support - vision - body position - open to field - decision making - verbal and visual communication - accuracy

Handball Tag

Click Here To View The Drill Animation!
Age Group: (5-7yrs) (8-11yrs) (12-15yrs) (16-Adult)
Emphasis: passing - dribbling
Description:
- if runner gets tagged he becomes the tagger / picks up tagger's pinnie
- runner is save if he has a ball in his hands
- runners can throw the ball around to save each other

Variation:
- same game as before but all players dribble a ball
- adjust size of field and/or number of taggers/balls if necessary

Coaching Points:
communication - vision

Handball Tag 2

Click Here To View The Drill Animation!
Age Group: (5-7yrs) (8-11yrs) (12-15yrs) (16-Adult)
Emphasis: passing
Description:
- players move inside the area without a ball
- two taggers carry a ball with their hands
- tagger holding the ball can tag the closest player
- tagger with the ball cannot take more than 2 steps
- if tagged, players become one of the taggers
- last two players standing become the taggers for the next round

Variation:
- taggers pass by volleying the ball
- adjust spacing depending on the age and ability of the group

Coaching Points:
angle, distance and timing of support - vision - decision making - verbal and visual communication

Heading Warm Up

Click Here To View The Drill Animation!
Age Group: (8-11yrs) (12-15yrs) (16-Adult)
Emphasis: heading - passing - possession
Description:
- teams score if a player heads the ball back to the pass giver
- possession changes if the ball is dropped or the other team intercepts the pass

Variation:
- player must head the ball to another player (not the pass giver) in order to score
- adjust spacing depending on the age and ability of the group

Coaching Points:
angle, distance and timing of support - vision - decision making - verbal and visual communication

Hit The Gate

Click Here To View The Drill Animation!
Age Group: (5-7yrs) (8-11yrs) (12-15yrs)
Emphasis: passing
Description:
- players are awarded a point if the ball goes through the goal
- player that scores 10 points first wins

Variation:
- specify how players must pass (left foot, right foot, high or low etc.)
- adjust spacing depending on the age and ability of the group

Coaching Points:
body mechanics - balance - weight of pass - accuracy - focus

In The Open Space

Click Here To View The Drill Animation!
Age Group: (8-11yrs) (12-15yrs) (16-Adult)
Emphasis: possession - passing - defending
Description:
- play 4v4
- grid is divided into four smaller grids as shown
- teams score by passing to a teammate who runs into an open grid to receive the pass
- players cannot wait inside a grid to receive the pass

Variation:
- play 5v3, 4v2, 6v3 etc.
- limit number of touches
- multiple 1v1s (players can only defend a designated player and cannot tackle another attacker)
- adjust spacing depending on the age and ability of the group

Coaching Points:
communication - create supporting angles - vision - body position – open to field - decision making

In the Open Space 2

Click Here To View The Drill Animation!
Age Group: (8-11yrs) (12-15yrs) (16-Adult)
Emphasis: possession - passing
Description:
- play 4v4
- grid is divided into four smaller grids as shown
- teams score by making a pass to a teammate who is in a different grid than the passer

Variation:
- play 4v2, 5v2, 6v3 etc.
- limit number of touches
- multiple 1v1s (players can only defend a designated player and cannot tackle another attacker)
- teams score by making a lofted pass to a teammate who is in a different grid than the passer
- adjust size of field if necessary

Coaching Points:
communication - create supporting angles - vision - body position – open to field - decision making

In the Open Space 3

Click Here To View The Drill Animation!
Age Group: (8-11yrs) (12-15yrs) (16-Adult)
Emphasis: possession - passing
Description:
- play 4v4
- grid is divided into four smaller grids as shown
- teams score by making a pass to a teammate who is in a different grid diagonally than the passer

Variation:
- play 4v2, 5v2, 6v3 etc.
- limit number of touches
- teams score by making a lofted pass to a teammate who is in a different grid diagonally than the passer
- multiple 1v1s (players can only defend a designated player and cannot tackle another attacker)
- adjust spacing depending on the age and ability of the group

Coaching Points:
communication - create supporting angles - vision - body position – open to field - decision making

In the Open Space 4

Click Here To View The Drill Animation!
Age Group: (8-11yrs) (12-15yrs) (16-Adult)
Emphasis: possession - passing
Description:
- play 4v4
- grid is divided into four smaller grids as shown
- teams score by connecting three passes and then making a pass to a teammate who is in a different grid than the passer

Variation:
- play 5v5, 6v6, 4v2, 5v2, 6v3 etc.
- limit number of touches
- multiple 1v1s (players can only defend a designated player and cannot tackle another attacker)
- teams score by connecting three passes and then making a lofted pass to a teammate who is in a different grid than the passer
- adjust spacing depending on the age and ability of the group

Coaching Points:
communication - create supporting angles - vision - body position – open to field - decision making

Keep Away

Click Here To View The Drill Animation!
Age Group: (5-7yrs) (8-11yrs) (12-15yrs) (16-Adult)
Emphasis: possession - passing
Description:
- attackers attempt to keep ball away from defender by passing
- if the ball goes out of bounce or is won by the defender last attacker to have touched the ball switches role with defender

Variation:
- 5v2, 5v3, 4v2, 3v1
- if defender allows a certain number of (one-touch) passes or nutmeg he is to stay in the middle one extra round
- limited number of touches
- adjust spacing depending on the age and ability of the group

Coaching Points:
constant movement - angle, distance and timing of support - vision - body position – open to field - decision making - verbal and visual communication

Keep Away in 2 Grids

Click Here To View The Drill Animation!
Age Group: (8-11yrs) (12-15yrs) (16-Adult)
Emphasis: possession - passing
Description:
- players in red keep the ball away from the two white players inside the grid
- if defenders win the ball, they pass it to the other grid, join their teammates and play 4v2 against two red players in that grid

Variation:
- limit number of touches
- play 5v2, 5v3 etc.
- adjust spacing depending on the age and ability of the group

Coaching Points:
vision - communication - quick decision making - constant movement - first touch - create supporting angles

Keep Away w Supporting Player

Click Here To View The Drill Animation!
Age Group: (8-11yrs) (12-15yrs) (16-Adult)
Emphasis: dribbling - passing
Description:
- all attackers except for one dribble a ball
- defender attempts to win the ball
- attackers keep the ball away from the defender and have the option to pass to the attacker who doesn't have a ball
- if the defender wins the ball, he switches roles with the attacker who made the mistake

Variation:
- play with 2 attackers who don't have a ball
- play with 2 defenders
- adjust spacing depending on the age and ability of the group if necessary

Coaching Points:
angle, distance and timing of support - decision making - verbal and visual communication - vision - awareness - change of direction and speed - deception - set up defender - protect the ball - close control

Keep Away w Transition

Click Here To View The Drill Animation!
Age Group: (8-11yrs) (12-15yrs) (16-Adult)
Emphasis: passing - possession
Description:
- 5 attackers versus 2 defenders
- attackers try to make lofted passes to a target player at the opposite end of the grid as shown
- attackers must complete 5 passes before passing to target player on opposite end to be awarded a point
- once the ball is controlled by the target player all attackers and defenders must move into the other half of the playing area where the game resumes
- rotate defenders often

Variation:
- limit number of touches
- play 4v2, 5v3, 6v3 etc.
- adjust spacing depending on the age and ability of the group

Coaching Points:
vision - communication - quick decision making - constant movement - first touch - create supporting angles

Key Possession

Click Here To View The Drill Animation!
Age Group: (5-7yrs) (8-11yrs) (12-15yrs) (16-Adult)
Emphasis: possession - passing
Description:
- each team defends and attacks a goal
- teams must complete 5 passes before they can score

Variation:
- teams must connect 3 one-touch passes before they can score
- teams must play a 1-2 combination before they can score
- add a neutral player
- adjust size of field if necessary

Coaching Points:
angle, distance and timing of support - vision - body position – open to field - decision making - verbal and visual communication - first touch

Key Possession 2

Click Here To View The Drill Animation!
Age Group: (5-7yrs) (8-11yrs) (12-15yrs) (16-Adult)
Emphasis: possession - passing
Description:
- each team defends and attacks a goal
- each player of a team must touch the ball once before the team is allowed to score
- if ball goes out of bounce goalkeeper always restarts play

Variation:
- vary number of players that must touch the ball before scoring
- adjust spacing depending on the age and ability of the group

Coaching Points:
angle, distance and timing of support - vision - body position – open to field - decision making - verbal and visual communication - first touch

King of the Castle

Click Here To View The Drill Animation!
Age Group: (8-11yrs) (12-15yrs) (16-Adult)
Emphasis: passing - possession
Description:
- teams try to keep possession by throwing the ball to each other
- each team has a designated target player (blue shorts - red shirt)
- teams score one point by connecting 7 passes without losing possession and two points if the team's target receives a pass
- players are allowed to take two or fewer steps with the ball
- change of possession is when a pass is intercepted, ball drops to ground or players takes too many steps
- players cannot wrestle the ball from opponent
- rotate target players

Variation:
- play with 2 or 3 balls simultaneously
- players pass the ball with their feet
- players pass the ball by volleying (drop kicking) it to each other
- passer must call out the receiver's name before making a pass
- teams score only by passing to the target player
- adjust spacing depending on the age and ability of the group if necessary

Coaching Point:
angle, distance and timing of support - vision - decision making - verbal and visual communication - weight of pass - accuracy - disguise - first touch - protect the king

King Target Player

Click Here To View The Drill Animation!
Age Group: (5-7yrs) (8-11yrs) (12-15yrs) (16-Adult)
Emphasis: possession - passing
Description:
- each team has one designated "King" who carries a ball in his hand
- teams score by having their "King" receive a pass from a teammate
- switch target players every 3-5 minutes

Variation:
- teams score by playing a 'give and go' combination with the designated target player
- each team has two designated players that are the "Kings"
- adjust spacing depending on the age and ability of the group

Coaching Points:
constant movement - angle, distance and timing of support - vision - body position – open to field - decision making - verbal and visual communication

Knock Off 1

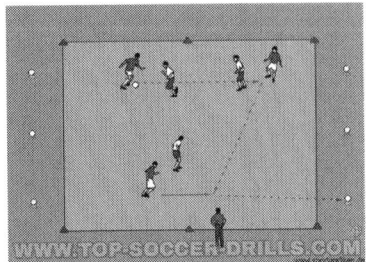

Click Here To View The Drill Animation!
Age Group: (5-7yrs) (8-11yrs) (12-15yrs) (16-Adult)
Emphasis: passing - finishing - attacking - defending
Description:
- 3v3
- each team defends and attacks a line of balls
- players attempt to keep possession and knock down balls which are placed on flat cones as shown
- players can only score from inside the opponent's half

Variation:
- teams can knock off balls on both sides of the field
- balls placed on all four sides of grid
- adjust spacing depending on the age and ability of the group

Coaching Points:
constant movement - communication - angle, distance and timing of support - first touch - quick decision making - aggressive and positive mentality - vision and anticipation - placement versus power

Knock Off 2

Click Here To View The Drill Animation!
Age Group: (5-7yrs) (8-11yrs) (12-15yrs) (16-Adult)
Emphasis: passing - finishing - attacking - defending
Description:
- 3v3
- teams score by knocking off balls which are placed on flat cones inside playing area

Variation:
- add a third or fourth ball as a target
- adjust spacing depending on the age and ability of the group

Coaching Points:
players should accelerate towards the ball - constant movement - communication is vital - good angle and distance of support to receive ball - first touch - quick decision making - accuracy over power

Knock Out 1

Click Here To View The Drill Animation!
Age Group: (5-7yrs) (8-11yrs) (12-15yrs) (16-Adult)
Emphasis: dribbling - ball control
Description:
- players dribble inside the playing area
- taggers carry the ball with their hands and attempt to knock everybody's ball out of the grid
- if a player's ball gets kicked out, he stays out of the game and dribbles around the grid until the round is over
- switch taggers after each round
- fastest group of taggers wins

Variation:
- specify how players must dribble (inside or outside of foot, sole, left or right foot only etc.)
- vary number of taggers
- players who are out of the game practice juggling
- taggers must try to throw their ball and hit the other player's ball- adjust spacing depending on the age and ability of the group

Coaching Points:
agility and balance - deception - setting up defender - change of speed & direction - protecting the ball

Knock Out 2

Click Here To View The Drill Animation!
Age Group: (5-7yrs) (8-11yrs) (12-15yrs) (16-Adult)
Emphasis: dribbling
Description:
- on coach's command two players knock their own balls out of the grid and attempt to knock out everybody else's ball for 30 seconds
- switch pair of taggers each round
- the pair with the most points wins

Variation:
- vary number of taggers
- taggers must carry their balls
- mark off a save zone for dribblers to be in for 5 seconds max
- adjust spacing depending on the age and ability of the group

Coaching Points:
agility and balance - deception - set up defender - change of speed & direction - protect the ball - vision - close control

Knock Out 3

Click Here To View The Drill Animation!
Age Group: (5-7yrs) (8-11yrs) (12-15yrs) (16-Adult)
Emphasis: dribbling - passing
Description:
- players dribble inside the playing area
- on coach's command all players attempt to knock out everybody else's ball while protecting their own ball
- if a player's ball gets kicked out of the grid, he retrieves the ball and dribbles around the grid or performs any other task (like juggling etc.)
- last player with a ball inside the grid wins

Variation:
- specify how players must dribble (inside or outside of foot, left or right foot only etc.)
- specify how players must pass, shoot (left or right foot, inside or outside foot etc.)
- adjust spacing depending on the age and ability of the group

Coaching Points:
agility and balance - contact surface of foot - deception - change of speed & direction - protect the ball - weight of pass - accuracy

Lay Off Shooting 2

Click Here To View The Drill Animation!
Age Group: (8-11yrs) (12-15yrs) (16-Adult)
Emphasis: finishing - passing
Description:
- pass and shoot sequence as shown
- first pass can be to either side - left or right
- lay off must pass to other side beyond coach/assistant who is in the middle
- players has only one or two touches before getting a shot off
- players have to get a shot off inside blue shooting zone

Variation:
- players are allowed to go for a rebound
- player has to shoot on first touch
- specify how players must pass to player on the side (high or low etc.)
- adjust spacing depending on the age and ability of the group

Coaching Points:
get the shot off as quickly as possible - aggressive and positive mentality - eye on ball - accuracy before power - try to be deceptive with the shot - don't switch off – recover as soon as you shoot

Lay Off Shooting 3

Click Here To View The Drill Animation!
Age Group: (8-11yrs) (12-15yrs) (16-Adult)
Emphasis: finishing - passing
Description:
- pass and shoot sequence as shown
- first pass always goes to the middle player who decides to pass it to
- lay off must to other side beyond the player in the middle as shown
- players has only one or two touches before getting a shot off
- players have to get a shot off inside blue shooting zone

Variation:
- players are allowed to go for a rebound
- player has to shoot on first touch
- specify how players must pass to player in the middle (high or low etc.)
- adjust spacing depending on the age and ability of the group

Coaching Points:
aggressive and positive mentality - eye on ball - accuracy over power - quality of preparation touch - quick finish

Lofted Passes

Click Here To View The Drill Animation!
Age Group: (8-11yrs) (12-15yrs) (16-Adult)
Emphasis: passing
Description:
- players make lofted passes to the other grid
- players must strike the ball moving

Variation:
- specify how players must pass/receive (left or right foot, inside, laces
-   or outside foot etc.)
- play with multiple players within the grid
- adjust spacing depending on the age and ability of the group

Coaching Points:
communication - constant movement - accuracy - first touch

Lofted Passes Over No-Go Zone

Click Here To View The Drill Animation!
Age Group: (8-11yrs) (12-15yrs) (16-Adult)
Emphasis: passing
Description:
- players make lofted pass to each other over the middle zone in the sequence as shown (two-touch)
- players must stay in their designated zones
- one point for a player if the ball doesn't bounce inside the no-go zone

Variation:
- one-touch passing
- specify how players must pass/receive (left or right foot, inside or outside foot etc.)
- adjust spacing depending on the age and ability of the group

Coaching Points:
body mechanics - balance - accuracy - weight of pass

Lofted Passes To Targets

Click Here To View The Drill Animation!
Age Group: (8-11yrs) (12-15yrs) (16-Adult)
Emphasis: possession - passing
Description:
- play 4v4
- teams score by making a lofted pass over the middle zone to their target player who controls the ball (ball cannot bounce in the middle zone!)
- no players allowed in the middle (dark) zones

Variation:
- play 3v3, 4v4 etc.
- teams must complete one pass in the middle zone before they pass to the target
- limit number of touches
- adjust spacing depending on the age and ability of the group

Coaching Points:
vision - good first touch - constant movement - accuracy - angle, distance and timing of support - decision making - verbal and visual communication

Making Runs

Click Here To View The Drill Animation!
Age Group: (8-11yrs) (12-15yrs) (16-Adult)
Emphasis: passing - possession
Description:
- teams score by making a pass through a goal and a teammate making a run to receive the ball as shown
- player must run around goal to receive the ball
- scoring team restarts play from goal that was just scored on
- team cannot score on same goal twice in a row

Variation:
- player is allowed to run through goal to receive pass
- limited number of touches
- adjust spacing depending on the age and ability of the group

Coaching Points:
weight of pass - accuracy - angle, distance and timing of support - vision - body position – open to field - decision making - verbal and visual communication

Middle Target Zone 1

Click Here To View The Drill Animation!
Age Group: (8-11yrs) (12-15yrs) (16-Adult)
Emphasis: finishing - passing - possession - attacking - defending
Description:
- each team defends and attacks a goal
- all players must stay out of middle zone until attacking player who makes a run into zone receives a pass from a teammate
- players cannot pass through middle zone into attacking zone

Variation:
- attacking players only have two touches
- adjust spacing depending on the age and ability of the group

Coaching Points:
quick finish - lead passes into space - vision - time your runs - communication - constant movement - angles of support to receive ball

Middle Target Zone 2

Click Here To View The Drill Animation!
Age Group: (8-11yrs) (12-15yrs) (16-Adult)
Emphasis: passing - possession
Description:
- 4 attackers vs. 2 defenders
- attackers attempt to keep possession and combine with target player as often as possible
- defenders cannot enter the target zone
- switch roles after 4-5 minutes or if defenders intercept 5 passes

Variation:
- defenders and attackers cannot enter the target zone
- limit number of touches for attacker and/or target player
- vary number of attackers and defenders (6v3, 5v3, 5v2 etc.)
- target player inside middle target zone acts as a neutral player
- adjust spacing depending on the age and ability of the group

Coaching Points:
constant movement - angle, distance and timing of support - vision - body position – open to field - decision making - verbal and visual communication

Middle Target Zone 5v3

Click Here To View The Drill Animation!
Age Group: (8-11yrs) (12-15yrs) (16-Adult)
Emphasis: passing - possession
Description:
- attacking team scores by passing to target player who controls the ball
- defenders cannot enter the target zone
- switch roles after 4-5 minutes or if defenders intercept 5 passes

Variation:
- attacking team scores by passing to the target player who
-   passes the ball to a third player
- limit number of touches for attacker and/or target player
- vary number of attackers and defenders (6v3, 5v3, 5v2 etc.)
- adjust spacing depending on the age and ability of the group

Coaching Points:
constant movement on and off the ball - angle, distance and timing of support - vision - body position – open to field - decision making - verbal and visual communication

Middle Target Zones

Click Here To View The Drill Animation!
Age Group: (8-11yrs) (12-15yrs) (16-Adult)
Emphasis: finishing - passing - attacking - defending
Description:
- each team defends and attacks a goal with goalie
- players stay in their designated half
- teams must pass to neutral player in target zone
- neutral player then moves into attacking zone to create numbers-up situation (4v3) as shown
- switch roles regularly

Variation:
- vary number of neutral players and target zones
- attacking players only have two touches
- adjust spacing depending on the age and ability of the group

Coaching Points:
quick finish - communication - first touch - vision - constant movement - angles of support to receive ball

Middle Third Transition

Click Here To View The Drill Animation!
Age Group: (5-7yrs) (8-11yrs) (12-15yrs) (16-Adult)
Emphasis: passing - possession - attacking - defending
Description:
- each team defends and attacks a goal
- players can move ball into next zone only by passing it to a teammate

Variation:
- 2 touches max. in defending and attacking third (free play in middle zone)
- adjust spacing depending on the age and ability of the group

Coaching Points:
vision - constant movement - angles of support to receive ball - good ball movement

Middle Zone Crossing

Click Here To View The Drill Animation!
Age Group: (5-7yrs) (8-11yrs) (12-15yrs)
Emphasis: passing
Description:
- play with four balls
- players in outer zones attempt to pass through middle zone
- if a player/ defender prevents the ball from going into another zone his team is awarded a point switch roles after 3-5 minutes
- team with most points wins

Variation:
- team inside middle zone is awarded a point if a ball leaves the grid
- specify how players must pass (left foot, right foot, high or low etc.)
- adjust size of field and/or number of balls/players if necessary

Coaching Points:
weight of pass - accuracy - vision - selection of pass & timing of pass

Moveable Goal 1

Click Here To View The Drill Animation!
Age Group: (5-7yrs) (8-11yrs)
Emphasis: dribbling - passing
Description:
- target players hold a pinnie between them and move around the grid
- players dribble and try to score by passing between target players
- rotate target players
- player to score most goals within 90 seconds wins

Variation:
- add one or two defenders
- no point is awarded once the ball leaves the grid after a pass
- attackers have only one or two balls which they have pass to each other and between targets to score a point
- adjust spacing depending on the age and ability of the group if necessary

Coaching Points:
vision - head up - close control - soft touches - move away from pressure - target players always keep same distance - accuracy - weight of pass

Moveable Goal 2

Click Here To View The Drill Animation!
Age Group: (5-7yrs) (8-11yrs) (12-15yrs)
Emphasis: dribbling - passing
Description:
- target players hold a pinnie between them and move around the grid
- players dribble and try to score by passing between target players from opposing team
- rotate target players
- team to score most goals within 90 seconds wins

Variation:
- add one or two defenders
- no point is awarded once the ball leaves the grid after a pass
- attackers have only one or two balls which they have pass to each other and between targets to score a point
- adjust spacing depending on the age and ability of the group if necessary

Coaching Points:
vision - head up - close control - soft touches - move away from pressure - target players always keep same distance - accuracy - weight of pass

Moveable Goal 3

Click Here To View The Drill Animation!
Age Group: (5-7yrs) (8-11yrs) (12-15yrs)
Emphasis: dribbling - passing
Description:
- target players from each team hold on to pinnie and move around inside playing area
- each team tries to score by passing between target players from opposing team
- team to score most goals within 5 minutes wins

Variation:
- each team has a designated defender who only tries to win the ball from the player from the opposing team (he cannot block the goal)
- adjust spacing depending on the age and ability of the group if necessary

Coaching Points:
head up - close control - soft touch - move away from pressure - target players always keep same distance - accuracy - weight of pass - angle, distance and timing of support - vision - decision making - verbal and visual communication

Moveable Goal 4

Click Here To View The Drill Animation!
Age Group: (5-7yrs) (8-11yrs) (12-15yrs) (16-Adult)
Emphasis: passing - possession
Description:
- neutral target players hold a pinnie between them and move around the grid
- teams score by passing through the moveable goal to a teammate who controls the ball
- rotate target players

Variation:
- limit number of touches
- adjust spacing depending on the age and ability of the group

Coaching Points:
constant movement - communication - vision - accurate passes

Moveable Goal 5

Click Here To View The Drill Animation!
Age Group: (5-7yrs) (8-11yrs)
Emphasis: dribbling - passing
Description:
- players dribble inside playing area
- coaches or players hold hands or a pinnie between them, forming a goal
- players try to pass their ball through the goal (moving target)
- players must receive their own pass to earn a point
- player with most points wins

Variation:
- specify how players must dribble (left or right foot, inside or outside foot etc.)
- specify how players must pass (left or right foot, inside or outside foot etc.)
- coach determines speed of targets (slow, medium, fast etc.)
- in pairs, players pass through the goal to their partner to earn a point
- vary number of targets (switch roles)
- adjust spacing depending on the age and ability of the group if necessary

Coaching Points:
head up - weight of pass - accuracy - change of speed & direction - vision - close control

Multiple 1v1 Plus 4

Click Here To View The Drill Animation!
Age Group: (8-11yrs) (12-15yrs) (16-Adult)
Emphasis: passing - possession
Description:
- 4 pairs inside the grid
- 4 neutral players around the grid
- each pair plays a separate 1v1 inside the grid
- players inside the grid score by passing to a neutral player who doesn't have a ball
- once a goal is scored only the passer/goalscorer can run to receive a new ball from another neutral player who has ball as shown
- switch roles after appr. 2 minutes

Variation:
- vary number of pairs inside the grid
- vary number of neutral players around the grid
- adjust spacing depending on the age and ability of the group

Coaching Points:
disguise - vision - first touch away from pressure - communication - quick decision making - accuracy over power

Multiple 1v1 Plus 4 Vol.2

Click Here To View The Drill Animation!
Age Group: (8-11yrs) (12-15yrs) (16-Adult)
Emphasis: passing
Description:
- servers with the ball positioned around the grid
- one player from each team pairs up with a player from the other team
- each pair plays a separate 1v1 inside the grid
- one team are designated defenders and the other team designated attackers
- attackers score by receiving a pass and playing it back to the server without losing possession

Variation:
- attackers must play one touch
- attackers must take the ball to a different target player
- adjust spacing depending on the age and ability of the group

Coaching Points:
disguise - vision - first touch away from pressure - verbal and visual communication - quick decision making - accuracy over power - explosiveness

Multiple 1v1 Plus 4+4

Click Here To View The Drill Animation!
Age Group: (8-11yrs) (12-15yrs) (16-Adult)
Emphasis: passing - possession
Description:
- 4 pairs inside the grid
- 4 players from each team around the grid as shown
- 2-3 target players outside the grid also have balls
- each pair plays a separate 1v1 inside the grid
- players inside the grid score by passing to a target player who doesn't have a ball
- once a goal is scored only the passer/goalscorer can run to receive a new ball from another target player as shown
- switch roles after appr. 2 minutes

Variation:
- vary number of pairs inside the grid
- vary number of target players with a ball
- adjust spacing depending on the age and ability of the group

Coaching Points:
disguise - vision - first touch - communication - quick decision making - accuracy over power

Multiple 1v1s With Neutrals

Click Here To View The Drill Animation!
Age Group: (8-11yrs) (12-15yrs) (16-Adult)
Emphasis: passing - dribbling - finishing - attacking - defending
Description:
- player with ball attempts to make a wall pass or any other combination with the neutral player before finishing on any goal
- after each finish pairs switch with another waiting at the sideline

Variation:
- limited touches for neutral players
- adjust size of field and number of pairs/neutral players if necessary

Coaching Points:
accuracy - quick decision making - quick finish - protect the ball - good angle of support - movement on and off the ball

Multiple Grids

Click Here To View The Drill Animation!
Age Group: (12-15yrs) (16-Adult)
Emphasis: passing
Description:
- one player from each team in a grid
- each team passes two balls around the grid with two-touches making sure that both balls don't end up in the same grid

Variation:
- one-touch passing only
- adjust spacing depending on the age and ability of the group

Coaching Points:
vision - first touch - communication - quick decision making - accuracy over power

Multiple Grids 2

Click Here To View The Drill Animation!
Age Group: (8-11yrs) (12-15yrs) (16-Adult)
Emphasis: passing
Description:
- 2 neutral players in middle grid
- one player from each team in all other grids
- each team passes a ball two-touch around the grid making sure that
- two balls don't end up in the same grid

Variation:
- one-touch passing only
- adjust spacing depending on the age and ability of the group

Coaching Points:
vision - first touch - communication - quick decision making - accuracy over power

Multitasking

Click Here To View The Drill Animation!
Age Group: (8-11yrs) (12-15yrs) (16-Adult)
Emphasis dribbling - passing
Description:
- players of one team dribble inside playing area
- players of the other team around the grid as shown
- players on the outside throw the ball to a dribbling player who receives and passes it back while keeping his own ball close
- players cannot go to the same outside player twice in a row
- players must accelerate into space for three touches after their pass back to the outside player

Variation:
- vary distribution by outside player (high/low throw, high/low pass)
- inside players must call outside player's name for a pass
- inside players catch the ball and then throw it back to the outside player
- inside players head/volley/drop kick it back to outside player
- inside players don't have to dribble a ball
- adjust spacing depending on the age and ability of the group if necessary

Coaching Points:
communication - vision - awareness - close control - contact surface of foot - change of direction and speed - weight of pass - accuracy - first touch

Neutral Channel Players

Click Here To View The Drill Animation!
Age Group: (8-11yrs) (12-15yrs) (16-Adult)
Emphasis: passing - possession - finishing - attacking - defending
Description:
- neutral channel player must stay inside designated area until he receives the ball
- neutral channel players can only be challenged if they have the ball
- goals off a cross count 2 points
- switch channel players regularly

Variation:
- channel player without the ball can enter the field to support the team in possession once the player in the other channel receives the ball
- only one team can utilize channel players
- adjust spacing depending on the age and ability of the group

Coaching Points:
constant movement - communication is vital - good angle and distance of support to receive ball - create supporting angles - look to combine - keep the ball moving with quick accurate passing

Neutral Wing Players

Click Here To View The Drill Animation!
Age Group: (5-7yrs) (8-11yrs) (12-15yrs) (16-Adult)
Emphasis: dribbling - passing - attacking - defending
Description:
- each team defends and attacks one goal
- each team has two neutral players on the side line
- neutrals on the side line help the team that has possession
- neutrals cannot be challenged unless they dribble into the grid
- neutrals must return to their side line after a shot on goal or if the team in possession loses the ball

Variation:
- maximum of three (two) touches for neutrals
- adjust spacing depending on the age and ability of the group if necessary

Coaching Points:
create space for others - attack space behind defense - supporting angle and distance to ball - support position behind ball - support position in advance of the ball - support position lateral to ball - combination play (1-2, double pass, overlap, take over)

No Go Zone 1

Click Here To View The Drill Animation!
Age Group: (5-7yrs) (8-11yrs) (12-15yrs) (16-Adult)
Emphasis: possession - passing - attacking - defending
Description:
- players cannot pass, dribble nor move through square in middle
- no high passes over square

Variation:
- allow passes on the ground (in the air) to go through the square
- adjust spacing depending on the age and ability of the group

Coaching Points:
accurate passes - quick decision making - good angle of support - movement on and off the ball - quick transitions

No Go Zone 2

Click Here To View The Drill Animation!
Age Group: (8-11yrs) (12-15yrs) (16-Adult)
Emphasis: attacking - defending - possession - passing
Description:
- teams must pass to neutral player inside middle zone before they can score

Variation:
- limited touches for neutral player in middle zone
- adjust spacing depending on the age and ability of the group

Coaching Points:
accurate passes - quick decision making - good angle of support - vision - quick transitions

No Go Zone 3

Click Here To View The Drill Animation!
Age Group: (8-11yrs) (12-15yrs) (16-Adult)
Emphasis: attacking - defending - possession - passing
Description:
- teams must pass to neutral player inside middle zone before they can score

Variation:
- limited touches for neutral player in middle zone
- adjust spacing depending on the age and ability of the group

Coaching Points:
accurate passes - quick decision making - good angle of support - vision - quick transitions

No Go Zone 4

Click Here To View The Drill Animation!
Age Group: (5-7yrs) (8-11yrs) (12-15yrs) (16-Adult)
Emphasis: attacking - defending - passing - finishing
Description:
- play 4v4
- each team defends and attacks a mini goal
- players must be in the attacking half and outside the no-go zone in order to score for their team

Variation:
- limit number of touches
- the ball can't bounce in the no-go zone (lofted passes only)
- teams must connect 3 passes before they can score
- adjust spacing depending on the age and ability of the group

Coaching Points:
quick finish - vision - communication - constant movement - angles of support to receive ball

Numbers Game

Click Here To View The Drill Animation!
Age Group: (5-7yrs) (8-11yrs) (12-15yrs)
Emphasis: dribbling - attacking - defending
Description:
- each team lines up on own goal line
- each player on each team is assigned a number (1-4)
- when coach calls out a number the player with that number runs into the grid to compete for a ball being distributed by the coach
- both players play 1v1 and try to score in the opponents' mini goal

Variation:
- team that last conceded a goal gets to have one more player on the grid than the opponent to make it a 2v1 situation
- one teammate of the player that wins the ball distributed by the coach enters the grid to make it a 2v1 situation
- call out more than just one number to create a 2v2, 3v3s, 4v4s etc.
- adjust spacing depending on the age and ability of the group if necessary

Coaching Points:
vision - change of speed & direction - close control - communication - set up defender

Numbers Passing

Click Here To View The Drill Animation!
Age Group: (5-7yrs) (8-11yrs) (12-15yrs) (16-Adult)
Emphasis: passing
Description:
- each player from both teams is assigned a number from 1-5
- players pass to their teammate in a sequence (1-2, 2-3, 3-4, 4-5, 5-1 etc.)
- team that is making the most passes within 90 sec. wins
- two touch passing

Variation:
- players must run around the nearest cone after completing a pass
- reverse sequence (5-4, 4-3, 3-2 etc.)
- limit number of touches
- add a second ball for each team
- adjust spacing depending on the age and ability of the group

Coaching Points:
weight of pass - accuracy - vision - timing of pass - teams move around grid constantly - importance of first touch to control and prepare ball

Numbers Up Dribble Game

Click Here To View The Drill Animation!
Age Group: (5-7yrs) (8-11yrs) (12-15yrs) (16-Adult)
Emphasis: dribbling - transition
Description:
- 4-6 attackers versus 1-3 defenders
- attackers attempt to dribble through as many goals as possible
- defenders try to win the ball and prevent attackers from dribbling through goals by keeping possession
- attackers cannot go through same goal twice in a row
- goals can scored from both sides
- players switch roles after 2-3 minutes

Variation:
- attackers must pass to three different players before they can score
- attackers must take three touches before they can score
- attackers score by passing through a goal to another attacker
- adjust spacing depending on the age and ability of the group

Coaching Points:
Attacking: deception - set up defender - change of speed & direction - protect the ball - vision - close control - angle, distance and timing of support - decision making - verbal and visual communication - quick transitions
Defending: angle and distance of cover - tracking (recovery runs) - changing role of pressure and cover - visual and verbal communication

Numbers Up Game

Click Here To View The Drill Animation!
Age Group: (5-7yrs) (8-11yrs) (12-15yrs) (16-Adult)
Emphasis: finishing - attacking - defending
Description:
- play 4v4 without steady goalies
- one designated player on the defending team becomes the goalie who can only block shots with his feet

Variation:
- two players on the defending team become the goalies
- limit number of touches
- adjust spacing depending on the age and ability of the group

Coaching Points:
quality of preparation touch - aggressive and positive mentality - vision and anticipation - placement versus power - positioning to gain an advantage - quick finish - quick transition - create space for others - attack space behind defense

Numbers Up Scrimmage

Click Here To View The Drill Animation!
Age Group: (5-7yrs) (8-11yrs) (12-15yrs) (16-Adult)
Emphasis: dribbling - attacking - defending
Description:
- teams play 4v4 on the larger grid and 1v1 on the smaller grid
- if a player dribbles across opponent's end line in the 1v1 he is allowed to join his team on the larger grid (5v4)

Variation:
- player must stop his ball dead on opponent's end line on smaller grid
- if a player dribbles across end line in the 1v1 he switches with a teammate from the larger grid
- limit number of touches for team with more players on the field
- team with more players must connect 4 passes before they can score

Coaching Points:
change of direction and speed - deception - set up defender - protect the ball - vision - close control - angle, distance and timing of support - decision making - verbal and visual communication

Numbers Up w Restrictions

Click Here To View The Drill Animation!
Age Group: (5-7yrs) (8-11yrs) (12-15yrs) (16-Adult)
Emphasis: dribbling - passing - attacking - defending
Description:
- each teams defends and attacks one goal with goalie
- team with 5 players has unlimited touches
- team with 6 players must have minimum of 2-3 touches
- switch roles after 5 minutes

Variation:
- play 4v3, 5v3, 7v6, 8v7 etc.
- adjust spacing depending on the age and ability of the group if necessary

Coaching Points:
change of direction and speed - deception - set up defender - vision - close control - quick finish - decision making - verbal and visual communication - angle, distance and timing of support

One Goal Plus Target Zones

Click Here To View The Drill Animation!
Age Group: (8-11yrs) (12-15yrs) (16-Adult)
Emphasis: passing - finishing - attacking - defending
Description:
- defenders defend goal with goalkeeper
- attackers' objective is to score on big goal
- defenders try to counterattack by passing to a teammate who is inside one of the target zones
- switch roles after 5-10 minutes

Variation:
- direction of play changes each time defenders score by passing to a teammate who is inside one of the target areas
- add a player to the attacking team (5v4)
- add neutral player
- adjust spacing depending on the age and ability of the group

Coaching Points:
angle, distance and timing of support - vision - body position – open to field - decision making - verbal and visual communication - spread out - quick finish - switch point of attack

One Touch Passing In Triangle

Click Here To View The Drill Animation!
Age Group: (5-7yrs) (8-11yrs) (12-15yrs)
Emphasis: passing
Description:
- players pass to each other as shown
- players cannot pass through same side twice in a row

Variation:
- limit number of touches
- adjust spacing depending on the age and ability of the group

Coaching Points:
body mechanics - balance - weight of pass - accuracy - first touch

Open Goals

Click Here To View The Drill Animation!
Age Group: (5-7yrs) (8-11yrs) (12-15yrs) (16-Adult)
Emphasis: attacking - defending - passing - possession - goalkeeping
Description:
- each team defends a cone goal
- goal can be scored from both sides of the goal

Variation:
- goalies can only move side to side on goal line
- goals only count if knee high
- goals can only be scored with the first touch
- adjust spacing depending on the age and ability of the group

Coaching Points:
accurate passes - quick decision making - protect the ball - good angle of support - movement on and off the ball

Open Up Space

Click Here To View The Drill Animation!
Age Group: (5-7yrs) (8-11yrs) (12-15yrs) (16-Adult)
Emphasis: passing - possession - attacking - defending
Description:
- each team defends 2 mini goals
- every time a pass is made, that player must sprint 4yrds in any direction to support their pass
- if a player forgets to sprint after his pass the opposing team automatically wins possession

Variation:
- goals can only be scored with the first touch
- limit number of touches for field players
- adjust spacing depending on the age and ability of the group

Coaching Points:
quick decision making - constant movement - communication is vital - good angle and distance of support to receive ball - create space for others - attack space behind defense - support position lateral to ball

Open Up Space 2

Click Here To View The Drill Animation!
Age Group: (8-11yrs) (12-15yrs) (16-Adult)
Emphasis: passing - possession - attacking - defending
Description:
- each team defends and attacks a goal
- every time a pass is made, that player must sprint 4yrds in any direction to support their pass
- if a player forgets to sprint after his pass the opposing team automatically wins possession

Variation:
- goals can only be scored on a one touch finish
- limit number of touches for field players
- adjust spacing depending on the age and ability of the group

Coaching Points:
quick decision making - constant movement - communication is vital - good angle and distance of support to receive ball - create space for others - attack space behind defense - support position lateral to ball

Organized Attack

Click Here To View The Drill Animation!
Age Group: (8-11yrs) (12-15yrs) (16-Adult)
Emphasis: passing - possession - attacking - defending
Description:
- play 6v6
- if a team loses possession they must recover defensively and cannot try to win the ball back until it gets back to their defensive half

Variation:
- limit number of touches
- adjust spacing depending on the age and ability of the group

Coaching Points:
constant movement - communication is vital - good angle and distance of support to receive ball - shift as a unit - defenders must transition quickly - quick recovery - build your attack slowly

Ouchee

Click Here To View The Drill Animation!
Age Group: (5-7yrs)
Emphasis: dribbling - passing
Description:
- coach moves around the playing area and players try to kick their balls against the coach
- coach calls out "Ouchee" each time he gets hit by a ball

Variation:
- start the game by having the kids throw the ball at you below the waist line as a warm up
- each time the coach is hit the player receives disc cone as an incentive
- players receive a disc cone if they pass the ball through the coach's legs
- each time the coach is hit the player receives disc cone as an incentive

Coaching Points:
accuracy - weight of pass - vision - constant movement - change of direction and speed - close control

Over The Edge

Click Here To View The Drill Animation!
Age Group: (5-7yrs) (8-11yrs)
Emphasis: passing
Description:
- players of each team position themselves around grid as shown
- players attempt to shoot against beach ball in order to push it across opponent's goal line
- each beach ball pushed across goal line is awarded a point
- players are allowed to enter grid only to retrieve balls

Variation:
- vary number/type of balls in the middle
- specify how players must pass (left or right foot, inside or outside foot etc.)
- adjust size of field if necessary

Coaching Points:
weight of pass - accuracy - quick decision making

Overlapping Run with Finish 1

Click Here To View The Drill Animation!
Age Group: (8-11yrs) (12-15yrs) (16-Adult)
Emphasis: finishing - passing
Description:
- players pass and shoot on goal in the sequence as shown
- shooters decide where to make the first pass

Variation:
- specify how players must shoot (left or right foot, inside or laces, high or low etc.)
- limit number of touches
- adjust spacing depending on the age and ability of the group

Coaching Points:
body mechanics and control of body - body position and balance - eye on ball - quality of preparation touch - contact surface - aggressive and positive mentality - placement versus power

Overlapping Run with Finish 2

Click Here To View The Drill Animation!
Age Group: (8-11yrs) (12-15yrs) (16-Adult)
Emphasis: finishing - passing
Description:
- players pass and shoot on goal in the sequence as shown
- players move to next position after each sequence

Variation:
- specify how players must shoot (left or right foot, inside or laces, high or low etc.)
- limit number of touches
- adjust spacing depending on the age and ability of the group

Coaching Points:
body mechanics and control of body - body position and balance - eye on ball - quality of preparation touch - contact surface - aggressive and positive mentality - placement versus power

Pac Man

Click Here To View The Drill Animation!
Age Group: (5-7yrs) (8-11yrs) (12-15yrs)
Emphasis: dribbling - passing
Description:
- two players (Pacmen) start with a ball
- Pacmen try to pass against other players below the knee
- if player is hit he takes a ball and becomes a "Pacman" as well
- last player without a ball wins and starts as a Pacman the next round

Variation:
- player without a ball switches role with Pac Man once hit by a pass (players who are not Pacmen at the end of the game win)
- adjust spacing depending on the age and ability of the group if necessary

Coaching Points:
stay within bounds - keep ball rolling - head up - vision - change direction and speed - fake passes - close control - agility and balance

Partner Passing

Click Here To View The Drill Animation!
Age Group: (8-11yrs) (12-15yrs) (16-Adult)
Emphasis: passing
Description:
- players pass to their partner in various ways:
- players pass to each other while moving
- players make one touch lead passes into space
- players make high passes
- players make 2 short, 2 long passes etc.
- players perform a move after receiving a pass
- players dribble with speed 3-4 steps in any direction with the ball after receiving a pass
- players turn with the ball in the opposite direction from where the pass came from

Variation:
- add one or more defenders who attempt to intercept passes only
- specify how players must pass/receive (left or right foot, receive with one foot and pass with another, inside, outside of foot, laces, high or low)
- adjust spacing depending on the age and ability of the group

Coaching Points:
accuracy - weight of pass - vision - body position and balance - first touch

Partner Passing Up and Down

Click Here To View The Drill Animation!
Age Group: (8-11yrs) (12-15yrs) (16-Adult)
Emphasis: passing
Description:
- one players (red) is going forward and his partner (white) is going backwards as shown
- player (red) makes a pass to his partner (white) who traps the ball with his sole
- switch roles each time players get to a touchline

Variation:
- specify how players must pass (left or right foot, high or low pass, hands etc.)
- specify how players must receive (chest, head, thigh, left or right foot, laces, inside foot etc.)

Coaching Points:
body mechanics - balance - weight of pass - accuracy - develop a rhythm

Partner Tag 2

Click Here To View The Drill Animation!
Age Group: (5-7yrs) (8-11yrs) (12-15yrs)
Emphasis: dribbling - finishing - passing
Description:
- taggers dribble a ball inside playing area and try to hit targets with their ball below the knees
- targets stay connected by holding a pinnie
- switch targets often

Variation:
- specify how players must pass/receive (left or right foot, inside or outside foot, high or low etc.)
- adjust size of field if necessary depending on the age and ability of the group

Coaching Points:
weight of pass - accuracy - quality of preparation touch - contact surface - aggressive and positive mentality - placement versus power - change of direction and speed - deception - vision - close control

Pass and Shoot Competition

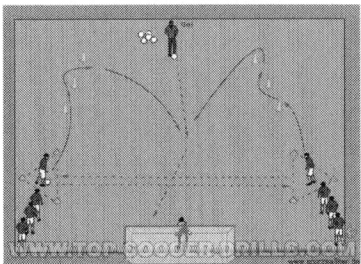

Click Here To View The Drill Animation!
Age Group: (8-11yrs) (12-15yrs) (16-Adult)
Emphasis: passing - finishing
Description:
- players inside triangles pass back and forth (2 touch passing)
- on coach's command players run zic-zac around cones and first player to the ball takes a shot at goal

Variation:
- various ways of distribution by the coach (high/low throw, high/low pass)
- specify how players must pass (left or right foot, high or low etc.)

Coaching Points:
weight of pass - accuracy - body position and balance - quick finish - aggressive and positive mentality - placement versus power

Pass and Shoot Sequence 1

Click Here To View The Drill Animation!
Age Group: (12-15yrs) (16-Adult)
Emphasis: passing - finishing
Description:
- players pass to players at cones and then make a lead pass to the shooter as shown
- switch pass givers(white-blue) every 3-4 min.

Variation:
- one touch passing
- switch setup to other side
- adjust spacing depending on the age and ability of the group

Coaching Points:
accuracy over power - importance of first touch to control and prepare ball

Pass and Shoot Sequence 2

Click Here To View The Drill Animation!
Age Group: (8-11yrs) (12-15yrs) (16-Adult)
Emphasis: finishing - passing
Description:
- players pass and finish on goal as shown

Variation:
- one touch for passers
- adjust spacing depending on the age and ability of the group

Coaching Points:
body mechanics and control of body - body position and balance - eye on ball - quality of preparation touch - contact surface - aggressive and positive mentality - placement versus power

Pass and Shoot Sequence 3

Click Here To View The Drill Animation!
Age Group: (8-11yrs) (12-15yrs) (16-Adult)
Emphasis: finishing - passing
Description:
- players pass and finish on goal as shown

Variation:
- one touch for all players
- adjust spacing depending on the age and ability of the group

Coaching Points:
body mechanics and control of body - body position and balance - eye on ball - quality of preparation touch - contact surface - aggressive and positive mentality - placement versus power

Pass and Shoot Sequence 4

Click Here To View The Drill Animation!
Age Group: (5-7yrs) (8-11yrs) (12-15yrs) (16-Adult)
Emphasis: finishing - passing
Description:
- players pass and finish on goal in the sequence as shown
- players switch sides after 4-5 minutes

Variation:
- one touch for all players
- adjust spacing depending on the age and ability of the group

Coaching Points:
body mechanics and control of body - body position and balance - eye on ball - quality of preparation touch - contact surface - aggressive and positive mentality - placement versus power

Pass and Shoot Sequence 5

Click Here To View The Drill Animation!
Age Group: (8-11yrs) (12-15yrs) (16-Adult)
Emphasis: finishing - passing
Description:
- players pass and finish on goal as shown
- players switch sides after 4-5 minutes

Variation:
- one touch for all players
- adjust spacing depending on the age and ability of the group

Coaching Points:
body mechanics and control of body - body position and balance - eye on ball - quality of preparation touch - contact surface - aggressive and positive mentality - placement versus power

Pass and Shoot Sequence 6

Click Here To View The Drill Animation!
Age Group: (8-11yrs) (12-15yrs) (16-Adult)
Emphasis: finishing - passing
Description:
- players pass and finish on goal as shown
- players switch sides after 4-5 minutes

Variation:
- one touch for all players
- adjust spacing depending on the age and ability of the group

Coaching Points:
body mechanics and control of body - body position and balance - eye on ball - quality of preparation touch - contact surface - aggressive and positive mentality - placement versus power

Pass and Shoot Sequence 7

Click Here To View The Drill Animation!
Age Group: (8-11yrs) (12-15yrs) (16-Adult)
Emphasis: finishing - passing
Description:
- players pass and finish on goal as shown
- players switch sides after 4-5 minutes

Variation:
- one touch for all players
- adjust spacing depending on the age and ability of the group

Coaching Points:
body mechanics and control of body - body position and balance - eye on ball - quality of preparation touch - contact surface - aggressive and positive mentality - placement versus power

Pass and Shoot Sequence 8

Click Here To View The Drill Animation!
Age Group: (8-11yrs) (12-15yrs) (16-Adult)
Emphasis: finishing - passing
Description:
- players pass and finish on goal in the sequence as shown
- players follow their passes
- shooter must finish at goal with his second touch

Variation:
- one touch for all players
- adjust spacing depending on the age and ability of the group

Coaching Points:
body mechanics and control of body - body position and balance - eye on ball - quality of preparation touch - contact surface - aggressive and positive mentality - placement versus power

Pass and Shoot Sequence 9

Click Here To View The Drill Animation!
Age Group: (8-11yrs) (12-15yrs) (16-Adult)
Emphasis: finishing - passing
Description:
- players pass and finish on goal in the sequence as shown
- players follow their passes
- shooter must finish at goal with his second touch

Variation:
- one touch for all players
- adjust size of grid if necessary

Coaching Points:
body mechanics and control of body - body position and balance - eye on ball - quality of preparation touch - contact surface - aggressive and positive mentality - placement versus power

Pass and Shoot Sequence 10

Click Here To View The Drill Animation!
Age Group: (8-11yrs) (12-15yrs) (16-Adult)
Emphasis: finishing - passing
Description:
- players pass and finish on goal in the sequence as shown
- player A takes player B's position and B takes C's
- shooter must finish at goal with his second touch

Variation:
- one touch for all players
- adjust spacing depending on the age and ability of the group

Coaching Points:
body mechanics and control of body - body position and balance - eye on ball - quality of preparation touch - contact surface - aggressive and positive mentality - placement versus power

Pass and Shoot Sequence 11

Click Here To View The Drill Animation!
Age Group: (12-15yrs) (16-Adult)
Emphasis: finishing - passing
Description:
- players pass (two-touch) and finish on goal in the sequence as shown
- same sequence goes on the other side
- players make only lofted passes
- player number 4 finishes on goal
- players keep their positions
- players change positions after 2-3 minutes

Variation:
- players follow their passes
- player number 4 has to finish on the first touch
- adjust spacing depending on the age and ability of the group

Coaching Points:
body mechanics and control of body - body position and balance - eye on ball - quality of preparation touch - contact surface - aggressive and positive mentality - placement versus power - accuracy - weight of pass

Pass and Shoot Sequence 12

Click Here To View The Drill Animation!
Age Group: (8-11yrs) (12-15yrs) (16-Adult)
Emphasis: finishing - passing - dribbling
Description:
- players dribble, pass, run around cone and then shoot on goal as shown
- players switch sides after 4-8 min.
- switch pass givers often

Variation:
- ball cannot bounce before it goes into the goal
- players have to finish on goal one-touch
- specify how players must shoot (left or right foot, inside or laces, high or low etc.)
- adjust spacing depending on the age and ability of the group

Coaching Points:
body mechanics and control of body - body position and balance - eye on ball - quality of preparation touch - contact surface - aggressive and positive mentality - placement versus power

Pass and Shoot Sequence 13

Click Here To View The Drill Animation!
Age Group: (8-11yrs) (12-15yrs) (16-Adult)
Emphasis: finishing - passing
Description:
- players pass to each other in the sequence as shown
- once the sequence is completed all players move to the next position

Variation:
- last player to receive the ball must beat the goalie by dribbling around him
- one touch for all pass-givers
- adjust spacing depending on the age and ability of the group

Coaching Points:
body mechanics and control of body - body position and balance - eye on ball - quality of preparation touch - contact surface - aggressive and positive mentality - vision and anticipation - placement versus power - positioning to gain an advantage

Pass and Shoot Sequence 14

Click Here To View The Drill Animation!
Age Group: (8-11yrs) (12-15yrs) (16-Adult)
Emphasis: finishing
Description:
- players pass and shoot on goal in the sequence as shown
- players switch roles/positions after each turn

Variation:
- specify how players must shoot (left or right foot, inside or laces, high or low etc.)
- limit number of touches
- adjust spacing depending on the age and ability of the group

Coaching Points:
body mechanics and control of body - body position and balance - eye on ball - quality of preparation touch - contact surface - aggressive and positive mentality - placement versus power

Pass and Shoot Sequence 15

Click Here To View The Drill Animation!
Age Group: (8-11yrs) (12-15yrs) (16-Adult)
Emphasis: finishing - passing
Description:
- players pass and shoot on goal in the sequence as shown
- players move to next position after each shot on goal
- repeat sequence

Variation:
- specify how players must shoot (left or right foot, inside or laces, high or low etc.)
- limit number of touches
- adjust spacing depending on the age and ability of the group

Coaching Points:
body mechanics and control of body - body position and balance - eye on ball - quality of preparation touch - contact surface - aggressive and positive mentality - placement versus power

Pass and Shoot Sequence 16

Click Here To View The Drill Animation!
Age Group: (8-11yrs) (12-15yrs) (16-Adult)
Emphasis: finishing - passing - dribbling
Description:
- player 1 passes to player 2
- player 2 lays it off to the side for player 3 who tries beat player 1 who now becomes the defender
- if player 3 beats player 1 he finishes on goal
- if player 1 wins the ball he must pass it to player 2 to end the sequence
- players move to the next position after each turn

Variation:
- specify how players must shoot (left or right foot, inside or laces, high or low etc.)
- limit number of touches
- adjust spacing depending on the age and ability of the group

Coaching Points:
body mechanics and control of body - body position and balance - eye on ball - quality of preparation touch - contact surface - aggressive and positive mentality - vision and anticipation - placement versus power - positioning to gain an advantage

Pass and Shoot Sequence 17

Click Here To View The Drill Animation!
Age Group: (8-11yrs) (12-15yrs) (16-Adult)
Emphasis: finishing
Description:
- player 2 moves towards player 1 to receive the pass, turn and shoot on goal
- player 2 must finish on goal from in front of cone goal as shown

Variation:
- player 1 makes a lofted pass to player 2
- specify how players must shoot (left or right foot, inside or laces, high or low etc.)
- adjust spacing depending on the age and ability of the group

Coaching Points:
body mechanics and control of body - body position and balance - eye on ball - quality of preparation touch - contact surface - aggressive and positive mentality - placement versus power - accurate passes - first touch

Pass and Shoot Sequence 18

Click Here To View The Drill Animation!
Age Group: (8-11yrs) (12-15yrs) (16-Adult)
Emphasis: finishing - passing
Description:
- player 1 passes to player 2 who makes a lofted pass to player 3
- player 3 throws the ball to player 4 who receives the ball out of the air and finishes on goal on his third (second) touch
- players move to next position after each sequence

Variation:
- specify how players must shoot on goal (left or right foot, inside or laces, high or low etc.)
- limit number of touches
- adjust spacing depending on the age and ability of the group

Coaching Points:
body mechanics and control of body - body position and balance - eye on ball - quality of preparation touch - contact surface - aggressive and positive mentality - placement versus power

Pass and Shoot Sequence 19

Click Here To View The Drill Animation!
Age Group: (8-11yrs) (12-15yrs) (16-Adult)
Emphasis: finishing - defending
Description:
- player 1 passes to player 2 who tries to finish on goal
- once player 2 receives the pass player 3 starts from his cone to defend player 2 as shown

Variation:
- first pass must be lofted
- specify how the receiver must control the pass (chest, head, feet etc.)

Coaching Points:
Attacking: quality of preparation touch - aggressive and positive mentality - placement versus power - accurate passes
Defending: angle and speed of approach - body shape, balance, and foot positioning - timing and decision to tackle

Pass and Shoot Sequence 20

Click Here To View The Drill Animation!
Age Group: (8-11yrs) (12-15yrs) (16-Adult)
Emphasis: finishing - defending
Description:
- player 1 passes to player 2 who tries to finish on goal
- once player 2 receives the ball player 3 starts from his cone to defend player 2

Variation:
- defender can try to score if he wins the ball
- adjust spacing depending on the age and ability of the group

Coaching Points:
Attacking: quality of preparation touch - aggressive and positive mentality - placement versus power - accurate passes
Defending: angle and speed of approach - body shape, balance, and foot positioning - timing and decision to tackle

Pass and Shoot Sequence 21

Click Here To View The Drill Animation!
Age Group: (8-11yrs) (12-15yrs) (16-Adult)
Emphasis: finishing - passing
Description:
- players pass to each other in the sequence as shown
- passers have two touches
- switch passers after 5 minutes
- switch sides

Variation:
- passers (blue) must play one touch
- shooter must beat the goalie by dribbling around him
- adjust spacing depending on the age and ability of the group

Coaching Points:
body mechanics and control of body - body position and balance - eye on ball - quality of preparation touch - contact surface - aggressive and positive mentality - placement versus power - accurate passes

Pass and Shoot Sequence 22

Click Here To View The Drill Animation!
Age Group: (8-11yrs) (12-15yrs) (16-Adult)
Emphasis: finishing - passing
Description:
- players pass to each other in the sequence as shown
- passers have two touches
- switch passers after 5 minutes
- switch sides

Variation:
- passers have one touch
- specify how players must shoot (left or right foot, inside or laces, high or low etc.)
- adjust spacing depending on the age and ability of the group

Coaching Points:
body mechanics and control of body - body position and balance - eye on ball - quality of preparation touch - contact surface - aggressive and positive mentality - placement versus power - accurate passes

Pass and Shoot Sequence 23

Click Here To View The Drill Animation!
Age Group: (8-11yrs) (12-15yrs) (16-Adult)
Emphasis: finishing - passing
Description:
- player pass to each other in the sequence as shown
- after each sequence each player moves on to next cone in order

Variation:
- same setup from the other side
- players have to shoot on the first touch
- players must try to beat the goalkeeper in a 1v1 situation
- adjust spacing depending on the age and ability of the group

Coaching Points:
get the shot off as quickly as possible - aggressive and positive mentality - eye on ball - accuracy before power - try to be deceptive with the shot - shoot the ball where the goalkeeper just came from, low and hard - identify the goalkeepers starting position

Pass and Shoot Sequence 24

Click Here To View The Drill Animation!
Age Group: (8-11yrs) (12-15yrs) (16-Adult)
Emphasis: finishing - passing
Description:
- players pass and shoot on goal in the sequence as shown

Variation:
- specify how players must shoot / pass (left or right foot, inside or laces high or low etc.)
- limit number of touches
- adjust spacing depending on the age and ability of the group

Coaching Points:
eye on ball - quality of preparation touch - contact surface - aggressive and positive mentality - placement versus power - weight of pass

Pass and Shoot Sequence 25

Click Here To View The Drill Animation!
Age Group: (8-11yrs) (12-15yrs) (16-Adult)
Emphasis: finishing - passing
Description:
- players pass and shoot on goal in the sequence as shown
- repeat sequence from the other side
- players get one point for a shot on target and two for a goal

Variation:
- specify how players must shoot (left or right foot, inside or laces, high or low etc.)
- limit number of touches
- adjust spacing depending on the age and ability of the group

Coaching Points:
body mechanics and control of body - body position and balance - eye on ball - quality of preparation touch - contact surface - aggressive and positive mentality - vision and anticipation - placement versus power - positioning to gain an advantage

Pass and Shoot Sequence 27

Click Here To View The Drill Animation!
Age Group: (8-11yrs) (12-15yrs) (16-Adult)
Emphasis: finishing - passing
Description:
- players pass and shoot on goal in the sequence a shown

Variation:
- specify how players must shoot (left or right foot, inside or laces, high or low etc.)
- vary position of the wall player
- limit number of touches
- adjust spacing depending on the age and ability of the group

Coaching Points:
body mechanics and control of body - body position and balance - eye on ball - quality of preparation touch - contact surface - aggressive and positive mentality - vision and anticipation - placement versus power - positioning to gain an advantage

Pass and Shoot Sequence 28

Click Here To View The Drill Animation!
Age Group: (8-11yrs) (12-15yrs) (16-Adult)
Emphasis: finishing - passing
Description:
- players dribble, pass and shoot on goal in the sequence as shown

Variation:
- specify how players must shoot (left or right foot, inside or laces, high or low etc.)
- players must beat the goalie by dribbling around him
- limit number of touches
- adjust spacing depending on the age and ability of the group

Coaching Points:
body mechanics and control of body - body position and balance - eye on ball - quality of preparation touch - contact surface - aggressive and positive mentality - vision and anticipation - placement versus power - positioning to gain an advantage

Pass and Shoot Sequence 29

Click Here To View The Drill Animation!
Age Group: (8-11yrs) (12-15yrs) (16-Adult)
Emphasis: finishing - passing
Description:
- players pass and shoot on goal in the sequence as shown

Variation:
- specify how players must shoot (left or right foot, inside or laces, high or low etc.)
- the goalie punts or throws the ball back to the player
- players must beat the goalie by dribbling around him
- limit number of touches
- adjust spacing depending on the age and ability of the group

Coaching Points:
body mechanics and control of body - body position and balance - eye on ball - quality of preparation touch - contact surface - aggressive and positive mentality - placement versus power

Pass and Shoot Sequence 30

Click Here To View The Drill Animation!
Age Group: (8-11yrs) (12-15yrs) (16-Adult)
Emphasis: finishing - passing
Description:
- players pass and shoot on goal in the sequence as shown

Variation:
- specify how players must shoot (left or right foot, inside or laces, high or low etc.)
- limit number of touches
- adjust spacing depending on the age and ability of the group

Coaching Points:
body mechanics and control of body - body position and balance - eye on ball - quality of preparation touch - contact surface - aggressive and positive mentality - placement versus power - weight of pass - accuracy of pass

Pass and Shoot Sequence 31

Click Here To View The Drill Animation!
Age Group: (8-11yrs) (12-15yrs) (16-Adult)
Emphasis: finishing - passing
Description:
- players pass and shoot on goal in the sequence as shown

Variation:
- specify how players must shoot (left or right foot, inside or laces, high or low etc.)
- limit number of touches
- adjust spacing depending on the age and ability of the group

Coaching Points:
body mechanics and control of body - body position and balance - eye on ball - quality of preparation touch - contact surface - aggressive and positive mentality - placement versus power - weight of pass - accuracy of pass

Pass and Shoot Sequence 32

Click Here To View The Drill Animation!
Age Group: (8-11yrs) (12-15yrs) (16-Adult)
Emphasis: finishing - passing
Description:
- players pass and shoot on goal in the sequence as shown

Variation:
- specify how players must shoot (left or right foot, inside or laces, high or low etc.)
- limit number of touches
- adjust spacing depending on the age and ability of the group

Coaching Points:
body mechanics and control of body - body position and balance - eye on ball - quality of preparation touch - contact surface - aggressive and positive mentality - placement versus power - weight of pass - accuracy of pass

Pass and Shoot Sequence 33

Click Here To View The Drill Animation!
Age Group: (8-11yrs) (12-15yrs) (16-Adult)
Emphasis: finishing - passing
Description:
- players pass and shoot on goal in the sequence as shown

Variation:
- specify how players must shoot (left or right foot, inside or laces, high or low etc.)
- limit number of touches
- adjust spacing depending on the age and ability of the group

Coaching Points:
body mechanics and control of body - body position and balance - eye on ball - quality of preparation touch - contact surface - aggressive and positive mentality - placement versus power - weight of pass - accuracy of pass

Pass and Shoot Sequence 34

Click Here To View The Drill Animation!
Age Group: (8-11yrs) (12-15yrs) (16-Adult)
Emphasis: finishing - passing
Description:
- players pass and shoot on goal in the sequence as shown

Variation:
- vary ways of how the goalie and/or wall player feed the ball to the shooter (high, low, throw, punt etc.)
- specify how players must shoot (left or right foot, inside or laces, high or low etc.)
- limit number of touches
- adjust spacing depending on the age and ability of the group

Coaching Points:
quality of preparation touch - contact surface - aggressive and positive mentality - placement versus power - weight of pass - accuracy of pass

Pass and Shoot Sequence 35

Click Here To View The Drill Animation!
Age Group: (8-11yrs) (12-15yrs) (16-Adult)
Emphasis: finishing - passing
Description:
- players pass and shoot on goal in the sequence as shown

Variation:
- specify how players must shoot (left or right foot, inside or laces, high or low etc.)
- limit number of touches
- adjust spacing depending on the age and ability of the group

Coaching Points:
body mechanics and control of body - body position and balance - eye on ball - quality of preparation touch - contact surface - aggressive and positive mentality - placement versus power - accuracy of pass - weight of pass

Pass and Shoot Sequence 36

Click Here To View The Drill Animation!
Age Group: (8-11yrs) (12-15yrs) (16-Adult)
Emphasis: finishing - passing
Description:
- players pass and shoot on goal in the sequence as shown
- two touch passing

Variation:
- specify how players must pass (left or right foot, inside or outside foot, high or low etc.)
- player must try beat the goalie in a 1v1 situation
- one touch passing
- adjust spacing depending on the age and ability of the group

Coaching Points:
weight of pass - accuracy - first touch

Pass and Shoot Sequence 37

Click Here To View The Drill Animation!
Age Group: (8-11yrs) (12-15yrs) (16-Adult)
Emphasis: finishing - passing
Description:
- players pass and shoot on goal in the sequence as shown
- allow player D to go for a rebound
- players move to next position after each sequence
- one point for a shot on target and two for a goal

Variation:
- specify how players must shoot (left or right foot, inside or laces, high or low etc.)
- limit number of touches
- adjust spacing depending on the age and ability of the group

Coaching Points:
body mechanics and control of body - body position and balance - eye on ball - quality of preparation touch - contact surface - aggressive and positive mentality - placement versus power

Pass and Shoot Sequence 38

Click Here To View The Drill Animation!
Age Group: (8-11yrs) (12-15yrs) (16-Adult)
Emphasis: finishing - passing
Description:
- players pass and shoot on goal in the sequence as shown
- players move to next position after each sequence
- one point for a shot on target and two for a goal
- player with most goals wins (losers do 20 push-ups)

Variation:
- specify how players must shoot (left or right foot, inside or laces, high or low etc.)
- adjust spacing depending on the age and ability of the group

Coaching Points:
body mechanics and control of body - body position and balance - eye on ball - quality of preparation touch - contact surface - aggressive and positive mentality - vision and anticipation - placement versus power - positioning to gain an advantage

Pass and Shoot Sequence 39

Click Here To View The Drill Animation!
Age Group: (8-11yrs) (12-15yrs) (16-Adult)
Emphasis: finishing - passing
Description:
- players pass and shoot on goal in the sequence as shown
- player A takes player B's position
- repeat sequence from the other side
- player is awarded a point for a shot on target and two for a goal
- group with most points wins

Variation:
- specify how players must shoot (left or right foot, inside or laces, high or low etc.)
- limit number of touches
- adjust spacing depending on the age and ability of the group

Coaching Points:
body mechanics and control of body - body position and balance - eye on ball - quality of preparation touch - contact surface - aggressive and positive mentality - placement versus power

Pass and Shoot Sequence 40

Click Here To View The Drill Animation!
Age Group: (5-7yrs) (8-11yrs) (12-15yrs) (16-Adult)
Emphasis: finishing - passing
Description:
- players pass to each other as shown
- after receiving the pass players try to beat the goalie by dribbling around him

Variation:
- players have to shoot on the second touch / first touch
- same setup from the other side
- adjust spacing depending on the age and ability of the group

Coaching Points:
get the shot off as quickly as possible - aggressive and positive mentality - eye on ball - accuracy before power - try to be deceptive with the shot - identify the goalkeepers starting position - if the goalkeeper charges out - slot the ball under him or dribble around him

Pass and Shoot Sequence Coordination

Click Here To View The Drill Animation!
Age Group: (8-11yrs) (12-15yrs) (16-Adult)
Emphasis: finishing - passing - coordination
Description:
- players pass and shoot on goal in the sequence as shown

Variation:
- specify how players must shoot (left or right foot, inside or laces, high or low etc.)
- limit number of touches
- adjust spacing depending on the age and ability of the group

Coaching Points:
body mechanics and control of body - body position and balance - eye on ball - quality of preparation touch - contact surface - aggressive and positive mentality - placement versus power

Pass Receive Dribble

Click Here To View The Drill Animation!
Age Group: (5-7yrs) (8-11yrs) (12-15yrs)
Emphasis: dribbling - passing
Description:
- players inside squares move towards ball, receive it and dribble to next corner in a clockwise direction
- the first touch for the receiver must be inside the square and his second must be outside of it
- players then perform a move before they leave the grid
- player at the corner follows his pass into square
- next players goes when previous player stops his ball in front of him (and/or gives a high five)

Variation:
- specify how players must pass/receive/dribble the ball (left or right foot, inside or outside foot, high or low etc.)
- play with passive defenders inside the grid who block dribbler's path
- reverse direction
- adjust spacing depending on the age and ability of the group if necessary

Coaching Points:
close control - change of speed & direction - communication - protect your ball - deception - set up defender - weight of pass - accuracy - good first touch

Pass Receive Turn

Click Here To View The Drill Animation!
Age Group: (5-7yrs) (8-11yrs) (12-15yrs) (16-Adult)
Emphasis: passing
Description:
- players on the outside pass to a player inside the middle zone who receives and turns with the ball to pass it to the player on the opposite side
- switch roles after 20 passes

Variation:
- specify how players must pass/receive (left or right foot, inside or outside foot, high or low etc.)
- adjust spacing depending on the age and ability of the group

Coaching Points:
players should try to develop a rhythm with their passing - players should accelerate towards the ball - weight of pass - accuracy - good first touch

Pass Run Shoot

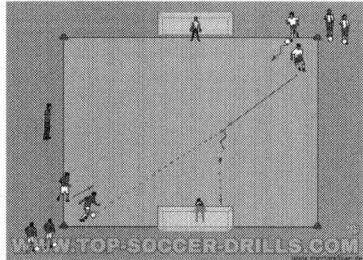

Click Here To View The Drill Animation!
Age Group: (8-11yrs) (12-15yrs) (16-Adult)
Emphasis: finishing - passing
Description:
- first player in line passes to player in opposite corner who moves towards the ball to receive and shoot on goal
- next a player from the white group makes a pass diagonally to a player from the red group

Variation:
- pass giver becomes a passive (active) defender
- specify how players must shoot (left or right foot, number of touches before shot etc.)

Coaching Points:
importance of first touch to control and prepare ball - timing of pass and run - accuracy - contact surface - aggressive and positive mentality - placement versus power

Pass Tag

Click Here To View The Drill Animation!
Age Group: (8-11yrs) (12-15yrs) (16-Adult)
Emphasis: passing
Description:
- tagger attempts to apply tag on runner
- runner is "save" if he is in possession of a ball
- in order to help other runners one is allowed to pass the ball around
- if a runner gets tagged he then becomes a tagger

Variation:
- vary number of balls
- vary number of taggers
- adjust spacing depending on the age and ability of the group

Coaching Points:
weight of pass - accuracy over power - vision - communication

Pass To Striker

Click Here To View The Drill Animation!
Age Group: (8-11yrs) (12-15yrs) (16-Adult)
Emphasis: passing - possession
Description:
- play 4v4 inside the grid
- each team has a target player in an end zone and a last defender from the other team behind the end zone
- if the ball is passed to the target player he attempts to dribble outside of the end zone to receive a point for his team
- the defending player can enter the zone and try to win the ball after the first touch has been made

Variation:
- play 3v3, 5v5 etc.
- adjust spacing depending on the age and ability of the group

Coaching Points:
explosiveness - look for open space - importance of first touch to control and prepare ball - communication - vision - accurate passes to feet - quick turn by player in end zone - don't let striker turn with the ball

Pass To Striker 2

Click Here To View The Drill Animation!
Age Group: (8-11yrs) (12-15yrs) (16-Adult)
Emphasis: passing - finishing - attacking - defending
Description:
- play 4v4
- each team has a target player in an end zone and a last defender from the other team behind the end zone
- if the ball is passed to the target player he attempts to control the ball and score on of the two mini goals to receive a point for his team
- defending player can enter the zone and try to win the ball after the first touch has been made

Variation:
- play with only one goal on each goal line
- play 3v3, 5v5 etc.
- adjust spacing depending on the age and ability of the group

Coaching Points:
explosiveness - first touch - communication - accurate passes to feet - quick turn by player in end zone - aggressive and positive mentality - vision and anticipation - placement versus power - positioning to gain an advantage

Passes Into Target Areas

Click Here To View The Drill Animation!
Age Group: (8-11yrs) (12-15yrs) (16-Adult)
Emphasis: passing - possession - attacking - defending
Description:
- teams score by passing into one of the target areas to a teammate
- players cannot wait inside target area to receive a pass

Variation:
- add a neutral player
- limit number of touches
- adjust spacing depending on the age and ability of the group

Coaching Points:
communication - selection & timing of pass - time your run into target area - get into line of flight of the ball - switch point of attack away from pressure - keep the ball moving with quick accurate passing

Passes Into Target Areas 2

Click Here To View The Drill Animation!
Age Group: (8-11yrs) (12-15yrs) (16-Adult)
Emphasis: passing - possession
Description:
- teams score by passing into an area to a target player who connects to a third teammate with a 1 or 2 touch pass
- switch roles once a team has five points

Variation:
- players must play a lofted pass to target player
- limit number of touches for field players
- adjust spacing depending on the age and ability of the group

Coaching Points:
communication - accuracy - selection & timing of pass - switch point of attack away from pressure - keep the ball moving with quick accurate passing

Passes Into Target Areas 3

Click Here To View The Drill Animation!
Age Group: (8-11yrs) (12-15yrs) (16-Adult)
Emphasis: passing - possession
Description:
- play 4 v 4, 5 v 5, 6 v 6 etc.
- neutral players are responsible for keeping balls in play from the middle line
- players attempt to pass into target area to player who connects to a third teammate with a 1 or 2 touch pass in order to score
- switch roles once a team has five points

Variation:
- players must play a lofted pass to target player
- limit number of touches for field players
- adjust spacing depending on the age and ability of the group

Coaching Points:
angle, distance and timing of support - vision - decision making - verbal and visual communication - switch point of attack away from pressure - keep the ball moving with quick accurate passing

Passes Into Target Areas 4

Click Here To View The Drill Animation!
Age Group: (8-11yrs) (12-15yrs) (16-Adult)
Emphasis: passing - possession
Description:
- play 4v4, 5v5, 6v6 etc.
- teams score by passing to a teammate who is making a run into the target area
- players cannot wait inside a target area to receive a pass

Variation:
- players must play a lofted pass into the target area
- limit number of touches
- adjust spacing depending on the age and ability of the group

Coaching Points:
angle, distance and timing of support - vision - communication - selection & timing of pass - switch point of attack away from pressure - keep the ball moving with quick accurate passing

Passes Into Target Areas 5

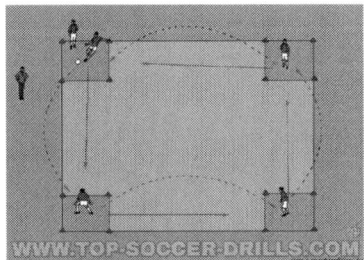

Click Here To View The Drill Animation!
Age Group: (8-11yrs) (12-15yrs) (16-Adult)
Emphasis: passing
Description:
- players make lofted passes and follow into the next target area
- group is awarded a point if a pass is completed into the target zone
- no point if the ball bounces before it gets into the target zone or if the receiver can't control the ball
- ball cannot come to a standstill
- team with most points after 5 minutes wins

Variation:
- limit number of touches
- ball can bounce before entering the target area
- adjust spacing depending on the age and ability of the group

Coaching Points:
accuracy - weight of pass - first touch - focus - communication

Passes Into Target Areas 6

Click Here To View The Drill Animation!
Age Group: (8-11yrs) (12-15yrs) (16-Adult)
Emphasis: passing - possession
Description:
- play 4v4, 5v5, 6v6 etc.
- teams score by making a lofted pass to a teammate who controls the ball inside the target area
- players cannot be challenged inside target areas

Variation:
- players can be challenged inside target area
- players must enter target area at the same as the ball to receive it
- each team can score in two designated areas plus a neutral zone
- limit number of touches
- adjust spacing depending on the age and ability of the group

Coaching Points:
vision - decision making - angle, distance and timing of support - communication - selection & timing of pass - switch point of attack away from pressure - keep the ball moving with quick accurate passing

Passing 4 Goal Game w Vertical Middle Line

Click Here To View The Drill Animation!
Age Group: (8-11yrs) (12-15yrs) (16-Adult)
Emphasis: passing - possession - attacking - defending
Description:
- each team defends two mini goals on the same goal line
- field is divided into two channels
- teams score if they win the ball and pass across the vertical middle line and then score on the mini goal

Variation:
- teams can score on any goal
- one point for scoring in the same channel (two points for scoring after switching channels)
- ball cannot be dribbled across vertical middle line
- limit number of touches
- adjust spacing depending on the age and ability of the group

Coaching Points:
shift as unit - constant movement - angle, distance and timing of support - vision - decision making - verbal and visual communication - switch point of attack

Passing 6 Goal Game

Click Here To View The Drill Animation!
Age Group: (5-7yrs) (8-11yrs) (12-15yrs) (16-Adult)
Emphasis: passing - attacking - defending
Description:
- each team defends 3 cone goals

Variation:
- teams score by connecting three passes before they can score
- limit number of touches
- adjust size of field or cone goals if necessary

Coaching Points:
quick decision making - constant movement - communication is vital - good angle and distance of support to receive ball - shift as a unit - switch point of attack

Passing 6 Goal Game 2

Click Here To View The Drill Animation!
Age Group: (8-11yrs) (12-15yrs) (16-Adult)
Emphasis: passing - possession - attacking - defending
Description:
- each team defends 3 cone goals
- one neutral target player in each of the outer channels
- target players must stay in their channel

Variation:
- neutral players can leave their channel but cannot be in the same channel simultaneously
- team must complete a pass to a neutral player before they can score
- use mini goals instead of cone goals
- adjust spacing depending on the age and ability of the group

Coaching Points:
quick decision making - constant movement - communication is vital - good angle and distance of support to receive ball - vision - shift as a unit - switch point of attack

Passing 6 Goal Game 3

Click Here To View The Drill Animation!
Age Group: (5-7yrs) (8-11yrs) (12-15yrs) (16-Adult)
Emphasis: passing - dribbling - attacking - defending
Description:
- each team defends three cone goals
- teams score by dribbling through the outer goals and passing through the middle goal

Variation:
- teams score by connecting three passes before they can score
- limit number of touches
- adjust size of field or cone goals if necessary

Coaching Points:
quick decision making - constant movement - communication is vital - good angle and distance of support to receive ball - shift as a unit - switch point of attack

Passing 6 Goal Game w Sweeper

Click Here To View The Drill Animation!
Age Group: (8-11yrs) (12-15yrs) (16-Adult)
Emphasis: passing - finishing - attacking - defending
Description:
- each team defends 3 cone goals
- sweeper acts as a defender/goalie who cannot leave the end zone

Variation:
- limit number of touches for field players and/or sweepers
- adjust spacing depending on the age and ability of the group

Coaching Points:
switch point of attack - awareness of goalkeeper's position - quick finish - attack open space - spread out attack - shift as unit - vision - communication

Passing 6 Goal Game w Target Player

Click Here To View The Drill Animation!
Age Group: (8-11yrs) (12-15yrs) (16-Adult)
Emphasis: passing - possession
Description:
- each team defends 3 cone goals
- each team scores by passing the ball through one of the 3 goals to a target player
- switch target player every 4-5 minutes

Variation:
- target players are neutral
- pass giver switches with target player
- limit number of touches
- adjust size of field if necessary

Coaching Points:
angle, distance and timing of support - vision - decision making - verbal and visual communication - switch point of attack - attack open space - spread out attack

Passing Accuracy

Click Here To View The Drill Animation!
Age Group: (5-7yrs) (8-11yrs)
Emphasis: passing
Description:
- each team must stay in their zone
- no player is allowed inside middle zone
- both teams attempt to score on the other team's goals
- ball has to be moving when players strike it
- players cannot block shots
- teams with most goals wins

Variation:
- players can play defense
- vary number of goals
- specify how players must pass (left or right foot, inside or outside foot, laces, high or low etc.)
- adjust spacing depending on the age and ability of the group

Coaching Points:
accurate passes - body mechanics - balance - weight of pass

Passing Activity 1

Click Here To View The Drill Animation!
Age Group: (5-7yrs) (8-11yrs) (12-15yrs)
Emphasis: passing
Description:
- players stand in front of cones
- players pass back and forth (two touch passing)

Variation:
- one touch passing
- specify how players must pass (left or right foot, inside or outside foot, high or low etc.)
- adjust spacing depending on the age and ability of the group

Coaching Points:
body mechanics - accuracy - weight of pass - first touch

Passing Activity 2

Click Here To View The Drill Animation!
Age Group: (5-7yrs) (8-11yrs) (12-15yrs)
Emphasis: passing
Description:
- players pass to their partner who takes it to the other side of the cone to pass it back as shown

Variation:
- specify how players must pass (left or right foot, inside or outside foot)
- adjust spacing depending on the age and ability of the group

Coaching Points:
body mechanics - balance - weight of pass - accuracy - first touch

Passing Activity 3

Click Here To View The Drill Animation!
Age Group: (5-7yrs) (8-11yrs) (12-15yrs)
Emphasis: passing
Description:
- players pass to their partner who takes it to the other side of the cone to pass it back diagonally as shown

Variation:
- three (two) touch limitation
- specify how players must pass (left or right foot, inside or outside foot)
- adjust spacing depending on the age and ability of the group

Coaching Points:
body mechanics - balance - weight of pass - accuracy - first touch

Passing Activity 4

Click Here To View The Drill Animation!
Age Group: (5-7yrs) (8-11yrs) (12-15yrs)
Emphasis: passing
Description:
- players pass and follow their pass as shown
- last player at each station dribbles over to other station's start

Variation:
- specify how players must pass (left or right foot, inside or outside foot)
- adjust spacing depending on the age and ability of the group

Coaching Points:
body mechanics - balance - weight of pass - accuracy - first touch - communication

Passing Activity 5

Click Here To View The Drill Animation!
Age Group: (5-7yrs) (8-11yrs) (12-15yrs)
Emphasis: passing
Description:
- players pass back and forth amongst themselves
- players cannot pass through same channel that it came through

Variation:
- specify how players must pass/receive (left or right foot, laces, inside or outside foot etc.)
- adjust spacing depending on the age and ability of the group

Coaching Points:
body mechanics - balance - weight of pass - accuracy - first touch

Passing Activity 7

Click Here To View The Drill Animation!
Age Group: (5-7yrs) (8-11yrs) (12-15yrs)
Emphasis: passing
Description:
- players pass to each other in the sequence as shown

Variation:
- add a second ball
- reverse direction
- specify how players must pass/receive (left or right foot, inside or outside foot etc.)
- adjust spacing depending on the age and ability of the group

Coaching Points:
body mechanics - balance - weight of pass - accuracy - first touch - communication

Passing Activity 8

Click Here To View The Drill Animation!
Age Group: (5-7yrs) (8-11yrs) (12-15yrs)
Emphasis: passing
Description:
- blue player starts by passing the ball towards the next cone
- red player lays off the ball to the outside the square for the blue player to run to
- blue player continues to the next cone to repeat the sequence as shown
- sequence continues for 2 minutes with all players being involved in the activity

Variation:
- red players stand right in front of the cones and lay off the ball to either the outside or the inside of the square for the blue player to run to
- red player passes one-touch straight back to blue player for them to control around the cone
- red player picks up the ball and feeds it back to the blue player in the air for them to control
- adjust spacing depending on the age and ability of the group

Coaching Points:
body mechanics - balance - weight of pass - accuracy - vision - first touch - communication

Passing Activity 9

Click Here To View The Drill Animation!
Age Group: (5-7yrs) (8-11yrs)
Emphasis: passing
Description:
- 2 cones are placed in between two players as shown
- objective is to knock down the most cones within two minutes
- cones are being put up again after they get knocked down

Variation:
- two touch passing only
- add a third cone
- increase distance between partners

Coaching Points:
body mechanics - balance - weight of pass - accuracy

Passing Activity 10

Click Here To View The Drill Animation!
Age Group: (5-7yrs) (8-11yrs) (12-15yrs)
Emphasis: passing
Description:
- players in opposite corners start with a ball
- players pass and follow their pass in the same direction as shown

Variation:
- one-touch passing
- reverse direction
- specify how players must pass/receive (left or right foot, inside or outside foot, high or low etc.)
- adjust spacing depending on the age and ability of the group

Coaching Points:
body mechanics - balance - weight of pass - accuracy - first touch - ball speed

Passing Activity 11

Click Here To View The Drill Animation!
Age Group: (5-7yrs) (8-11yrs) (12-15yrs) (16-Adult)
Emphasis: passing
Description:
- players make lofted two-touch passes back and forth
- ball can bounce only once before receiver touches it

Variation:
- players must receive the ball out of the air
- specify how players must pass (left or right foot)
- adjust spacing depending on the age and ability of the group

Coaching Points:
body mechanics - balance - weight of pass - accuracy - first touch - communication

Passing Activity 12

Click Here To View The Drill Animation!
Age Group: (5-7yrs) (8-11yrs) (12-15yrs)
Emphasis: passing
Description:
- players switch sides after each pass as shown
- two-touch passing

Variation:
- only one pair switches sides while the other pair acts as the servers
- specify how players must pass/receive (left or right foot, inside or outside foot, high or low etc.)
- one touch passing
- adjust spacing depending on the age and ability of the group

Coaching Points:
constant movement - communication - balance - weight of pass - accuracy - first touch

Passing Activity 13

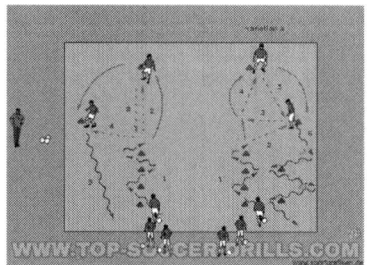

Click Here To View The Drill Animation!
Age Group: (8-11yrs) (12-15yrs)
Emphasis: passing - dribbling
Description:
- players pass to each other in the sequence as shown
- two-touch passing
- first group to complete 2-3 rounds wins (losers do 20x squat jumps)

Variation:
- variation a
- one-touch passing
- adjust spacing depending on the age and ability of the group

Coaching Points:
weight of pass - accuracy - first touch

Passing Activity 14

Click Here To View The Drill Animation!
Age Group: (8-11yrs) (12-15yrs)
Emphasis: passing - dribbling
Description:
- players pass to each other in the sequence as shown
- two-touch passing

Variation:
- specify how players must pass (left or right foot, inside or outside foot, high or low etc.)
- one-touch passing
- adjust spacing depending on the age and ability of the group

Coaching Points:
weight of pass - accuracy - first touch

Passing Activity 14.2

Click Here To View The Drill Animation!
Age Group: (8-11yrs) (12-15yrs) (16-Adult)
Emphasis: passing - dribbling
Description:
- players pass to each other in the sequence as shown
- last player shoots from distance into the mini goal
- two-touch passing

Variation:
- one-touch passing
- adjust spacing depending on the age and ability of the group

Coaching Points:
weight of pass - accuracy - first touch

Passing Activity 15

Click Here To View The Drill Animation!
Age Group: (5-7yrs) (8-11yrs) (12-15yrs)
Emphasis: passing - dribbling
Description:
- all four players pass and dribble simultaneously in the sequence as shown

Variation:
- players dribble diagonally to the next cone
- adjust spacing depending on the age and ability of the group

Coaching Points:
constant movement - communication - balance - weight of pass - accuracy - first touch

Passing Activity 16

Click Here To View The Drill Animation!
Age Group: (8-11yrs) (12-15yrs) (16-Adult)
Emphasis: passing
Description:
- players pass and run to each other in sequence as shown
- switch positions every 2 minutes

Variation:
- limit number of touches
- adjust spacing depending on the age and ability of the group

Coaching Points:
weight of pass - accuracy - first touch - good speed of play - communication

Passing Activity 17

Click Here To View The Drill Animation!
Age Group: (5-7yrs) (8-11yrs) (12-15yrs)
Emphasis: passing
Description:
- one player in each of the outer zones
- one players starts in the middle zone
- players must stay in their designated zones
- players in the outer zones try to pass to each other through the middle zone
- if a player in the middle zone intercepts a pass they switch roles with the player that made the pass
- players in the outer zones must try to keep the ball in bounce

Variation:
- limit number of touches for players in the outer zones
- specify how players must pass (left or right foot, inside or outside foot etc.)
- adjust spacing depending on the age and ability of the group

Coaching Points:
angle, distance and timing of support - vision - decision making - verbal and visual communication - accuracy - weight of pass - first touch

Passing Activity 18

Click Here To View The Drill Animation!
Age Group: (5-7yrs) (8-11yrs) (12-15yrs) (16-Adult)
Emphasis: passing
Description:
- players pass and follow their pass to opposite goal
- players must receive and pass the ball behind goal line
- team that completes most passes in one go wins

Variation:
- players must move through goal to receive and pass the ball in front of it
- limit number of touches
- specify how players must pass (left or right foot, high or low etc.)
- adjust spacing depending on the age and ability of the group

Coaching Points:
accuracy - weight of pass - good ball speed - body position and balance - importance of first touch to control and prepare ball - players should try to develop a rhythm with their passing

Passing Central 1

Click Here To View The Drill Animation!
Age Group: (5-7yrs) (8-11yrs) (12-15yrs)
Emphasis: passing - dribbling
Description:
- corner player passes to an inside player who then turns and dribbles the ball around the nearest cone and passes back to the next corner player
- corner player who passed the ball to the inside follows his pass and waits for a ball from another outside player

Variation:
- inside player receives the ball from corner and then does a specific move before he enters the square
- specify how players must pass/receive (left or right foot, inside or outside foot, high or low etc.)
- adjust spacing depending on the age and ability of the group

Coaching Points:
accuracy - weight of pass - communication - quick decision making - accelerate into square - tight turns

Passing Central 2

Click Here To View The Drill Animation!
Age Group: (5-7yrs) (8-11yrs) (12-15yrs)
Emphasis: passing - dribbling
Description:
- corner player passes to an inside player who then turns and dribbles the ball through the middle square and once he gets out of it he passes to the next available corner (not the one he received the pass from!)
- corner player who passed the ball to the inside follows his pass and waits for a ball from another outside player

Variation:
- inside player receives the ball from corner and then does a specific move before he enters the square
- vary number of balls
- specify how players must pass/receive (left or right foot, inside or outside foot, high or low etc.)
- adjust spacing depending on the age and ability of the group

Coaching Points:
accuracy - weight of pass - quick decision making - accelerate into square - tight turns

Passing Combinations 1

Click Here To View The Drill Animation!
Age Group: (5-7yrs) (8-11yrs) (12-15yrs)
Emphasis: passing
Description:
- players take two touches and lay the ball off to the side as shown
- players then run to pass partner's ball to opposite side on one touch

Variation:
- specify how players must pass (left or right foot, high or low etc.)
- adjust spacing depending on the age and ability of the group

Coaching Points:
body mechanics - balance - weight of pass - accuracy

Passing Combinations 2

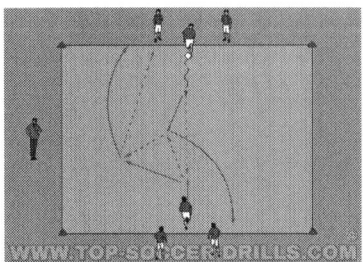

Click Here To View The Drill Animation!
Age Group: (8-11yrs) (12-15yrs) (16-Adult)
Emphasis: passing
Description:
- players pass to each other as shown

Variation:
- specify how players must pass (left or right foot, high or low etc.)
- adjust spacing depending on the age and ability of the group

Coaching Points:
body mechanics - balance - weight of pass - accuracy

Passing Corner with Neutral

Click Here To View The Drill Animation!
Age Group: (8-11yrs) (12-15yrs) (16-Adult)
Emphasis: passing
Description:
- one player from each team positioned in opposite corners as shown
- players in the middle play 1v1 and try to pass to teammate who can receive the ball only inside designated area (triangle)
- player must utilize neutral player before passing to a player in designated area

Variation:
- neutral player only has one touch
- adjust spacing depending on the age and ability of the group

Coaching Points:
communication - combination - accuracy - protect the ball - vision - close control

Passing Corner x 4

Click Here To View The Drill Animation!
Age Group: (5-7yrs) (8-11yrs) (12-15yrs) (16-Adult)
Emphasis: passing - dribbling
Description:
- players compete 1v1 to beat the defender and pass the ball into one of their team's corner
- players switch on successful passes into their teams zones
- defender remains in the middle until he wins the ball and passes it to one of his teams zones

Variation:
- add neutral player to create 2v1 situation
- adjust spacing depending on the age and ability of the group

Coaching Points:
accuracy - quick decision making - change of speed & direction - communication - get defender off balance - protect the ball

Passing Corner x 4 Vol.2

Click Here To View The Drill Animation!
Age Group: (8-11yrs) (12-15yrs) (16-Adult)
Emphasis: passing - possession
Description:
- one player from each team positioned in opposite corners as shown
- teams score by passing to their corner player
- corner player switches role with pass giver

Variation:
- limit number of touches
- after receiving a pass corner player must play to a third player in order to score a point for his team
- adjust spacing depending on the age and ability of the group

Coaching Points:
combination play - accuracy - quick decision making - changing the point of attack - good angle and distance of support to receive ball

Passing Face Off

Click Here To View The Drill Animation!
Age Group: (5-7yrs) (8-11yrs) (12-15yrs)
Emphasis: passing
Description:
- players inside triangles pass back and forth (two-touch passing)
- on coach's command players run zigzag around cones and first player to get to coach wins

Variation:
- specify how players must pass (left or right foot, high or low etc.)
- adjust spacing depending on the age and ability of the group

Coaching Points:
weight of pass - accuracy - body position and balance

Passing Gates

Click Here To View The Drill Animation!
Age Group: (5-7yrs) (8-11yrs) (12-15yrs)
Emphasis: passing
Description:
- players pass to each other as shown

Variation:
- three (two) touch limitation
- specify how players must pass/receive (left or right foot, inside or outside foot, high or low etc.)
- adjust spacing depending on the age and ability of the group

Coaching Points:
eye contact - body mechanics - balance - weight of pass - first touch

Passing Into End Zones

Click Here To View The Drill Animation!
Age Group: (8-11yrs) (12-15yrs) (16-Adult)
Emphasis: possession - passing
Description:
- play 4v4
- each team defends one designated end zone
- players attempt to make a pass to a teammate who is making a run into the end zone to receive the ball
- players cannot wait inside end zone to receive the ball

Variation:
- play 3v3, 5v5 etc.
- limit number of touches
- adjust spacing depending on the age and ability of the group

Coaching Points:
first touch - constant movement - angle, distance and timing of support - vision - decision making - verbal and visual communication

Passing Into End Zones w Targets

Click Here To View The Drill Animation!
Age Group: (8-11yrs) (12-15yrs) (16-Adult)
Emphasis: possession - passing
Description:
- play 3v3
- each team defends a designated end zone
- each team has two targets in the attacking half outside the grid
- targets have two touches
- players attempt to make a pass to a teammate who is making a run into the end zone to receive the ball
- players cannot wait inside end zone to receive the ball

Variation:
- teams must pass to a target player before they can score
- play 3v3, 5v5 etc.
- targets have one touch only
- limit number of touches
- adjust spacing depending on the age and ability of the group

Coaching Points:
vision - first touch takes ball away from pressure - constant movement - angles of support to receive ball - body position – open to field - decision making - verbal and visual communication

Passing Into Target Areas 3

Click Here To View The Drill Animation!
Age Group: (8-11yrs) (12-15yrs) (16-Adult)
Emphasis: passing - possession
Description:
- play 4 v 4, 5 v 5, 6 v 6 etc.
- neutral players are responsible for keeping balls in play from the middle line
- players attempt to pass into target area to player who connects to a third teammate with a 1 or 2 touch pass in order to score
- switch roles once a team has five points

Variation:
- players must play a lofted pass to target player
- limit number of touches for field players
- adjust spacing depending on the age and ability of the group

Coaching Points:
angle, distance and timing of support - vision - decision making - verbal and visual communication - switch point of attack away from pressure - keep the ball moving with quick accurate passing

Passing Into Target Areas 4

Click Here To View The Drill Animation!
Age Group: (8-11yrs) (12-15yrs) (16-Adult)
Emphasis: passing - possession - attacking - defending
Description:
- 2 players in each target zone and one neutral defender in the center
- the coach calls out a number 1 - 4
- one of the players with the number becomes the defender and helps the blue neutral player in the center of the square to defend his target zone (other player stays behind to be the target player)
- defender passes a ball to any of the other three players and all of them become attackers to make 3 v 2
- attackers (no. 1,3 & 4) score by passing to target player number 2 who is inside his target zone
- defenders score passing to any of the other three target players in their target zones
- kick-ins only

Variation:
- attackers must make a lofted pass to target player in order to score
- limit number of touches for attackers
- adjust spacing depending on the age and ability of the group

Coaching Points:
accuracy - angle, distance and timing of support - vision - decision making - verbal and visual communication - switch point of attack away from pressure - keep the ball moving with quick accurate passing

Passing Pattern 1

Click Here To View The Drill Animation!
Age Group: (8-11yrs) (12-15yrs)
Emphasis: passing
Description:
- players pass to each other in the sequence as shown
- players leave their designated area to receive and pass the ball
- players must return to their area (triangle) after each pass

Variation:
- one touch passing
- reverse direction
- adjust spacing depending on the age and ability of the group

Coaching Points:
body position and balance - weight of pass - first touch - accuracy

Passing Pattern 2

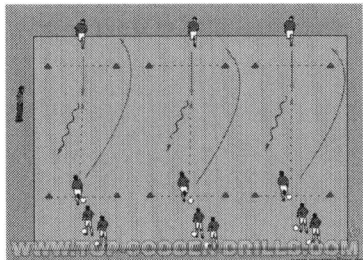

Click Here To View The Drill Animation!
Age Group: (5-7yrs) (8-11yrs) (12-15yrs)
Emphasis: passing
Description:
- players pass to partner who moves through gate to receive the ball
- pass giver follows his pass around gate as shown

Variation:
- specify how players must pass (left or right foot, inside or outside foot, high or low etc.)
- adjust spacing depending on the age and ability of the group

Coaching Points:
accuracy - weight of pass - eye contact - body mechanics

Passing Pattern 3

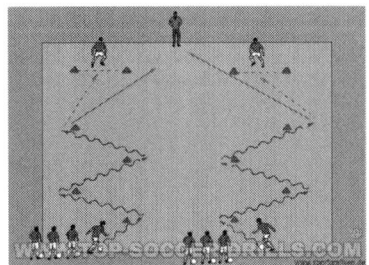

Click Here To View The Drill Animation!
Age Group: (5-7yrs) (8-11yrs) (12-15yrs)
Emphasis: passing - dribbling
Description:
- players dribble around cones as shown and pass to partner
- player to get to coach first after pass is awarded a point for his team
- team to score 20 points first wins

Variation:
- adjust spacing depending on the age and ability of the group

Coaching Points:
accuracy - eye contact - body mechanics

Passing Pattern 4

Click Here To View The Drill Animation!
Age Group: (5-7yrs) (8-11yrs) (12-15yrs) (16-Adult)
Emphasis: passing
Description:
- player passes to partner who runs to receive the ball in front of the cone and then moves back to make room for next player as shown

Variation:
- one-touch passing
- specify how players must pass (left or right foot, inside or outside foot, high or low etc.)
- adjust spacing depending on the age and ability of the group

Coaching Points:
accuracy - stay on your toes and always be prepared to receive the ball - players should accelerate towards the ball - players should try to develop a rhythm with their passing

Passing Pattern 5

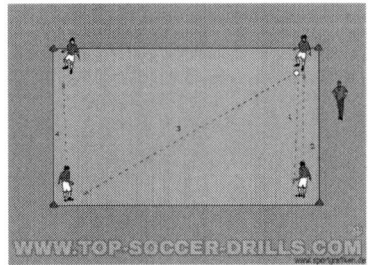

Click Here To View The Drill Animation!
Age Group: (5-7yrs) (8-11yrs) (12-15yrs) (16-Adult)
Emphasis: passing
Description:
- players pass to each other as shown
- sequence: short, short, long, short, short, long etc.

Variation:
- one-touch passing
- reverse direction
- specify how players must pass (left or right foot, inside or outside foot, high or low etc.)
- adjust spacing depending on the age and ability of the group

Coaching Points:
body mechanics - weight of pass - accuracy - first touch

Passing Pattern 6

Click Here To View The Drill Animation!
Age Group: (5-7yrs) (8-11yrs) (12-15yrs) (16-Adult)
Emphasis: passing
Description:
- players pass to each other as shown

Variation:
- one touch passing
- specify how players must pass (left or right foot, inside or outside foot, high or low etc.)
- adjust size of field if necessary

Coaching Points:
body mechanics - balance - weight of pass - accuracy - first touch

Passing Pattern 7

Click Here To View The Drill Animation!
Age Group: (5-7yrs) (8-11yrs) (12-15yrs) (16-Adult)
Emphasis: passing
Description:
- players pass to each other in the sequence as shown

Variation:
- one-touch passing
- specify how players must pass (left or right foot, inside or outside foot, high or low etc.)
- adjust spacing depending on the age and ability of the group

Coaching Points:
body mechanics - balance - weight of pass - accuracy - first touch

Passing Pattern 8

Click Here To View The Drill Animation!
Age Group: (8-11yrs) (12-15yrs) (16-Adult)
Emphasis: passing
Description:
- players pass to each other in sequence as shown
1. high pass over player in middle
2. player receives high pass and passes it on to player in middle
3. player in middle controls pass and passes it back to starting player

Variation:
- player who receives lofted pass can go through the following skills:(inside foot volley, top of the foot volley, thigh volley, chest volley, headers etc.)
- one-touch passing for player at outer cones
- adjust spacing depending on the age and ability of the group

Coaching Points:
accuracy - weight of pass - first touch - body position and balance - eye on ball - contact surface

Passing Pattern 9

Click Here To View The Drill Animation!
Age Group: (5-7yrs) (8-11yrs) (12-15yrs) (16-Adult)
Emphasis: passing
Description:
- play with two balls and place two or more players at each station
- players pass and follow using two touches

Variation:
- one-touch passing
- adjust spacing depending on the age and ability of the group

Coaching Points:
weight of pass - accuracy - first touch - communication

Passing Pattern 10

Click Here To View The Drill Animation!
Age Group: (5-7yrs) (8-11yrs) (12-15yrs) (16-Adult)
Emphasis: passing
Description:
- play with two balls and place two players at opposite corners as shown
- players pass and follow using two touch

Variation:
- one-touch passing
- specify how players must pass/receive (left or right foot, inside or outside foot, high or low etc.)
- adjust spacing depending on the age and ability of the group

Coaching Points:
weight of pass - accuracy - first touch - communication

Passing Pattern 11

Click Here To View The Drill Animation!
Age Group: (5-7yrs) (8-11yrs) (12-15yrs)
Emphasis: passing
Description:
- players pass and follow their pass

Variation:
- limit number of touches
- specify how players must pass/receive (left or right foot, inside or outside foot, high or low etc.)
- adjust spacing depending on the age and ability of the group

Coaching Points:
body mechanics - balance - weight of pass - accuracy - first touch - communication

Passing Pattern 12

Click Here To View The Drill Animation!
Age Group: (8-11yrs) (12-15yrs) (16-Adult)
Emphasis: passing
Description:
- players pass and follow their pass by running zig zag around cones

Variation:
- limit number of touches
- specify how players must pass/receive (left or right foot, inside or outside foot, high or low etc.)
- adjust spacing depending on the age and ability of the group

Coaching Points:
body mechanics - balance - weight of pass - accuracy - first touch - communication - accelerate towards cones

Passing Pattern 13

Click Here To View The Drill Animation!
Age Group: (8-11yrs) (12-15yrs) (16-Adult)
Emphasis: passing
Description:
- player A passes to player B who dribbles the ball to the next cone and passes to player C who passes back right away
- player B now repeats the sequence in the other direction
- player C + D simultaneously start the sequence on the other side
- which group can pass the ball the longest without making an error
- rotate positions after 2-3 minutes

Variation:
- specify how players must pass/receive (left or right foot, inside or outside foot etc.)
- adjust spacing depending on the age and ability of the group

Coaching Points:
body mechanics - balance - weight of pass - accuracy - first touch

Passing Pattern 14

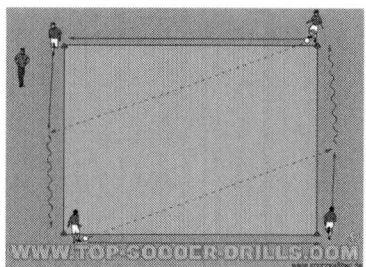

Click Here To View The Drill Animation!
Age Group: (5-7yrs) (8-11yrs) (12-15yrs) (16-Adult)
Emphasis: passing
Description:
- players pass to each other in the sequence as shown
- players pass 2 balls simultaneously

Variation:
- limit number of touches
- specify how players must pass/receive (left or right foot, inside or outside foot, high or low etc.)
- adjust spacing depending on the age and ability of the group

Coaching Points:
body mechanics - balance - weight of pass - accuracy - first touch

Passing Pattern 15

Click Here To View The Drill Animation!
Age Group: (5-7yrs) (8-11yrs) (12-15yrs)
Emphasis: passing
Description:
- players pass to each other in the sequence as shown
- players switch starting positions each turn

Variation:
- limit number of touches
- specify how players must pass/receive (left or right foot, inside or outside foot etc.)
- adjust spacing depending on the age and ability of the group

Coaching Points:
body mechanics - balance - weight of pass - accuracy - first touch

Passing Pattern 16

Click Here To View The Drill Animation!
Age Group: (5-7yrs) (8-11yrs) (12-15yrs)
Emphasis: passing
Description:
- players pass to each other as shown
- outside players play one touch

Variation:
- adjust spacing depending on the age and ability of the group

Coaching Points:
body mechanics - balance - weight of pass - accuracy - first touch

Passing Pattern 17

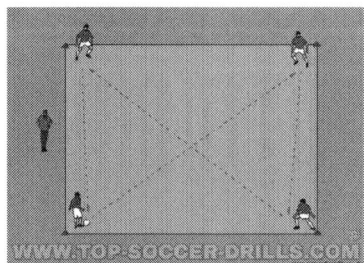

Click Here To View The Drill Animation!
Age Group: (5-7yrs) (8-11yrs) (12-15yrs)
Emphasis: passing
Description:
- players pass to each other in the sequence as shown
- switch positions every 2-3 minutes

Variation:
- one-touch passing
- specify how players must pass/receive (left or right foot, inside or outside foot, high or low etc.)
- adjust spacing depending on the age and ability of the group

Coaching Points:
body mechanics - balance - weight of pass - accuracy - first touch

Passing Pattern 18

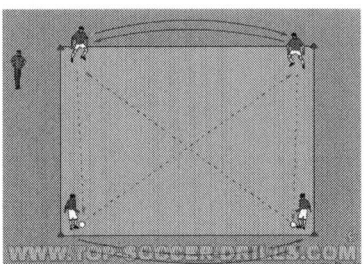

Click Here To View The Drill Animation!
Age Group: (8-11yrs) (12-15yrs)
Emphasis: passing
Description:
- players pass to each other and switch positions in the sequence as shown
- switch positions after 2-3 minutes

Variation:
- all players make diagonal passes
- adjust spacing depending on the age and ability of the group

Coaching Points:
body mechanics - balance - weight of pass - accuracy - first touch - time your passes - communication

Passing Pattern 19

Click Here To View The Drill Animation!
Age Group: (5-7yrs) (8-11yrs) (12-15yrs) (16-Adult)
Emphasis: passing
Description:
- players pass two balls in the same direction
- which group can pass the balls the longest without making error

Variation:
- one-touch passing
- specify how players must pass/receive (left or right foot, inside or outside foot etc.)
- adjust spacing depending on the age and ability of the group

Coaching Points:
body mechanics - balance - weight of pass - accuracy - first touch

Passing SSG Goals Back To Back

Click Here To View The Drill Animation!
Age Group: (8-11yrs) (12-15yrs) (16-Adult)
Emphasis: passing - finishing
Description:
- play 6v6
- each team defends and attacks a goal

Variation:
- teams can score on both goals
- 2 points are awarded for goals off a header, volley etc.
- goals only count off a header, volley etc.
- limit number of touches
- adjust spacing depending on the age and ability of the group

Coaching Points:
constant movement - communication - good angle and distance of support to receive ball - quality of preparation touch - contact surface - aggressive and positive mentality - vision and anticipation - placement versus power - positioning to gain an advantage

Passing SSG Middle Cone Goal

Click Here To View The Drill Animation!
Age Group: (5-7yrs) (8-11yrs) (12-15yrs) (16-Adult)
Emphasis: passing - possession
Description:
- teams can score by making a pass through cone goal that is received by a teammate (low passes only)
- players are not allowed to cross goal line

Variation:
- teams must complete a certain number of consecutive passes before they can pass through cone goal
- adjust spacing depending on the age and ability of the group

Coaching Points:
players should spread out - selection of pass & timing of pass - constant movement - communication is vital - good angle and distance of support to receive ball - switching point of attack

Passing SSG Middle Cone Goal 2

Click Here To View The Drill Animation!
Age Group: (5-7yrs) (8-11yrs) (12-15yrs) (16-Adult)
Emphasis: passing - possession - finishing
Description:
- teams score from both sides of the goal

Variation:
- each team can score only from one designated side of the goal
- adjust spacing depending on the age and ability of the group

Coaching Points:
ball must be kept on the ground - players should spread out - constant movement - communication - good angle and distance of support to receive ball

Passing SSG Middle Cone Goal 3

Click Here To View The Drill Animation!
Age Group: (5-7yrs) (8-11yrs) (12-15yrs) (16-Adult)
Emphasis: passing - possession
Description:
- teams can score on either goal and from both sides
- teams score by passing through a cone goal to a teammate

Variation:
- same rules as before but now each team defends one goal
- adjust spacing depending on the age and ability of the group

Coaching Points:
only low passes - players should spread out - selection of pass & timing of pass - constant movement - communication is vital - good angle and distance of support to receive ball - switching point of attack

Passing SSG Middle Cone Goal 4

Click Here To View The Drill Animation!
Age Group: (5-7yrs) (8-11yrs) (12-15yrs) (16-Adult)
Emphasis: possession - passing
Description:
- play 5v5
- teams can score on either goal and from both sides
- kick- ins only

Variation:
- play 3v3, 4v4 etc.
- each team defends and attacks one goal
- adjust size of field and cone goals if necessary

Coaching Points:
only low passes - players should spread out - selection of pass & timing of pass - constant movement - communication is vital - good angle and distance of support to receive ball - switch point of attack

Passing SSG Middle Cone Goal 5

Click Here To View The Drill Animation!
Age Group: (5-7yrs) (8-11yrs) (12-15yrs) (16-Adult)
Emphasis: possession - passing
Description:
- play 4v4
- teams can score from all sides
- each goalie defends two sides
- kick- ins only

Variation:
- play 3v3, 5v5 etc.
- limit number of touches
- adjust spacing depending on the age and ability of the group

Coaching Points:
only low passes - players should spread out - selection of pass & timing of pass - constant movement - communication is vital - good angle and distance of support to receive ball - switch point of attack

Passing to Team Captains

Click Here To View The Drill Animation!
Age Group: (5-7yrs) (8-11yrs) (12-15yrs) (16-Adult)
Emphasis: possession - passing
Description:
- play 4v4
- players score by passing to their team captain who is inside the goal zone
- passer then becomes team captain and takes over the role inside the goal zone

Variation:
- play 3v3, 5v5 etc.
- only passes below the waist allowed
- limit number of touches
- adjust spacing depending on the age and ability of the group

Coaching Points:
communication - vision - first touch takes ball away from pressure - constant movement - angles of support to receive ball - quick transitions

Passing Triangle 1

Click Here To View The Drill Animation!
Age Group: (5-7yrs) (8-11yrs) (12-15yrs)
Emphasis: passing
Description:
- players make a pass to player inside triangle
- receiver of pass must dribble out of triangle through another side of the triangle as shown
- pass giver takes receiver's spot in triangle
- player with most amount of passes within 2 min. wins

Variation:
- players inside triangle play a 1-2 pass with dribbler
- specify how players dribble, pass and receive the ball
- adjust spacing depending on the age and ability of the group

Coaching Points:
communication - good first touch into space - close control - accurate passes - first touch

Passing Triangle 2

Click Here To View The Drill Animation!
Age Group: (5-7yrs) (8-11yrs) (12-15yrs) (16-Adult)
Emphasis: passing
Description:
- players dribble inside playing area
- players make a pass to player inside the triangle who then dribbles out through a different side of the triangle as shown
- pass giver follows pass and takes receiver's spot inside triangle
- players switch role if defender wins ball (defender carries pinnie)

Variation:
- adjust spacing depending on the age and ability of the group

Coaching Points:
communication - good first touch - accuracy

Passing Triangle 3

Click Here To View The Drill Animation!
Age Group: (5-7yrs) (8-11yrs) (12-15yrs)
Emphasis: passing
Description:
- players inside triangle play wall passes
- passes come in through one side and go out another as shown
- player with most amount of passes within 2 min. wins
- switch roles every 2-3 minutes

Variation:
- specify how players must pass (left or right foot, inside or outside foot, high or low etc.)
- limit number of touches for players inside triangles
- adjust spacing depending on the age and ability of the group

Coaching Points:
communication - good first touch into space - accuracy

Passing Triangle 4

Click Here To View The Drill Animation!
Age Group: (5-7yrs) (8-11yrs) (12-15yrs)
Emphasis: passing
Description:
- players inside triangle play wall passes as shown
- passes come in through one side and go out another as shown
- players switch role if defender wins the ball (defender carries pinnie)
- player with most amount of passes within 2 min. wins
- switch roles every 2-3 minutes

Variation:
- specify how players must pass (left or right foot, inside or outside foot, high or low etc.)
- adjust spacing depending on the age and ability of the group

Coaching Points:
communication - good first touch into space - accuracy

Plus 1 Neutral Player

Click Here To View The Drill Animation!
Age Group: (5-7yrs) (8-11yrs) (12-15yrs) (16-Adult)
Emphasis: attacking - defending - possession - passing - finishing
Description:
- each team defends and attacks a goal
- neutral players must stay in designated half
- attacking team can only score if neutral player touches the ball first

Variation:
- neutral players only have one touch
- adjust spacing depending on the age and ability of the group

Coaching Points:
accurate passes - quick decision making - protect the ball - good angle of support - movement on and off the ball - vision

Plus 2 Channel Players

Click Here To View The Drill Animation!
Age Group: (8-11yrs) (12-15yrs) (16-Adult)
Emphasis: passing - finishing - attacking - defending
Description:
- 2v2 with 2 channel players on the attacking team in each half
- channel player with the ball attempts to make a cross
- opposite channel player must pinch in to create numbers up situation
- if ball is won by the defenders channel player must retreat back to his designated area
- defenders attempt to make a pass to their channel players or attackers
- goals off a cross count 2 points

Variation:
- adjust spacing depending on the age and ability of the group

Coaching Points:
constant movement - communication - good angle and distance of support to receive ball - create supporting angles - look to combine - keep the ball moving with quick accurate passing

Possess to Finish

Click Here To View The Drill Animation!
Age Group: (8-11yrs) (12-15yrs) (16-Adult)
Emphasis: attacking - defending - possession - passing - finishing
Description:
- play 6v6 in three zones
- teams have to connect 3 passes in the defending third
- teams have to connect 2 passes in the middle third
- free play in the attacking third
- free play if the ball is won in the middle or attacking third

Variation:
- if the ball is won in the defending third the goalie has to receive a pass to help switching the attack
- limit number of touches
- adjust spacing depending on the age and ability of the group

Coaching Points:
accuracy - selection of pass & timing of pass - angle, distance and timing of support - body position – open to field - decision making - verbal and visual communication - shape of team to maintain possession - aggressive and positive mentality - vision and anticipation

Possession (2v2 + 4) # 1

Click Here To View The Drill Animation!
Age Group: (8-11yrs) (12-15yrs) (16-Adult)
Emphasis: passing - possession
Description:
- 2v2 with 2 target players in each half
- team in possession has to make at least three passes in the grid before they can play to a target player of the other grid
- they can score again by repeating the feat and returning to the grid, following a pass to a target player

Variation:
- limit number of touches for target players
- adjust spacing depending on the age and ability of the group

Coaching Points:
importance of first touch to control and prepare ball - players should accelerate towards the ball - constant movement - communication is vital - good angle and distance of support to receive ball

Possession 7 2v2 + 4

Click Here To View The Drill Animation!
Age Group: (8-11yrs) (12-15yrs) (16-Adult)
Emphasis: passing - possession
Description:
- 2v2 with 2 target players in each half
- team in possession has to make at least three passes in the grid before they can play to a target player of the other grid
- they can score again by repeating the sequence and returning to the grid, following a pass to a target player

Variation:
- limit number of touches for target players
- adjust spacing depending on the age and ability of the group

Coaching Points:
first touch - accuracy - constant movement - angle, distance and timing of support - vision - decision making - verbal and visual communication

Possession 8 4v2

Click Here To View The Drill Animation!
Age Group: (5-7yrs) (8-11yrs) (12-15yrs) (16-Adult)
Emphasis: passing - possession
Description:
- players play 4v2 two-touch keep away
- two players in the middle need to touch the ball to get out
- defenders stay in the middle for another turn if a pass splits them
- players on the outside must stay on the line to pass and receive
- any player that gives away possession goes in the middle

Variation:
- one-touch passing only
- play 4v1, 5v2 etc.
- adjust spacing depending on the age and ability of the group

Coaching Points:
weight of pass - accuracy - disguise - communication - quick decision making

Possession Game

Click Here To View The Drill Animation!
Age Group: (8-11yrs) (12-15yrs) (16-Adult)
Emphasis: passing - possession - defending
Description:
- 5 attackers vs 2 defenders
- attackers keep possession and play from one to the other grid across middle zone
- one defender is allowed to pressure and win the ball
- other defender can only stay inside middle zone attempting to intercept a pass
- once the pass is made to the other grid the defenders switch roles
- pass giver must follow into other grid to support
- switch roles every 3-5 minutes

Variation:
- attackers must complete 2-3 passes before they can pass to other grid
- add an extra defender
- limit number of touches
- adjust spacing depending on the age and ability of the group

Coaching Points:
quick passing - angle, distance and timing of support - vision - body position – open to field - decision making - verbal and visual communication

Possession Game 2

Click Here To View The Drill Animation!
Age Group: (8-11yrs) (12-15yrs) (16-Adult)
Emphasis: passing - possession - defending
Description:
- 4 attackers play keep away from two defenders
- if defenders win possession they look to play the ball into the other grid to their teammates and then sprint into the other square to support them
- two attackers go into other square to try to win the ball back

Variation:
- limit number of touches
- adjust spacing depending on the age and ability of the group

Coaching Points:
quick passing - angle, distance and timing of support - vision - body position – open to field - decision making - verbal and visual communication - keep possession

Possession Game 3

Click Here To View The Drill Animation!
Age Group: (8-11yrs) (12-15yrs) (16-Adult)
Emphasis: passing - possession - defending
Description:
- red team starts with the ball and three blue players (defenders) go over to their area to try to win the ball
- red team plays one or two touch keep-away
- if a defender wins the ball, he has to pass it back over to his area on his first or second touch
- three red players then go into the blue team's area to do the same

Variation:
- vary number of defenders
- adjust spacing depending on the age and ability of the group

Coaching Points:
quick passing - angle, distance and timing of support - vision - body position – open to field - decision making - verbal and visual communication

Possession Game 4

Click Here To View The Drill Animation!
Age Group: (5-7yrs) (8-11yrs) (12-15yrs) (16-Adult)
Emphasis: passing - possession - defending
Description:
- red team plays keep-away (5v2)
- red team has to complete three passes before passing the ball (across middle zone) to the other red team to do the same

Variation:
- limit number of touches
- adjust spacing depending on the age and ability of the group

Coaching Points:
quick passing - angle, distance and timing of support - vision - body position – open to field - decision making - verbal and visual communication

Possession Game 5 (3v1)

Click Here To View The Drill Animation!
Age Group: (5-7yrs) (8-11yrs) (12-15yrs) (16-Adult)
Emphasis: passing - possession - defending
Description:
- red team plays keep-away (3v1)
- red team has to complete three passes before passing the ball (across middle zone) to the other red team to do the same

Variation:
- limit number of touches
- adjust spacing depending on the age and ability of the group

Coaching Points:
quick passing - angle, distance and timing of support - vision - body position – open to field - decision making - verbal and visual communication

Possession Game 6 w Squares

Click Here To View The Drill Animation!
Age Group: (8-11yrs) (12-15yrs) (16-Adult)
Emphasis: passing - possession
Description:
- play 4v4
- each team defends and attacks one square
- teams score by passing through the square to another teammate
- one defender is allowed inside the square who acts as a goalie
- after each goal ball starts with the team that was scored upon

Variation:
- play 5v5, 6v6 etc.
- teams can score on both squares
- limit number of touches
- adjust size of field and/or target areas

Coaching Points:
first touch - quick transition - aggressive and positive mentality - vision and anticipation - quick decision making - switch point of attack - spread out attack

Possession Game 7

Click Here To View The Drill Animation!
Age Group: (5-7yrs) (8-11yrs) (12-15yrs) (16-Adult)
Emphasis: passing - possession
Description:
- team in possession scores by passing the ball to knock off the ball which is placed on top of a cone in the center square
- kick-ins only

Variation:
- play 3v1, 4v1, 4v2, 5v2, 5v3 etc.
- limit number of touches
- adjust spacing depending on the age and ability of the group

Coaching Points:
angle, distance and timing of support - vision - body position – open to field - decision making - verbal and visual communication - shape of team to maintain possession - constant movement - quick decision making - quick finish - look to combine

Possession Game 8

Click Here To View The Drill Animation!
Age Group: (5-7yrs) (8-11yrs) (12-15yrs) (16-Adult)
Emphasis: passing - possession
Description:
- play 4v2
- attacking team must play two-touch and can only score if the goal scorer finishes on one-touch
- team in possession scores by passing the ball to knock off the ball which is placed on top of a cone in the center square
- if the defending team wins the ball or kicks it out of the grid then they switch with the attacking player who made the mistake
- kick-ins only

Variation:
- play 5v2, 5v3, 4v1 etc.
- attacking team must connect 3 passes before they can score
- one-touch passing
- adjust spacing depending on the age and ability of the group

Coaching Points:
angle, distance and timing of support - vision - body position – open to field - decision making - verbal and visual communication - shape of team to maintain possession - constant movement - quick decision making - quick finish - look to combine

Possession Passing Drill

Click Here To View The Drill Animation!
Age Group: (8-11yrs) (12-15yrs) (16-Adult)
Emphasis: passing
Description:
- players pass to each other and cannot leave an empty cone adjacent to the player with the ball
- players move quickly to the next supporting position
- players can only receive passes in the corners of the grid

Variation:
- limit number of touches
- add a defender (same rules apply)
- adjust spacing depending on the age and ability of the group

Coaching Points:
weight of pass - first touch - communication - quick decision making - accuracy

Possession Passing Game

Click Here To View The Drill Animation!
Age Group: (8-11yrs) (12-15yrs) (16-Adult)
Emphasis: possession - passing
Description:
- play 2v2 with a neutral player who plays for the team that is in possession
- teams score by connecting 3 passes before making a fourth pass to a teammate who makes a run outside the grid to receive the ball

Variation:
- limit number of touches
- fourth pass must be lofted
- adjust spacing depending on the age and ability of the group

Coaching Points:
angle, distance and timing of support - vision - decision making - verbal and visual communication - first touch - accuracy

Possession Winner

Click Here To View The Drill Animation!
Age Group: (5-7yrs) (8-11yrs) (12-15yrs) (16-Adult)
Emphasis: attacking - defending - passing - possession
Description:
- play 6v6
- if a team scores they cannot score again until the other team scores a goal
- team that is winning tries to keep possession for as long as possible but cannot score again until the losing team scores the equalizer
- winning team must play 1 or 2 touch

Variations:
- add a neutral player
- adjust spacing depending on the age and ability of the group

Coaching Points:
vision and awareness - concentration - angle, distance and timing of support - body position – open to field - decision making - verbal and visual communication - shape of team to maintain possession

Quick Finish

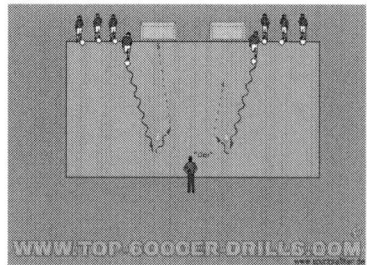

Click Here To View The Drill Animation!
Age Group: (5-7yrs) (8-11yrs) (12-15yrs)
Emphasis: finishing - passing - dribbling
Description:
- players dribble around cone and attempt to shoot the ball into their goal first
- 2 points to score first; 1 point for just scoring; 0 points for missing the goal
- team with most points after 5-7 minutes wins

Variation:
- use tall cones instead of mini goals as targets
- play with three groups (three goals) for more repetition
- specify how players must shoot (left or right foot, inside or laces, high or low etc.)
- adjust spacing depending on the age and ability of the group

Coaching Points:
body mechanics and control of body - body position and balance - eye on ball - quality of preparation touch - contact surface - aggressive and positive mentality - placement versus power

Quick Passing

Click Here To View The Drill Animation!
Age Group: (5-7yrs) (8-11yrs) (12-15yrs)
Emphasis: passing
Description:
- 4 players on the outside of the grid and 2 players in the center grid
- players in the center start by passing a ball to a player on the outside of the grid
- outside player who receives it plays the ball back one touch and calls out the name of another outside player
- player in the center receives the pass and turns to that player and repeats the sequence
- switch roles after 2-3 minutes

Variation:
- one-touch for outside players
- specify how players must pass/receive (left or right foot, inside or outside foot, high or low etc.)
- adjust spacing depending on the age and ability of the group

Coaching Points:
accuracy - good speed of play - vision - first touch - communication - quick decision making - awareness

Quick Passing 2

Click Here To View The Drill Animation!
Age Group: (5-7yrs) (8-11yrs) (12-15yrs)
Emphasis: passing
Description:
- one player stands in the center grid with four more players standing around the outside, each having a ball
- one outside player passes to the center player and calls out the name of another outside player before he receives the ball back
- player in the center turns and makes a run towards that player up to the edge of the grid and repeats the sequence

Variation:
- add another player to be in the center square
- one touch for player in the center
- specify how players must pass/receive (left or right foot, inside or outside foot, high or low etc.)
- adjust spacing depending on the age and ability of the group

Coaching Points:
accuracy - good ball speed - vision - first touch - communication - quick decision making - awareness

Quick Passing 3

Age Group: (5-7yrs) (8-11yrs) (12-15yrs) (16-Adult)
Emphasis: passing
Description:
- two players stand in the center grid with four more players standing around the outside, each having a ball
- one outside player passes to the center player and calls out the name of another outside player before he receives the ball back
- player in the center turns and makes a run towards that player up to the edge of the grid and repeats the sequence
- challenge to keep passing sequence going without errors for 60 sec.
- which grid can keep going the longest without an error?

Variation:
- one-touch for players in the center
- specify how players must pass/receive (left or right foot, inside or
-    outside foot, high or low etc.)
- adjust spacing depending on the age and ability of the group

Coaching Points:
accuracy - good ball speed - vision - first touch - communication - quick decision making - awareness

Relay Dribbling 1

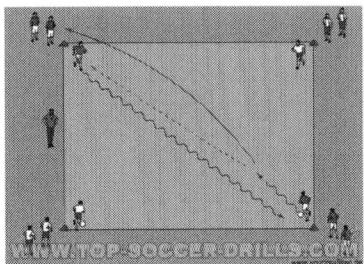

Click Here To View The Drill Animation!
Age Group: (5-7yrs) (8-11yrs) (12-15yrs) (16-Adult)
Emphasis: dribbling - passing
Description:
- first player touches ball twice before he passes and follows it as shown
- next player dribbles back and stops the ball dead in front of next the player
- next player repeats the sequence
- team to get back to its starting position first wins

Variation:
- specify how players must dribble (left or right foot, inside or outside foot etc.)
- specify how players must pass/receive (left or right foot, inside or outside foot, high or low etc.)
- adjust spacing depending on the age and ability of the group

Coaching Points:
weight of pass - accuracy - first touch - agility and balance - contact surface of foot - close control - soft touch

Relay Race 3

Click Here To View The Drill Animation!
Age Group: (5-7yrs) (8-11yrs)
Emphasis: dribbling
Description:
- relay race
- players dribble around cone and stop the ball dead in front of next player
- first team back to its original position wins

Variation:
- players dribble zig zac around cones (V1)
- payers dribble diagonally from cone to cone (v2)
- players run around cone with a ball in their hands and hand it over to the next player
- players dribble a ball around cone with a ball in their hands
- players dribble a ball backwards with a ball in their hands
- adjust spacing depending on the age and ability of the group if necessary

Coaching Points:
agility and balance - contact surface of foot - change of direction   - close control

Relay Race 4

Click Here To View The Drill Animation!
Age Group: (8-11yrs) (12-15yrs) (16-Adult)
Emphasis: passing
Description:
- each group has one designated wall player
- players dribble and pass in the sequence as shown
- the first group to be back to its original position after 2-3 rounds wins

Variation:
- specify how players must pass/receive (left or right foot, inside or outside foot, high or low etc.)
- one touch passing
- adjust spacing depending on the age and ability of the group if necessary

Coaching Points:
agility and balance - change of speed & direction - acceleration - close control - soft touches - weight of pass - accuracy - communication

Scoring with Restriction

Click Here To View The Drill Animation!
Age Group: (5-7yrs) (8-11yrs) (12-15yrs) (16-Adult)
Emphasis: passing - finishing - attacking - defending
Description:
- each team defends and attacks 2 goals
- players only are allowed to score from inside the playing area as shown
- ball must stay on the ground

Variation:
- goals only count if it was scored with the first touch
- goals only count after two passes
- adjust spacing depending on the age and ability of the group

Coaching Points:
ball movement - quick finish - combinations - switch point of attack - angle, distance and timing of support - aggressive and positive mentality - placement versus power

Scoring with Restriction 2

Click Here To View The Drill Animation!
Age Group: (5-7yrs) (8-11yrs) (12-15yrs) (16-Adult)
Emphasis: passing - finishing
Description:
- each team defends 2 adjacent goals or opposite from each other
- players only are allowed to score from inside the playing area as shown
- ball must stay on the ground

Variation:
- each team defends two designated goals
- goals only count if it was scored on the first touch
- goals only count after two passes
- adjust spacing depending on the age and ability of the group

Coaching Points:
quick finish - combinations 1-2 - switch point of attack

Scrimmage w Channel Players

Click Here To View The Drill Animation!
Age Group: (8-11yrs) (12-15yrs) (16-Adult)
Emphasis: dribbling - passing - attacking - defending
Description:
- each team defends and attacks one goal
- one neutral player in each channel
- 3 points for goals that come off a cross from one of the channel players
- one defender can come into channel after channel player's first (second) touch

Variation:
- players in the middle area have a maximum of three touches
- ball must go through both channels for a goal to count
- adjust spacing depending on the age and ability of the group if necessary

Coaching Points:
shift us a unit - pressure the ball - quick decision making - switch point of attack - vision - close control - verbal and visual communication - accuracy - weight of pass

Scrimmage w Channels

Click Here To View The Drill Animation!
Age Group: (8-11yrs) (12-15yrs) (16-Adult)
Emphasis: dribbling - attacking - defending
Description:
- each team defends and attacks one goal
- if the attacking team has the ball inside one channel the defending team must have all its players move out of the opposite channel (3x violations = 1x penalty)

Variation:
- add one or two neutral players who cannot score
- ball must go through one channel for a goal to count
- ball must go through both channels for a goal to count
- if the attacking team has the ball inside a channel it has to have all its players move out of the opposite channel

Coaching Points:
shift us a unit - pressure the ball - quick decision making - switch point of attack - change of direction and speed - deception - set up defender - protect the ball - vision - close control - verbal and visual communication

Scrimmage w Two Neutrals

Click Here To View The Drill Animation!
Age Group: (5-7yrs) (8-11yrs) (12-15yrs) (16-Adult)
Emphasis: dribbling - attacking - possession
Description:
- each defends and attacks one goal with goalie
- one neutral player on each side line as shown
- neutral players cannot be challenged unless they dribble into the grid
- neutral players must return to the side line after a shot on goal or if the attacking team loses the ball

Variation:
- players must take a maximum of three touches
- adjust spacing depending on the age and ability of the group if necessary

Coaching Points:
quick finish - good first touch - attack open space - angle, distance and timing of support - vision - decision making - verbal and visual communication - create space for others - attack space behind defense

Scrimmage w Two Neutrals 2

Click Here To View The Drill Animation!
Age Group: (5-7yrs) (8-11yrs) (12-15yrs) (16-Adult)
Emphasis: dribbling - attacking - possession
Description:
- each defends and attacks one goal with goalie
- wall players on the side line help one designated team to create a numbers up situation
- wall players cannot be challenged unless they dribble into the grid
- neutral players must return to the side line after a shot on goal or if the attacking team loses the ball
- after 5-10 minutes wall players play for the other team exclusively

Variation:
- players must take a maximum of three touches
- adjust spacing depending on the age and ability of the group if necessary

Coaching Points:
quick finish - good first touch - attack open space - angle, distance and timing of support - vision - decision making - verbal and visual communication - create space for others - attack space behind defense

Self Pass in Groups

Click Here To View The Drill Animation!
Age Group: (5-7yrs) (8-11yrs) (12-15yrs) (16-Adult)
Emphasis: passing
Description:
- players with the ball pass it through open legs of standing players
- player with most passes within 90 seconds wins

Variation:
- players make a half moon pass (i.e. pass it past a player to his right and run by him on his left to receive own pass)
- players perform a move before making a the self-pass through legs
- specify how players must pass (left or right foot etc.)
- adjust spacing depending on the age and ability of the group

Coaching Points:
body mechanics - balance - weight of pass - accuracy

Separate 1v1s With Targets

Click Here To View The Drill Animation!
Age Group: (5-7yrs) (8-11yrs) (12-15yrs) (16-Adult)
Emphasis: passing
Description:
- 2 pairs inside the grid
- 4 neutral players around the grid
- each pair plays a separate 1v1 inside the grid
- two of the four neutral players have soccer balls
- players inside the grid score by passing to a neutral player who doesn't have a ball
- once a goal is scored the passer runs to receive a new ball from another neutral player as shown
- switch roles after appr. 2 minutes

Variation:
- vary number of pairs inside the grid
- vary number of neutral players with a ball
- adjust spacing depending on the age and ability of the group

Coaching Points:
disguise - vision - first touch - communication - quick decision making - accuracy over power

Shooting Combination

Click Here To View The Drill Animation!
Age Group: (8-11yrs) (12-15yrs) (16-Adult)
Emphasis: finishing - passing
Description:
- player A passes to player B who lays it off to the side to player A who makes a lead pass to player B who has made a run towards the goal to receive the ball and finish
- once the sequence is completed player B gets back in line and player A takes player B's starting position
- switch sides after 8-10 min.

Variation:
- specify how players must shoot (left or right foot, inside or laces, high or low etc.)
- players must finish on goal one-touch
- ball cannot bounce before it goes into the goal
- adjust spacing depending on the age and ability of the group

Coaching Points:
body mechanics and control of body - body position and balance - eye on ball - quality of preparation touch - contact surface - aggressive and positive mentality - placement versus power - accurate passing

Shooting Competition

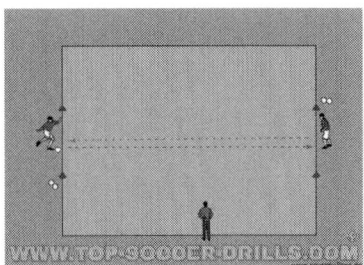

Click Here To View The Drill Animation!
Age Group: (5-7yrs) (8-11yrs) (12-15yrs)
Emphasis: finishing - passing
Description:
- players try to shoot the ball past their partner at the opposite side while keeping the ball in the channel
- the other player attempts to block/receive the ball before it goes past him through the cone goal
- if the ball gets past the player between the two cones, the shooting player is awarded a point
- low shots only

Variation:
- specify how players must shoot (left or right foot, inside foot or laces etc.)
- adjust size of grid depending on the age and ability of the group

Coaching Points:
body mechanics and control of body - body position and balance - eye on ball - quality of preparation touch - contact surface - aggressive and positive mentality - placement versus power

Shooting Coordination Drill 1

Click Here To View The Drill Animation!
Age Group: (8-11yrs) (12-15yrs) (16-Adult)
Emphasis: finishing - coordination
Description:
- players pass, do coordination exercises and shoot on goal in the sequence as shown

Variation:
- specify how players must shoot (left or right foot, inside or laces, high or low etc.)
- adjust spacing depending on the age and ability of the group

Coaching Points:
body mechanics and control of body - body position and balance - eye on ball - quality of preparation touch - contact surface - aggressive and positive mentality - vision and anticipation - placement versus power - positioning to gain an advantage

Shooting Coordination Drill 2

Click Here To View The Drill Animation!
Age Group: (8-11yrs) (12-15yrs) (16-Adult)
Emphasis: finishing - coordination
Description:
- players pass their ball along the line of hurdles and then they make two-footed (one-footed) jumps over the hurdles
- next they pass through the cone goal and finish on goal one-touch

Variation:
- specify how players must shoot (left or right foot, inside or laces, high or low etc.)
- adjust spacing depending on the age and ability of the group

Coaching Points:
body mechanics and control of body - body position and balance - eye on ball - quality of preparation touch - contact surface - aggressive and positive mentality - placement versus power

Shooting Coordination Drill 4

Age Group: (5-7yrs) (8-11yrs) (12-15yrs) (16-Adult)
Emphasis: finishing - coordination
Description:
- players jump one-footed (two-footed) over the hurdle and receive a pass from either the left or right side and then take a touch and finish on goal
- switch pass-givers after 5 minutes

Variation:
- pass-givers make a lofted pass
- specify how players must shoot (left or right foot, inside or laces, high or low etc.)
- adjust spacing depending on the age and ability of the group

Coaching Points:
body mechanics and control of body - body position and balance - eye on ball - quality of preparation touch - contact surface - aggressive and positive mentality - placement versus power

Shooting Coordination Drill 5

Click Here To View The Drill Animation!
Age Group: (8-11yrs) (12-15yrs) (16-Adult)
Emphasis: finishing - coordination
Description:
- players pass, do coordination exercises and shoot on goal in the sequence as shown
- players must finish on goal with their second (first) touch

Variation:
- specify how players must shoot (left or right foot, inside or laces, high or low etc.)
- adjust spacing depending on the age and ability of the group

Coaching Points:
body mechanics and control of body - body position and balance - eye on ball - quality of preparation touch - contact surface - aggressive and positive mentality - vision and anticipation - placement versus power - positioning to gain an advantage

Shooting Drill 1

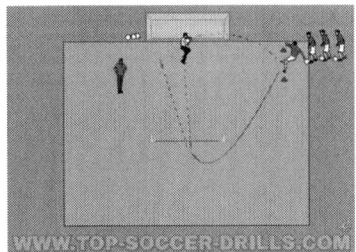

Click Here To View The Drill Animation!
Age Group: (8-11yrs) (12-15yrs) (16-Adult)
Emphasis: finishing - passing
Description:
- first player in line makes a lofted pass to the goalkeeper who catches it and then rolls the ball through the yellow cone goal
- passer runs around the yellow cone goal to receive the ball and finish on goal

Variation:
- shooter must finish one-touch
- first pass is on the ground and the goalie passes it through cone goal
- specify how players must shoot (left or right foot, inside or laces, high or low etc.)
- adjust spacing depending on the age and ability of the group

Coaching Points:
body mechanics and control of body - body position and balance - eye on ball - quality of preparation touch - contact surface - aggressive and positive mentality - vision and anticipation - placement versus power - positioning to gain an advantage

Shooting Drill w Center Grid 3

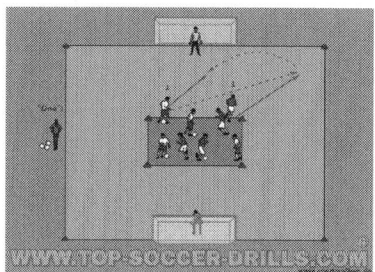

Click Here To View The Drill Animation!
Age Group: (8-11yrs) (12-15yrs) (16-Adult)
Emphasis: finishing - passing
Description:
- each pairing is assigned a number
- players pass to their partners inside the grid
- on coach's command the player with the ball in that moment dribbles out of the center grid and passes to his partner who makes a run towards one of the corner flags
- the player then crosses it back in front of the goal to his partner

Variation:
- players must finish on goal with a header or volley
- limit number of touches inside the center grid
- players throw the ball to each other inside the center grid
- adjust spacing depending on the age and ability of the group

Coaching Points:
quality of preparation touch - aggressive and positive mentality - vision and anticipation - placement versus power - positioning to gain an advantage

Shooting Drill w Center Grid 5

Click Here To View The Drill Animation!
Age Group: (8-11yrs) (12-15yrs) (16-Adult)
Emphasis: finishing
Description:
- all players from each group are assigned a number from 1-4
- each group is assigned a goal which to score on
- players dribble inside playing area
- when coach calls out a number the players with that number pass to a target player who lays it of for a shot on goal
- players are awarded a point if they score and an extra point if the shot is on target
- first player to shoot is awarded an extra point
- the group with most points wins

Variation:
- specify how players must shoot (left or right foot, inside or laces, high or low etc.)
- players juggle in center grid and then pass to the target player
- the shot cannot touch the ground before it goes into the goal
- adjust spacing depending on the age and ability of the group

Coaching Points:
body mechanics and control of body - body position and balance - eye on ball - quality of preparation touch - contact surface - aggressive and positive mentality - vision and anticipation - placement versus power - positioning to gain an advantage

Shooting Exercise 6

Click Here To View The Drill Animation!
Age Group: (8-11yrs) (12-15yrs) (16-Adult)
Emphasis: finishing - passing
Description:
- players pass and shoot in the sequence as shown
- first shot is taken with the laces and second shot with the inside foot

Variation:
- limit number of touches
- adjust spacing depending on the age and ability of the group

Coaching Points:
body mechanics and control of body - body position and balance - eye on ball - quality of preparation touch - contact surface - aggressive and positive mentality - vision and anticipation - placement versus power - positioning to gain an advantage

Short Passing 1

Click Here To View The Drill Animation!
Age Group: (8-11yrs) (12-15yrs) (16-Adult)
Emphasis: passing
Description:
- two players in between red cones move back and forth to receive the ball and pass to players standing behind blue cones

Variation:
- only one player moves back and forth between red cones
- one-touch passing
- adjust spacing depending on the age and ability of the group

Coaching Points:
body mechanics - balance - weight of pass - accuracy - first touch

Short Passing 2

Click Here To View The Drill Animation!
Age Group: (5-7yrs) (8-11yrs) (12-15yrs)
Emphasis: passing
Description:
- players in between red line of cones move back and forth to receive the ball and pass to players who stand behind blue line of cones
- middle player to complete most passes within 60 seconds wins
- switch roles often

Variation:
- one-touch passing
- adjust spacing depending on the age and ability of the group

Coaching Points:
body mechanics - balance - weight of pass - accuracy - first touch - go faster gradually - make eye contact

Short Passing 3

Click Here To View The Drill Animation!
Age Group: (5-7yrs) (8-11yrs) (12-15yrs) (16-Adult)
Emphasis: passing
Description:
- players pass back and forth from inside a designated square
- players cannot leave square to receive or pass the ball
- pair to complete most passes within 2 minutes wins

Variation:
- one-touch passing
- specify how players must pass/receive (left or right foot, inside or outside foot, high or low etc.)
- adjust spacing depending on the age and ability of the group

Coaching Points:
body mechanics - balance - weight of pass - accuracy - first touch - make eye contact

Short Passing 4

Click Here To View The Drill Animation!
Age Group: (5-7yrs) (8-11yrs) (12-15yrs) (16-Adult)
Emphasis: passing
Description:
- players pass back and forth from inside a designated square
- players cannot leave square to receive or pass the ball
- players must run around one of the cones after each pass
- pair to complete most passes within 2 minutes wins

Variation:
- one-touch passing
- specify how players must pass/receive (left or right foot, inside or outside foot, high or low etc.)
- adjust spacing depending on the age and ability of the group

Coaching Points:
body mechanics - balance - weight of pass - accuracy - first touch - make eye contact

Short Passing 5

Click Here To View The Drill Animation!
Age Group: (5-7yrs) (8-11yrs) (12-15yrs) (16-Adult)
Emphasis: passing
Description:
- players pass to each other as shown
- after each pass players run around cones before receiving next pass
- pair to complete most passes within 2 minutes wins

Variation:
- one-touch passing
- specify how players must run around cones
- specify how players must pass and receive
- adjust spacing depending on the age and ability of the group

Coaching Points:
accuracy over power - first touch - make eye contact - move towards the ball - go faster gradually

Short Passing 6

Click Here To View The Drill Animation!
Age Group: (5-7yrs) (8-11yrs) (12-15yrs) (16-Adult)
Emphasis: passing
Description:
- one player runs between the cones back and forth to receive his partner's pass which he then returns to him
- switch roles every 1-2 minutes
- player to complete most passes within 90 seconds wins

Variation:
- one-touch passing for running player
- adjust spacing depending on the age and ability of the group

Coaching Points:
accuracy over power - first touch - make eye contact - go faster gradually

Short Passing 7

Click Here To View The Drill Animation!
Age Group: (5-7yrs) (8-11yrs) (12-15yrs) (16-Adult)
Emphasis: passing
Description:
- each player stand in front of a blue cone and pass in between white cones to their partner on the opposite side
- two touch passing (1.receive 2. pass)
- practice for 90 seconds and then make it competitive
- pair to complete most passes within 90 seconds wins

Variation:
- one-touch passing
- specify how players must pass/receive (left or right foot, inside or outside foot, etc.)
- adjust spacing depending on the age and ability of the group

Coaching Points:
accuracy over power - first touch - make eye contact - go faster gradually

Short Passing 8

Click Here To View The Drill Animation!
Age Group: (5-7yrs) (8-11yrs) (12-15yrs) (16-Adult)
Emphasis: passing
Description:
- players pass back and forth as shown
- players run back and forth between cones before and after each pass as shown

Variation:
- one-touch passing
- specify how players must pass/receive (left or right foot, inside or outside foot, high or low etc.)
- adjust spacing depending on the age and ability of the group

Coaching Points:
body mechanics - balance - weight of pass - accuracy - first touch - communication

Short Passing 9

Click Here To View The Drill Animation!
Age Group: (8-11yrs) (12-15yrs) (16-Adult)
Emphasis: passing
Description:
- player with the ball dribbles to open corner cone
- once he gets to the cone he passes to his partner while moving (ball cannot come to a standstill)
- the receiver now dribbles to the open corner cone and passes to his partner while moving
- continue sequence
- team to complete most passes in 90 seconds wins

Variation:
- three or four touch max for each player
- adjust spacing depending on the age and ability of the group

Coaching Points:
body mechanics - balance - weight of pass - accuracy - first touch

Short Passing 10

Click Here To View The Drill Animation!
Age Group: (8-11yrs) (12-15yrs) (16-Adult)
Emphasis: passing
Description:
- target player in the middle of the square starts by passing to any player standing by a cone
- corner player with the ball passes to any other available player
- target player moves towards corner player to receive the ball back from the player he just passed it to

Variation:
- one-touch passes back to target player
- adjust spacing depending on the age and ability of the group

Coaching Points:
body mechanics - balance - weight of pass - accuracy - first touch

Short Passing 11

Click Here To View The Drill Animation!
Age Group: (5-7yrs) (8-11yrs) (12-15yrs) (16-Adult)
Emphasis: passing
Description:
- players pass and run to the end of their line
- which group can keep on passing without making an error
- repeat setup to accommodate the entire team

Variation:
- limit number of touches
- specify how players must pass/receive (left or right foot, inside or outside foot, high or low etc.)
- adjust spacing depending on the age and ability of the group

Coaching Points:
body mechanics - balance - weight of pass - accuracy - first touch

Shot Set Up

Click Here To View The Drill Animation!
Age Group: (8-11yrs) (12-15yrs) (16-Adult)
Emphasis: finishing
Description:
- player A passes to player B who lets the ball run through his legs for player C
- player C lays off for B and then spins outside to attack the far post

Variation:
- specify how players must shoot (left or right foot, inside or laces, high or low etc.)
- player A chips the ball over player B to player C who lays off for player B
- shooter must finish with his first touch
- adjust spacing depending on the age and ability of the group

Coaching Points:
body mechanics and control of body - body position and balance - eye on ball - quality of preparation touch - contact surface - aggressive and positive mentality - placement versus power - accuracy of pass - weight of pass

Small Sided Finishing Game

Click Here To View The Drill Animation!
Age Group: (8-11yrs) (12-15yrs) (16-Adult)
Emphasis: finishing - attacking - defending
Description:
- 4 defenders vs. 2 attackers in each half
- players must stay in their designated area
- the defenders shoot from their own half of the field and the forwards can only score on rebounds

Variation:
- defenders must connect 2 passes before they can score
- limit number of touches for defenders
- adjust spacing depending on the age and ability of the group

Coaching Points:
body mechanics and control of body - body position and balance - eye on ball - quality of preparation touch - contact surface - aggressive and positive mentality - vision and anticipation - placement versus power - positioning to gain an advantage

Small Sided Shooting Game 2

Click Here To View The Drill Animation!
Age Group: (8-11yrs) (12-15yrs) (16-Adult)
Emphasis: finishing - passing - attacking - defending
Description:
- 3 neutral ball feeders positioned around the grid as shown
- play 3v3 with a neutral goalie
- the ball is fed in if the game ball goes out of bounce or goal is scored
- players feed the ball in following order (1, 2, 3, 1, 2, 3 ....)

Variation:
- specify how players must shoot (left or right foot, inside or laces, high or low etc.)
- vary number of ball feeders
- play 4v4, 5v5 etc.
- balls are played in various ways (thrown, rolled, high pass etc.)
- ball feeders play in the ball randomly (communication)
- limit number of touches
- adjust spacing depending on the age and ability of the group

Coaching Points:
body mechanics and control of body - body position and balance - eye on ball - quality of preparation touch - contact surface - aggressive and positive mentality - vision and anticipation - placement versus power - positioning to gain an advantage

Small Sided Shooting Game 4

Click Here To View The Drill Animation!
Age Group: (8-11yrs) (12-15yrs) (16-Adult)
Emphasis: finishing - passing - attacking - defending
Description:
- play 4v4 plus goalies
- each team must stay in their own half
- objective is to score a goal by shooting from your own half
- one defender is allowed into the opponent's half to pressure the ball
- the defending team can try and block shots

Variation:
- two defenders can enter the opponent's half to pressure the ball
- teams must connect 5 passes before they can score
- limit number of touches
- adjust spacing depending on the age and ability of the group

Coaching Points:
good ball movement - body mechanics and control of body - body position and balance - eye on ball - quality of preparation touch - contact surface - aggressive and positive mentality - placement versus power - switch point of attack

Small Sided Shooting Game 5

Click Here To View The Drill Animation!
Age Group: (8-11yrs) (12-15yrs) (16-Adult)
Emphasis: finishing - passing - attacking - defending
Description:
- play 5v5
- each team must stay in their own half
- objective is to score a goal by shooting from your own half
- one attacker is allowed into the opponent's half to go for a rebound
- the defending team tries to block all shots

Variation:
- teams must connect 5 passes before they can score
- limit number of touches
- adjust spacing depending on the age and ability of the group

Coaching Points:
body mechanics and control of body - body position and balance - eye on ball - quality of preparation touch - contact surface - aggressive and positive mentality - placement versus power - switch point of attack

Small Sided Shooting Game 6

Click Here To View The Drill Animation!
Age Group: (8-11yrs) (12-15yrs) (16-Adult)
Emphasis: finishing - passing - attacking - defending
Description:
- play 3v1 in each half
- players must stay in their designated half
- objective is to score a goal by shooting from your own half
- three players in possession may play back to their goalkeeper
- the forward in the attacking half pressures the ball
- the defending team tries to block all shots
- no throw ins, corners or goal kicks
- ball always starts with the goalie

Variation:
- teams must connect 5 passes before they can score
- limit number of touches
- adjust spacing depending on the age and ability of the group

Coaching Points:
body mechanics and control of body - body position and balance - eye on ball - quality of preparation touch - contact surface - aggressive and positive mentality - placement versus power - switch point of attack

Soccer Targets

Click Here To View The Drill Animation!
Age Group: (5-7yrs) (8-11yrs) (12-15yrs)
Emphasis: dribbling
Description:
- 2-6 designated (blue) target players (depending on group size)
- shooters attempt to pass their ball against the target's ball
- targets try to get away from shooters
- shooters are awarded a point for each hit
- switch roles every 2-3 min.

Variation:
- specify how players must pass (left or right foot, inside or outside foot etc.)
- group of shooters only has two (one) balls to pass around to each other with the objective to hit a target's ball
- vary number of target players
- target players are without a ball and can only be hit below the knees for a point to count
- adjust spacing depending on the age and ability of the group if necessary

Coaching Points:
accuracy over power - vision - first touch - deception - change of speed & direction - protect the ball - close control

Speed Dribbling

Click Here To View The Drill Animation!
Age Group: (5-7yrs) (8-11yrs) (12-15yrs)
Emphasis: dribbling - passing
Description:
- first player dribbles up to the far cone and passes it to the next player
- the passing player follows his pass as shown
- activity continues until all players have returned to their original starting positions

Variation:
- specify how players must dribble and receive (inside or outside of foot, sole, left or right foot only etc.)
- specify how players must pass/receive (left or right foot, inside or outside foot, high or low etc.)
- adjust spacing depending on the age and ability of the group if necessary

Coaching Points:
weight of pass - accuracy - eye contact - close control

Steady Wing Players

Click Here To View The Drill Animation!
Age Group: (5-7yrs) (8-11yrs) (12-15yrs) (16-Adult)
Emphasis: dribbling - passing - attacking - defending
Description:
- each team defends and attacks one goal
- one team has two neutral players on the side line as shown
- neutrals on the side line help the team that has possession
- neutrals cannot be challenged unless they dribble into the grid
- neutrals must return to their side line after a shot on goal or if the team in possession loses the ball
- switch roles 5-10 minutes

Variation:
- maximum of three (two) touches for neutrals
- adjust spacing depending on the age and ability of the group if necessary

Coaching Points:
switch point of attack - attack open space - change of direction and speed - deception - set up defender - vision - close control - quick finish - decision making - verbal and visual communication

Striker in Attacking Zone 1

Click Here To View The Drill Animation!
Age Group: (8-11yrs) (12-15yrs) (16-Adult)
Emphasis: finishing - passing - attacking
Description:
- play 4v4 in the middle zone
- one attacker in each end zone
- all players must stay in their zone initially
- teams score by connecting a pass to their attacker in the attacking end zone who then tries to finish on goal
- the defenders can enter the end zone once the attacker receives the ball
- switch players in end zones

Variation:
- play 5v5, 6v6, 7v7 in the middle zone etc.
- limit number of touches for players in the end zones
- adjust spacing depending on the age and ability of the group

Coaching Points:
weight of pass - accuracy - disguise - quality of preparation touch - aggressive and positive mentality - vision and anticipation - placement versus power - positioning to gain an advantage - angle, distance and timing of support
body position – open to field
decision making
verbal and visual communication

Striker in Attacking Zone 2

Click Here To View The Drill Animation!
Age Group: (8-11yrs) (12-15yrs) (16-Adult)
Emphasis: finishing - passing - attacking
Description:
- play 4v4 in the middle zone
- one attacker in each end zone
- all players must stay in their designated zone
- teams must connect three passes before they can pass to the attacking player in the end zone
- the attacking player then lays off for a shot on goal as shown
- switch players in end zones

Variation:
- play 5v5, 6v6, 7v7 in the middle zone etc.
- striker lays off the ball for another attacking player who is followed by a defender inside the end zone
- strikers inside the end zone are neutral which allows teams to score on both goals
- limit number of touches for strikers
- adjust spacing depending on the age and ability of the group

Coaching Points:
weight of pass - accuracy - disguise - quality of preparation touch - aggressive and positive mentality - vision and anticipation - placement versus power - positioning to gain an advantage - angle, distance and timing of support - body position – open to field - decision making - verbal and visual communication

Striker in Attacking Zone 3

Click Here To View The Drill Animation!
Age Group: (8-11yrs) (12-15yrs) (16-Adult)
Emphasis: finishing - passing - attacking
Description:
- each team defends one goal
- play 4v4 in the middle zone
- one striker in each end zone
- all players must stay in their designated zone
- teams must connect three passes before they can pass to the attacking player in the end zone
- the attacking player then lays off for a shot on goal as shown
- switch players in end zones

Variation:
- play with 2 mini goals on each goal line
- play 5v5, 6v6, 7v7 in the middle zone etc.
- strikers inside the end zone are neutral which allows teams to score on both goals
- limit number of touches for strikers
- adjust spacing depending on the age and ability of the group

Coaching Points:
weight of pass - accuracy - disguise - quality of preparation touch - aggressive and positive mentality - vision and anticipation - placement versus power - positioning to gain an advantage - angle, distance and timing of support - body position – open to field - decision making - verbal and visual communication

Striker in Attacking Zone 4

Click Here To View The Drill Animation!
Age Group: (8-11yrs) (12-15yrs) (16-Adult)
Emphasis: finishing - passing - attacking
Description:
- play 4v4 in the middle zone
- one neutral player in each end zone
- all players must stay in their designated zone
- teams must connect three passes before they can pass to the neutral player in the end zone
- the neutral player then lays off for a shot on goal as shown
- switch players in end zones

Variation:
- play 5v5, 6v6, 7v7 in the middle zone etc.
- play with 2 mini goals on each goal line
- limit number of touches for neutral players
- adjust spacing depending on the age and ability of the group

Coaching Points:
weight of pass - accuracy - disguise - quality of preparation touch - aggressive and positive mentality
vision and anticipation
placement versus power
positioning to gain an advantage
angle, distance and timing of support
body position – open to field
decision making
verbal and visual communication

Stuck in the Mud

Click Here To View The Drill Animation!
Age Group: (5-7yrs) (8-11yrs) (12-15yrs)
Emphasis: dribbling - passing
Description:
- game of tag with 2 taggers
- all players dribble a ball except for the taggers
- taggers carry a pinnie with which they apply a tag
- if a player is tagged, he picks up his ball and opens his legs
- teammates can unfreeze a tagged player by making a pass through their legs
- taggers win if they tag all players within 2-4 minutes
- switch pair of taggers

Variation:
- specify how players must dribble (inside or outside of foot, left or right foot only etc.)
- vary number of taggers
- adjust spacing depending on the age and ability of the group

Coaching Points:
close control - head up - attack the open space - change of speed & direction - agility and balance - accurate passes

Sudden Transition

Click Here To View The Drill Animation!
Age Group: (5-7yrs) (8-11yrs) (12-15yrs) (16-Adult)
Emphasis: passing - attacking - defending
Description:
- play 6v6
- each team defends a goal
- on coach's command the attacking team leaves the ball to the defending team who quickly attacks

Variations:
- limit number of touches for attacking team
- adjust spacing depending on the age and ability of the group

Coaching Points:
Defending: quick transition - positioning to provide cover and balance - defend vital space – squeeze toward center (compactness-concentration) - defend space behind - track players
Attacking: support position lateral to ball - combination play (1-2, double pass, overlap, take over) - unbalancing the defense - create space for others - attack space behind defense - supporting angle and distance to ball

Switch Point Of Attack 1

Click Here To View The Drill Animation!
Age Group: (5-7yrs) (8-11yrs) (12-15yrs) (16-Adult)
Emphasis: possession - passing
Description:
- each team defends 2 goals
- one neutral player in each grid
- teams score by connecting 3 passes and switching to the neutral player in the adjacent grid who lays off for a player of the possessing team to score a goal
- neutral players are not allowed to score
- repeat sequence
- kick ins only

Variation:
- limit number of touches
- goals can only be scored with a first touch
- the pass to switch the grid must be lofted
- adjust size of grid depending on the age and ability of the group

Coaching Points:
switch point of attack - ball movement - angle, distance and timing of support - vision - decision making - verbal and visual communication - quick transitions

Switch Point Of Attack 2

Click Here To View The Drill Animation!
Age Group: (8-11yrs) (12-15yrs) (16-Adult)
Emphasis: passing - possession - attacking - defending
Description:
- each team defends and attacks a goal with goalie
- teams must make a pass across the middle line before they can score

Variation:
- attacking team can score on both goals only after making a pass across the middle line, defending team attempts to keep possession
- switch roles after 8-10 minutes

Coaching Points:
angle, distance and timing of support - vision - body position (open to field) - decision making - verbal and visual communication

Switching Keep Away

Click Here To View The Drill Animation!
Age Group: (8-11yrs) (12-15yrs) (16-Adult)
Emphasis: passing - possession - defending
Description:
- five players try to keep the ball away from the two defenders
- after three (four) passes they are allowed to pass the ball to a player from the other grid who makes a run into the area between the two grids to receive the ball
- once he touches the ball the other two defenders from outside are allowed to enter the grid to pressure the ball
- the attacking team that loses possession or makes a mistake then switches roles with the defending team

Variation:
- play 4v1, 5v3, 5v1 etc.
- pass to switch the grid must be one-touch
- player that switches the ball to the other grid must chip the ball
- allow the defenders to enter the grid as soon as the pass is made
- limit number of touches
- adjust spacing depending on the age and ability of the group

Coaching Points:
Attacking: angle, distance and timing of support - vision - body position – open to field - decision making - verbal and visual communication
Defending: angle and distance of cover - changing role of pressure and cover - angle and speed of approach - body shape, balance, and foot positioning - delay and channel

Target Passing With Defenders

Click Here To View The Drill Animation!
Age Group: (8-11yrs) (12-15yrs) (16-Adult)
Emphasis: passing
Description:
- players on the outside of grid attempt to knock off balls from cones
- defenders on the inside of grid attempt to block shots
- balls which end up inside the grid can be retrieved by players
- team to knock off most balls within 2 min. wins

Variation:
- vary number of defenders
- vary number of targets
- use tall cones as targets
- players run around nearest corner cone after each shot/pass
- adjust spacing depending on the age and ability of the group

Coaching Points:
dribble around grid to find clear path towards target - aggressive and positive mentality - placement versus power - positioning to gain an advantage

Target Players 2

Click Here To View The Drill Animation!
Age Group: (5-7yrs) (8-11yrs) (12-15yrs) (16-Adult)
Emphasis: possession - passing
Description:
- each team has 2 players positioned outside the grid on adjacent sides as shown
- teams can score by passing to a target player and receiving a pass back from him
- teams cannot score on same target player twice in a row

Variation:
- target player only has one touch
- target player switches with pass giver
- adjust spacing depending on the age and ability of the group

Coaching Points:
angle, distance and timing of support - vision - body position – open to field - decision making - verbal and visual communication - good ball movement

Target Players 3

Click Here To View The Drill Animation!
Age Group: (5-7yrs) (8-11yrs) (12-15yrs) (16-Adult)
Emphasis: possession - passing
Description:
- teams score by passing to neutral target player inside middle box

Variation:
- team score a point only if they play a wall pass with target player
- adjust size of field and middle box if necessary

Coaching Points:
angle, distance and timing of support - vision - body position – open to field - decision making - verbal and visual communication

Target Players 4

Click Here To View The Drill Animation!
Age Group: (5-7yrs) (8-11yrs) (12-15yrs) (16-Adult)
Emphasis: possession - passing
Description:
- players score by passing to a teammate through middle box or by making 5 consecutive passes among teammates
- players cannot run through middle box

Variation:
- limit number of touches
- adjust spacing depending on the age and ability of the group

Coaching Points:
quick ball movement - angle, distance and timing of support - vision - body position (open to field) - decision making - verbal and visual communication

Target Players 5

Click Here To View The Drill Animation!
Age Group: (8-11yrs) (12-15yrs) (16-Adult)
Emphasis: possession - passing
Description:
- each team has a target player positioned inside the middle box
- teams score by passing to teams target player
- target player who receives a pass switches with pass giver as shown

Variation:
- team score a point only if they play a wall pass with target player
- adjust spacing depending on the age and ability of the group

Coaching Points:
angle, distance and timing of support - vision - body position – open to field - decision making - verbal and visual communication - quick ball movement

Target Players 6

Click Here To View The Drill Animation!
Age Group: (8-11yrs) (12-15yrs) (16-Adult)
Emphasis: possession - passing
Description:
- players attempt to pass to a teammate who is making a run into the middle box to receive the ball
- players cannot wait inside the box to receive the ball

Variation:
- add a neutral player
- limit number of touches
- adjust spacing depending on the age and ability of the group

Coaching Points:
angle, distance and timing of support - vision - body position – open to field - decision making - verbal and visual communication

Target Players 7

Click Here To View The Drill Animation!
Age Group: (8-11yrs) (12-15yrs) (16-Adult)
Emphasis: possession - passing
Description:
- two neutral players start with a ball
- attackers attempt to receive passes from neutral players from outside the grid and then pass it back to a different neutral player
- defenders try prevent attackers from receiving/completing passes
- if defenders win the ball they give it to the nearest neutral player
- attacking team to complete most passes within 3 minutes wins
- switch roles often

Variation:
- attackers are limited to one touch
- add another ball
- adjust spacing depending on the age and ability of the group

Coaching Points:
angle, distance and timing of support - vision - decision making - verbal and visual communication - first touch

Target Players 8

Click Here To View The Drill Animation!
Age Group: (5-7yrs) (8-11yrs) (12-15yrs) (16-Adult)
Emphasis: possession - passing
Description:
- 2 teams play 4v4 inside the playing area
- 2 neutral players are positioned opposite from each other
- teams score a point by passing the ball to a neutral player
- teams cannot score on same target player twice in a row

Variation:
- target players must play one (two) touch
- teams score by passing to both target players in one possession
- adjust spacing depending on the age and ability of the group

Coaching Points:
angle, distance and timing of support - vision - decision making - verbal and visual communication - first touch

Target Players 9

Click Here To View The Drill Animation!
Age Group: (8-11yrs) (12-15yrs) (16-Adult)
Emphasis: possession - passing
Description:
- each team has 2 players positioned outside the grid on opposite sides as shown
- teams score by passing to a target player
- teams cannot score on same target player twice in a row

Variation:
- limit number of touches for target players or field players
- target player switches with pass giver
- adjust spacing depending on the age and ability of the group

Coaching Points:
angle, distance and timing of support - vision - decision making - verbal and visual communication

Target Players 10

Click Here To View The Drill Animation!
Age Group: (5-7yrs) (8-11yrs) (12-15yrs) (16-Adult)
Emphasis: passing - possession
Description:
- 2 teams play 4v4
- each team has a target player positioned in a designated zone
- team score by passing to their target player

Variation:
- teams can only score if their target player can control a lofted pass
- adjust spacing depending on the age and ability of the group

Coaching Points:
communication - create supporting angles - weight of pass - accuracy - disguise - vision - first touch

Target Players 11

Click Here To View The Drill Animation!
Age Group: (8-11yrs) (12-15yrs) (16-Adult)
Emphasis: passing - possession
Description:
- 2 teams play 4v4
- each team has a target player positioned in each zone
- team score by passing to their target player who then must pass to a third player on the same team
- opposing player in target zone prevents other player from receiving or completing a pass

Variation:
- teams can only score if their target player can control a lofted pass
- adjust spacing depending on the age and ability of the group

Coaching Points:
angle, distance and timing of support - decision making - verbal and visual communication - weight of pass - accuracy - disguise - vision - first touch

Target Players 12

Click Here To View The Drill Animation!
Age Group: (5-7yrs) (8-11yrs) (12-15yrs) (16-Adult)
Emphasis: passing - possession
Description:
- teams play 4v4, 5v5 or 6v6 etc.
- teams score by getting the ball from one target player and play it to the other without losing possession to the defending team

Variation:
- teams score if one or both target players can control a lofted pass
- adjust spacing depending on the age and ability of the group

Coaching Points:
communication - create supporting angles - weight of pass - accuracy - vision - first touch

Target Players 13

Click Here To View The Drill Animation!
Age Group: (8-11yrs) (12-15yrs) (16-Adult)
Emphasis: passing - possession
Description:
- two target players and one defender in each end zone
- teams play 3v3, 4v4, 5v5 or 6v6 etc. in the middle
- teams score by getting the ball from one target player and play it to the other without losing possession to the defending team

Variation:
- target players have one or two touches
- teams score if one or both target players can control a lofted pass
- adjust spacing depending on the age and ability of the group

Coaching Points:
communication - create supporting angles - weight of pass - accuracy - vision - first touch

Target Players 14

Click Here To View The Drill Animation!
Age Group: (8-11yrs) (12-15yrs) (16-Adult)
Emphasis: passing - possession
Description:
- one target player and one defender in each end zone
- teams play 3v3, 4v4, 5v5 or 6v6 etc. in the middle
- teams score by getting the ball from one target player and play it to the other without losing possession to the defending team

Variation:
- target players have one or two touches
- teams score if one or both target players can control a lofted pass
- adjust spacing depending on the age and ability of the group

Coaching Points:
communication - create supporting angles - weight of pass - accuracy - vision - first touch

Target Players 15

Click Here To View The Drill Animation!
Age Group: (8-11yrs) (12-15yrs) (16-Adult)
Emphasis: passing - possession
Description:
- play 6v4 with one target in each end zone
- the attacking team with six players scores by passing to a target player in the end zone who passes to a third player
- the defending team with 4 players scores by passing into either of the four mini goals (players must take shot from inside the grid for the goal to count)

Variation:
- play 4v2, 5v3, 5v2, 6v3 etc.
- use cone goals instead of mini goals (vary number of goals)
- target players are limited to one or two touches
- the attacking team scores if one target players can control a lofted pass and then connects a pass to a third player
- adjust spacing depending on the age and ability of the group

Coaching Points:
angle, distance and timing of support - vision - decision making - verbal and visual communication - weight of pass
accuracy
vision
first touch

Target Players 16

Click Here To View The Drill Animation!
Age Group: (8-11yrs) (12-15yrs) (16-Adult)
Emphasis: finishing - possession - passing
Description:
- play 4v4
- each team has one target player in their attacking zone
- players must stay in their designated zone
- teams score by passing to their target player who passes back to a third player who then tries to score on either of the two goals

Variation:
- limit number of touches for targets
- goals must be scored off a first touch
- both targets are neutral which allows the teams to score on all four goals
- normal size goals with goalies instead of mini goals
- adjust spacing depending on the age and ability of the group

Coaching Points:
communication - create supporting angles - weight of pass - accuracy - vision - first touch

Target Players 17

Click Here To View The Drill Animation!
Age Group: (8-11yrs) (12-15yrs) (16-Adult)
Emphasis: finishing - passing - possession
Description:
- play 4v4, 5v5, 6v6, 7v7 etc.
- each team has one target player in their attacking zone
- players must stay in their designated zone
- teams try to make a pass to their target who lays the ball back for a shot on goal

Variation:
- limit number of touches for targets
- goals must be scored off a first touch
- target must lay back to a third player who takes a shot on goal
- both targets are neutral which allows the teams to score on both goals
- allow shots from the middle zone with the target being able to go for a rebound after a shot on goal
- adjust size of field and / or target zone if necessary

Coaching Points:
quick finish - communication - create supporting angles - weight of pass - accuracy - vision - first touch
aggressive and positive mentality
placement versus power

Target Players In Each Half

Click Here To View The Drill Animation!
Age Group: (8-11yrs) (12-15yrs) (16-Adult)
Emphasis: dribbling - passing - attacking - defending
Description:
- each team has two target players in the attacking half
- if a target player receives the ball from a teammate he dribbles it onto the field (passer takes the target players position)
- goals scored after a target player touches the ball are awarded 3 points

Variation:
- minimum of two (three) touches for all players
- target players can move around corner flag to opponent's goal line to support teammates
- adjust spacing depending on the age and ability of the group if necessary

Coaching Points:
attack open space - set up defender - protect the ball - vision - switch point of attack - communication - decision making - create space for others

Targets in Goals 1

Click Here To View The Drill Animation!
Age Group: (5-7yrs) (8-11yrs) (12-15yrs) (16-Adult)
Emphasis: passing - dribbling
Description:
- play 1v1 inside the grid and try to complete a penetrating shot, pass or dribble through the cone goals to the target player
- whoever plays the ball to the target player must replace them

Variation:
- one designated attacker and one designated defender who switch roles after 90 seconds
- adjust spacing depending on the age and ability of the group

Coaching Points:
quick decision making - accuracy - change of direction and speed - deception - set up defender - protect the ball - vision - close control

Targets in Goals 2

Click Here To View The Drill Animation!
Age Group: (5-7yrs) (8-11yrs) (12-15yrs) (16-Adult)
Emphasis: passing - possession
Description:
- play 4v4 inside the grid
- teams score by dribbling the ball to target players
- team starts with the ball from the goal it just scored upon
- losing team after 4-5 minutes switches with target players

Variation:
- teams score by completing pass through the cone goals to the target player
- each team can score on two designated targets
- adjust spacing depending on the age and ability of the group

Coaching Points:
vision - first touch - angle, distance and timing of support - decision making - verbal and visual communication - accuracy

Targets in Goals 3

Click Here To View The Drill Animation!
Age Group: (5-7yrs) (8-11yrs) (12-15yrs) (16-Adult)
Emphasis: passing - dribbling
Description:
- play 4v4 inside the grid
- teams score by passing it into one of the target players
- team starts with the ball from the goal it just scored upon
- that team cannot score into that goal again until they score in the 3 remaining corners first
- losing team after 4-5 minutes switches with target players

Variation:
- each team can score on two designated targets
- limit number of touches
- add neutral player on the field
- adjust spacing depending on the age and ability of the group

Coaching Points:
angle, distance and timing of support - vision - decision making - verbal and visual communication - set up defender - protect the ball - close control - first touch - accuracy

Targets in Goals 4

Click Here To View The Drill Animation!
Age Group: (5-7yrs) (8-11yrs) (12-15yrs) (16-Adult)
Emphasis: passing - dribbling
Description:
- play 5v4
- teams score by playing through any of the three remaining cone goals
- team with five players must always have a player in cone goal that was scored upon last
- switch roles after 5 minutes
- kick-ins only

Variation:
- limit number of touches for team with 5 players
- adjust spacing depending on the age and ability of the group

Coaching Points:
vision - first touch - quick decision making - constant movement - communication - good angle and distance of support to receive ball - spread out attack - switch point of attack

Team Knock Out

Click Here To View The Drill Animation!
Age Group: (5-7yrs) (8-11yrs) (12-15yrs)
Emphasis: dribbling - passing
Description:
- all players from one team dribble inside the grid
- players of the other group around the grid attempt to pass and hit the player's balls on the inside
- if a ball is hit, the player with that ball has to dribble around the grid one time before he can rejoin the game
- switch roles after 3-5 minutes
- group with most hits wins

Variation:
- vary number of balls for group on the outside
- specify how players must dribble (inside or outside of foot, left or right foot only etc.)
- specify how players must pass (left or right foot, inside or outside foot etc.)
- adjust spacing depending on the age and ability of the group

Coaching Points:
weight of pass - accurate passes - change of speed & direction - shielding the ball - protecting the ball - vision

Team Passing

Click Here To View The Drill Animation!
Age Group: (5-7yrs) (8-11yrs) (12-15yrs) (16-Adult)
Emphasis: passing
Description:
- players pass the ball to a teammate after they call out their name

Variation:
- players must run around the nearest cone after they complete a pass
- players only pass to a player from the other team after they call out the player's name
- specify how players must pass (left foot, right foot, high or low etc.)
- adjust spacing depending on the age and ability of the group

Coaching Points:
communication - body mechanics - balance - weight of pass - accuracy - first touch

Team Steal

Click Here To View The Drill Animation!
Age Group: (5-7yrs) (8-11yrs) (12-15yrs) (16-Adult)
Emphasis: dribbling - possession
Description:
- one team starts to dribble with 2-3 balls less than # of players
- players try to win and maintain possession
- team with most balls in their possession at the end wins
- alternate team that starts with the balls

Variation:
- vary number of balls
- adjust spacing depending on the age and ability of the group if necessary

Coaching Points:
Attacking: deception - set up defender - change of speed & direction - protect the ball - close control - angle, distance and timing of support - vision - decision making - verbal and visual communication
Defending: angle and distance of cover - intercept pass - track recovery runs - changing role of pressure and cover - visual and verbal communication - angle and speed of approach - body shape, balance, and foot positioning - control and restraint - delay and channel

Team Tag 2

Click Here To View The Drill Animation!

Age Group: (5-7yrs) (8-11yrs) (12-15yrs) (16-Adult)
Emphasis: passing - dribbling
Description:
- one team (taggers) attempts to tag the players on the other team by passing their soccer ball at them below their knee or on their soccer ball
- players keep score of how many times they tag the other team
- passes must below the knees
- teams switch roles after 3-5 minutes
- team with better score wins

Variation:
- adjust spacing depending on the age and ability of the group

Coaching Points:
vision - move away from pressure - change of speed & direction - awareness of surrounding - accuracy over power

Team Tag 3

Click Here To View The Drill Animation!
Age Group: (5-7yrs) (8-11yrs) (12-15yrs)
Emphasis: passing - dribbling
Description:
- all players dribble inside playing area and the players of one team try to tag (freeze) the other team
- if a player is tagged he must freeze, put the ball in his hands and open his legs
- players can unfreeze their teammate by passing the ball through the frozen player's legs
- objective for the taggers is to freeze all players of the opposing team
- teams switch roles once taggers freeze all opponents or after 3-4 minutes

Variation:
- coach or some other player can be the only "freezer"; players continue to unfreeze each other
- adjust spacing depending on the age and ability of the group

Coaching Points:
vision - move away from pressure - change of speed & direction - awareness of surrounding - accuracy over power - keep ball on ground - communication

Through Pass Finish

Click Here To View The Drill Animation!
Age Group: (8-11yrs) (12-15yrs) (16-Adult)
Emphasis: finishing
Description:
- players dribble along the line of the blue cones to pass down along the line of the red cones to his partner who makes a run to receive and finish on goal
- if the pass isn't on target the goalie is allowed to come out of the goal
- players switch roles on the next turn

Variation:
- switch sides after 5-10 minutes
- players must finish one-touch
- adjust spacing depending on the age and ability of the group

Coaching Points:
body mechanics and control of body - body position and balance - eye on ball - quality of preparation touch - contact surface - aggressive and positive mentality - vision and anticipation - placement versus power - positioning to gain an advantage

Through The Middle 1

Click Here To View The Drill Animation!
Age Group: (5-7yrs) (8-11yrs) (12-15yrs)
Emphasis: passing
Description:
- players position themselves around grid as shown
- players (red) attempt to hit ball that is being passed back and forth between (white) players

Variation:
- limit number of touches
- specify how players must pass (left or right foot, inside or outside foot etc.)
- adjust spacing depending on the age and ability of the group

Coaching Points:
weight of pass - accuracy - quick decision making

Through The Middle 2

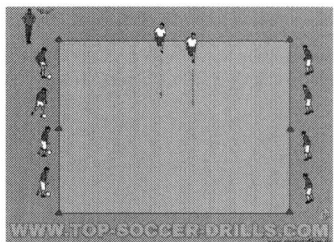

Click Here To View The Drill Animation!
Age Group: (5-7yrs) (8-11yrs) (12-15yrs)
Emphasis: passing
Description:
- players position themselves around grid as shown
- players (red) attempt to shoot at players who try running across grid without getting hit

Variation:
- vary number of players who run across grid
- specify how players must pass (left or right foot, inside or outside foot etc.)
- adjust spacing depending on the age and ability of the group

Coaching Points:
weight of pass - accuracy - quick decision making

Touch Restriction 1

Click Here To View The Drill Animation!
Age Group: (8-11yrs) (12-15yrs) (16-Adult)
Emphasis: dribbling - attacking - defending
Description:
- each team defends and attacks one goal
- maximum of 3 touches in defending third
- maximum of 2 touches in middle third
- maximum of 1 touch in attacking third
- if rule is broken automatic free kick for the other team

Variation:
- vary number of touches allowed in each third
- players must stay in their designated half
- each team selects one player who has unlimited touches
- adjust spacing depending on the age and ability of the group if necessary

Coaching Points:
Attacking: protect the ball - close control - angle, distance and timing of support - vision - decision making - verbal and visual communication - weight of pass - accuracy - first touch - aggressive and positive mentality in front of goal - placement versus power in front of goal
Defending: angle and speed of approach - control and restraint - delay and channel - angle and distance of cover - intercept pass - change role of pressure and cover - visual and verbal communication

Touch Restriction 2

Click Here To View The Drill Animation!
Age Group: (5-7yrs) (8-11yrs) (12-15yrs) (16-Adult)
Emphasis: dribbling - attacking - defending
Description:
- each teams defends and attacks one goal with goalkeeper
- team with 5 players has unlimited touches
- team with 6 players must have minimum of 2-3 touches
- switch roles after 5 minutes

Variation:
- play 4v3, 5v3, 7v6, 8v7 etc.
- adjust spacing depending on the age and ability of the group if necessary

Coaching Points:
Attacking: protect the ball - close control - angle, distance and timing of support - vision - decision making - verbal and visual communication - weight of pass - accuracy- first touch - aggressive and positive mentality in front of goal - placement versus power in front of goal
Defending: angle and speed of approach - control and restraint - delay and channel - angle and distance of cover - intercept pass - change role of pressure and cover - visual and verbal communication

Touchline Passing 1

Click Here To View The Drill Animation!
Age Group: (8-11yrs) (12-15yrs) (16-Adult)
Emphasis: passing
Description:
- players pass and follow their pass to take receiver's position

Variation:
- specify how players must pass (left foot, right foot, high or low etc.)
- adjust spacing depending on the age and ability of the group

Coaching Points:
constant movement - communication is vital - stay on your toes and always be prepared to receive the ball - accuracy - weight of pass - first touch away from pressure

Touchline Passing 2

Click Here To View The Drill Animation!
Age Group: (8-11yrs) (12-15yrs) (16-Adult)
Emphasis: passing
Description:
- players inside the grid play a wall pass with a player around the grid
- switch roles after 2-3 minutes

Variation:
- specify how players must pass (left foot, right foot, high or low etc.)
- adjust spacing depending on the age and ability of the group

Coaching Points:
players accelerate into space after receiving the ball - constant movement - communication is vital - stay on your toes and always be prepared to receive the ball - accuracy - weight of pass - first touch away from pressure

Touchline Passing 3

Click Here To View The Drill Animation!
Age Group: (8-11yrs) (12-15yrs) (16-Adult)
Emphasis: passing - heading
Description:
- servers distribute/throw the ball from the outside
- players head the ball back
- switch roles after 2-3 minutes

Variation:
- players volley it back
- players are awarded a point if the server can catch the ball with his hands (player with most points within 90 seconds wins)
- adjust spacing depending on the age and ability of the group

Coaching Points:
constant movement - communication is vital - accuracy of pass and service - weight of pass - shielding - explosiveness

Touchline Passing 4

Click Here To View The Drill Animation!
Age Group: (8-11yrs) (12-15yrs) (16-Adult)
Emphasis: passing - dribbling
Description:
- players inside the grid receive a ball from an outside player, dribble around a cone and pass it back as shown
- next they have to go and receive a pass from a different player
- switch roles after 2-3 minutes

Variation:
- outside players distribute the ball by throwing
- specify how players must pass (left foot, right foot, high or low etc.)
- adjust spacing depending on the age and ability of the group

Coaching Points:
players accelerate into space after receiving the ball - constant movement - communication - stay on your toes and always be prepared to receive the ball - accuracy - weight of pass - tight turns

Touchline Passing 5

Click Here To View The Drill Animation!
Age Group: (5-7yrs) (8-11yrs) (12-15yrs) (16-Adult)
Emphasis: passing
Description:
- players inside the grid receive passes from players outside the grid
- after receiving the ball and taking a couple of touches they pass to a different player outside the grid
- switch roles every 90 sec.

Variation:
- two players distribute low passes; other two players high passes by throwing the ball
- specify how players must pass/receive (left or right foot, inside or outside foot, high or low etc.)
- adjust spacing depending on the age and ability of the group

Coaching Points:
accuracy over power - first touch - players should accelerate towards the ball - constant movement

Touchline Passing 6

Click Here To View The Drill Animation!
Age Group: (5-7yrs) (8-11yrs) (12-15yrs) (16-Adult)
Emphasis: passing
Description:
- players inside the grid receive passes from players outside the grid
- after receiving the ball and taking a couple of touches they pass to a different player outside the grid
- defender who carries a pinnie attempts to win the ball from a player on the inside of the grid
- players switch roles if defender wins ball (defender carries pinnie)
- switch roles every 2-3 minutes

Variation:
- vary number of defenders
- two players distribute low passes; other two players high passes by throwing the ball
- specify how players must pass/receive (left or right foot, inside or outside foot, high or low etc.)
- adjust spacing depending on the age and ability of the group

Coaching Points:
accuracy over power - first touch - players should accelerate towards the ball - constant movement

Touchline Passing 7

Click Here To View The Drill Animation!
Age Group: (8-11yrs) (12-15yrs) (16-Adult)
Emphasis: passing - defending
Description:
- each attacker pairs up with a defender
- servers distribute/throw the ball from the outside
- attackers head the ball back
- defenders can challenge their partner for the ball
- switch roles after 2-3 minutes

Variation:
- attackers volley it back
- players are awarded a point if the server can catch the ball with
- adjust spacing depending on the age and ability of the group

Coaching Points:
constant movement - communication - accuracy of pass and service - weight of pass - explosiveness

Transition Game

Click Here To View The Drill Animation!
Age Group: (8-11yrs) (12-15yrs) (16-Adult)
Emphasis: passing - finishing - attacking
Description:
- team shape for both teams is 3-2-2 to begin
- players must stay in designated zones to begin
- now allow players to cross over zones to support each other but must be replaced by another player from that zone
- players change back to their positions as soon as they can within the game

Variation:
- vary team shape (3-3-1, 2-3-2 etc.)
- adjust spacing depending on the age and ability of the group

Coaching Points:
quick transition - verbal and visual communication - keep team shape - unbalancing the defense on offense - create space for others on offense - attack space behind defense

Transition Game 1

Click Here To View The Drill Animation!
Age Group: (8-11yrs) (12-15yrs) (16-Adult)
Emphasis: finishing - attacking
Description:
- play 6v6
- the defending team always must have two players on goal line and defend the goal without using their hands (4v6)
- goal can only be scored below knee height
- goalies are not allowed to move out off goal line (penalty kick for the attacking team if they do)

Variation:
- goals count only if it the shot comes off a first touch
- limit number of touches
- adjust spacing depending on the age and ability of the group

Coaching Points:
quick transitions - quick finish - angle, distance and timing of support - decision making - verbal and visual communication - quality of preparation touch - aggressive and positive mentality - vision and anticipation - placement versus power - positioning to gain an advantage

Triangle Passing

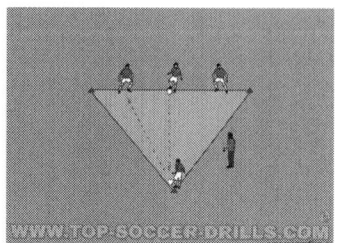

Click Here To View The Drill Animation!
Age Group: (5-7yrs) (8-11yrs) (12-15yrs) (16-Adult)
Emphasis:
- passing

Description:
- players are positioned on opposite sides as shown (3v1)
- players pass around 2 balls simultaneously
- players must pass up or down to available player

Variation:
- one-touch passing
- start with only one ball
- specify how players must pass/ receive (left or right foot, inside or outside foot etc.)
- adjust spacing depending on the age and ability of the group

Coaching Points:
weight of pass - accuracy - first touch - vision - communication - quick decision making

Two Neutrals w Restrictions

Click Here To View The Drill Animation!
Age Group: (8-11yrs) (12-15yrs) (16-Adult)
Emphasis: finishing - passing - possession - attacking - defending
Description:
- play 5v5 with two neutral players
- goals are awarded 3 points if the final pass comes from a neutral player otherwise only one
- neutral players cannot score

Variation:
- limit number of touches for neutral players
- adjust spacing depending on the age and ability of the group

Coaching Points:
quality of preparation touch - aggressive and positive mentality - vision and anticipation - placement versus power - positioning to gain an advantage - angle, distance and timing of support - body position – open to field - decision making - verbal and visual communication - quick transitions

Two Shots On Goal

Click Here To View The Drill Animation!
Age Group: (5-7yrs) (8-11yrs) (12-15yrs) (16-Adult)
Emphasis: finishing
Description:
- on coach's (goalie's) command both servers pass towards the first player of their group
- the shooters run towards the ball and attempt to finish on goal on their first touch
- the player who scores a goal is awarded a point for his group
- the player whose shot is on target is also awarded a point for his group
- group with most points wins

Variation:
- player must shoot the ball without a bounce in the net (ball must not bounce)
- specify how players must shoot (left or right foot, inside or laces, high or low etc.)
- adjust spacing depending on the age and ability of the group

Coaching Points:
body mechanics and control of body - body position and balance - eye on ball - quality of preparation touch - contact surface - aggressive and positive mentality - placement versus power

Ultimate Frisbee

Click Here To View The Drill Animation!
Age Group: (8-11yrs) (12-15yrs) (16-Adult)
Emphasis: passing - attacking - defending
Description:
- each team defends one end zone
- players score by catching frisbee inside end zone
- player with the frisbee can take two steps before the throw

Variation:
- scoring team keeps possession and direction of play changes
- frisbee can only be thrown forwards or sideways
- adjust spacing depending on the age and ability of the group if necessary

Coaching Points:
angle, distance and timing of support - vision - decision making - verbal and visual communication - weight of pass - accuracy

Unit Shift 1

Click Here To View The Drill Animation!
Age Group: (8-11yrs) (12-15yrs) (16-Adult)
Emphasis: passing - attacking - defending
Description:
- each team defends and attacks a goal with goalie
- teams can only score if all attacking players have moved out of defending third

Variation:
- 2 touch restriction in defending and attacking third
- if ball goes out of bounce goalkeeper restarts play
- adjust spacing depending on the age and ability of the group

Coaching Points:
quick ball movement - shift as a unit - quick finish - lead passes into space - vision - constant movement - angles of support to receive ball

Unit Shift 2

Click Here To View The Drill Animation!
Age Group: (8-11yrs) (12-15yrs) (16-Adult)
Emphasis: passing - attacking - defending
Description:
- each team defends and attacks a goal
- teams can only score if all attacking players have moved out of their own half

Variation:
- if a goal is scored and the defending team doesn't have all of their players in their half of the field the goal counts double
- if ball goes out of bounce goalkeeper restarts play
- adjust spacing depending on the age and ability of the group

Coaching Points:
attack open space - protect the ball - quick counterattacking - communication - fast transition - shift as a unit - movement on and off the ball

Unit Shift 3

Click Here To View The Drill Animation!
Age Group: (8-11yrs) (12-15yrs) (16-Adult)
Emphasis: passing - attacking - defending
Description:
- no defender is allowed inside the channel on one side if the ball is in the channel on the other side
- if a defender is caught 'sleeping' the other team is awarded a penalty kick or a free-kick close to the goal

Variation:
- limit number of touches
- adjust spacing depending on the age and ability of the group

Coaching Points:
constant movement - communication is vital - good ball movement - shift as a unit - defenders must transition quickly - keep team shape

Unit Shift 4

Click Here To View The Drill Animation!
Age Group: (8-11yrs) (12-15yrs) (16-Adult)
Emphasis: passing - attacking - defending
Description:
- teams can score only if all players of the team are in the attacking half
- a goal counts 2 points if not all defenders are inside the defending half at the moment the goal is scored

Variation:
- limit number of touches
- adjust spacing depending on the age and ability of the group

Coaching Points:
constant movement - communication - quick ball movement - good angle and distance of support to receive ball - keep the ball moving with quick accurate passing - shift as a unit - defenders must transition quickly

Unit Shift 5

Click Here To View The Drill Animation!
Age Group: (5-7yrs) (8-11yrs) (12-15yrs) (16-Adult)
Emphasis: passing - possession
Description:
- play 4v4 with target players in each end zone and wall players along side line
- teams score by passing into end zone to a target player who must connect to another player of the team that had possession
- all players must be in one half
- players cannot enter the other half until the ball does (dribble or pass)
- if defending team wins possession they score in that half before crossing over

Variation:
- play 3v3, 5v5 etc.
- attacking team must enter other half with a pass
- adjust spacing depending on the age and ability of the group

Coaching Points:
explosiveness - vision - get defender off balance - lead passes - quick transitions - focus - communication

Unit Shift 6

Click Here To View The Drill Animation!
Age Group: (8-11yrs) (12-15yrs) (16-Adult)
Emphasis: passing - possession
Description:
- play 4v4 with neutral players
- each team tries to score by getting ball in other end zone under control, pass or dribble
- all players must be in one half
- players cannot enter the other half until the ball does (dribble or pass)
- if defending team wins possession they score in that half before crossing over

Variation:
- play 3v3, 5v5 etc.
- attacking team must utilize neutral players before they can score
- adjust spacing depending on the age and ability of the group

Coaching Points:
explosiveness - look for open space - lead passes - quick transitions - focus - communication - shift as a unit - supporting runs

Vertical Pass Plus Finish 1

Click Here To View The Drill Animation!
Age Group: (8-11yrs) (12-15yrs) (16-Adult)
Description:
- players pass to the player in the middle who relays the ball through the middle cone goal
- player who made the first pass then makes a run through one of outer cone goals to the receive the ball and finish on goal

Variation:
- specify how players must shoot (left or right foot, inside or laces, high or low etc.)
- the receiver in the middle decides in which direction to lay off the ball
- players must finish by dribbling around the goalkeeper
- adjust spacing depending on the age and ability of the group

Coaching Points:
body mechanics and control of body - body position and balance - eye on ball - quality of preparation touch - contact surface - aggressive and positive mentality - anticipation - placement versus power - accurate passing

Vertical Pass Plus Finish 2

Click Here To View The Drill Animation!
Age Group: (8-11yrs) (12-15yrs) (16-Adult)
Emphasis: finishing
Description:
- players pass to the player in the middle who relays the ball through the middle or one of the outer cone goals
- player who made the first pass then makes a run through the neighboring cone goal to receive the ball and finish on goal

Variation:
- specify how players must shoot (left or right foot, inside or laces, high or low etc.)
- players must finish by dribbling around the goalkeeper
- adjust spacing depending on the age and ability of the group

Coaching Points:
body mechanics and control of body - body position and balance - eye on ball - quality of preparation touch - contact surface - aggressive and positive mentality - anticipation - placement versus power - attack the goalkeeper at pace

Volleys and Headers

Click Here To View The Drill Animation!
Age Group: (8-11yrs) (12-15yrs) (16-Adult)
Emphasis: finishing - passing - attacking - defending
Description:
- teams can score on both goals
- goals count only off headers and volley shots
- the team that scores maintains possession but has to move the ball across the middle line before it can score again

Variation:
- no goalies
- goals count only if the last pass was made on a first touch
- adjust spacing depending on the age and ability of the group

Coaching Points:
quality of preparation touch - aggressive and positive mentality - vision and anticipation - placement versus power - positioning to gain an advantage

Wall Passes 1

Click Here To View The Drill Animation!
Age Group: (5-7yrs) (8-11yrs) (12-15yrs)
Emphasis: passing
Description:
- first player with a ball decides with which player (left or right) to play a 1-2 pass
- after receiving the ball back he lays it off to next player as shown

Variation:
- specify how players must pass/ receive (left or right foot, inside or outside foot etc.)
- adjust spacing depending on the age and ability of the group

Coaching Points:
weight of pass - accuracy - first touch - eye contact

Wall Passes 2

Click Here To View The Drill Animation!
Age Group: (5-7yrs) (8-11yrs) (12-15yrs)
Emphasis: passing
Description:
- first player from each group plays a wall pass with the player to his right
- after receiving the ball back he lays it off to next player as shown

Variation:
- specify how players must pass/ receive (left or right foot, inside or outside foot etc.)
- adjust spacing depending on the age and ability of the group

Coaching Points:
weight of pass - accuracy - first touch - eye contact

Wall Passes 3

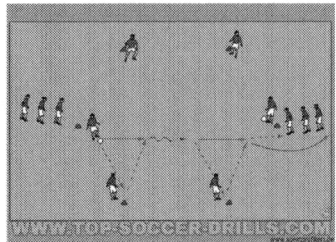

Click Here To View The Drill Animation!
Age Group: (8-11yrs) (12-15yrs) (16-Adult)
Emphasis: passing
Description:
- first player from each group plays a wall pass with the player to his right
- after receiving the ball back from the second passer he lays it off fro next player in line

Variation:
- 3 or 4 passers positioned on each side
- specify how players must pass/ receive (left or right foot, inside or outside foot etc.)
- adjust spacing depending on the age and ability of the group

Coaching Points:
weight of pass - accuracy - first touch - eye contact

Wall Passes 4

Click Here To View The Drill Animation!
Age Group: (8-11yrs) (12-15yrs) (16-Adult)
Emphasis: passing
Description:
- players play a wall pass with each player til they get an open cone where they take their position to play wall passes with other players

Variation:
- one-touch passing

Coaching Points:
weight of pass - accuracy - first touch - eye contact

Wall Players Shooting Drill 1

Click Here To View The Drill Animation!
Age Group: (8-11yrs) (12-15yrs) (16-Adult)
Emphasis: finishing - passing
Description:
- players play 1-2 passes with wall players one after the other and then shoot on goal with the first touch
- first player with 5 goals wins
- switch roles and sides after 5-7 minutes

Variation:
- specify how players must shoot (left or right foot, inside or laces, high or low etc.)
- adjust spacing depending on the age and ability of the group

Coaching Points:
body mechanics and control of body - body position and balance - eye on ball - quality of preparation touch - contact surface - aggressive and positive mentality - placement versus power

Wall Players Shooting Drill 2

Click Here To View The Drill Animation!
Age Group: (8-11yrs) (12-15yrs) (16-Adult)
Emphasis: finishing
Description:
- players play 1-2 passes with wall players one after the other and then shoot on goal with the first touch
- first player with 5 goals wins
- switch roles and sides after 5-7 minutes

Variation:
- specify how players must shoot (left or right foot, inside or laces, high or low etc.)
- adjust spacing depending on the age and ability of the group

Coaching Points:
body mechanics and control of body - body position and balance - eye on ball - quality of preparation touch - contact surface - aggressive and positive mentality - placement versus power

Wall Players Shooting Drill 3

Click Here To View The Drill Animation!
Age Group: (8-11yrs) (12-15yrs) (16-Adult)
Emphasis: finishing
Description:
- players pass and shoot in the sequence as shown
- first player with 5 goals wins
- switch roles and sides after 5-7 minutes

Variation:
- specify how players must shoot (left or right foot, inside or laces, high or low etc.)
- limit number of touches
- adjust spacing depending on the age and ability of the group

Coaching Points:
body mechanics and control of body - body position and balance - eye on ball - quality of preparation touch - contact surface - aggressive and positive mentality - placement versus power

Wall Players Shooting Drill 4

Click Here To View The Drill Animation!
Age Group: (8-11yrs) (12-15yrs) (16-Adult)
Emphasis: finishing - passing
Description:
- players play 1-2 passes with wall players one after the other and then shoot on goal with the first touch (second touch)
- first player with 5 goals wins
- switch roles after 5-7 minutes

Variation:
- specify how players must shoot (left or right foot, inside or laces, high or low etc.)
- adjust spacing depending on the age and ability of the group

Coaching Points:
body mechanics and control of body - body position and balance - eye on ball - quality of preparation touch - contact surface - aggressive and positive mentality - placement versus power

Warm Up 1

Click Here To View The Drill Animation!
Age Group: (8-11yrs) (12-15yrs) (16-Adult)
Emphasis: dribbling - ball control - warm up
Description:
- player without the ball performs various physical exercises (jumping jacks, squat jumps, push ups, stretches etc.)
- the players with the ball dribble around the grid and make self-passes around the players without a ball
- the players are awarded a point for each pass
- switch roles after 2-3 minutes
- player/group with most points wins

Variation:
- specify how players must dribble (inside or outside of foot, sole, left or right foot only etc.)
- the players without the ball are laying on their stomach (the players with the ball flick the ball over the players laying and jump over their legs)
- players without the ball are in a push up position with their hands and feet on the ground like a bridge (the players with the ball pass the ball underneath and receive the ball at the other end)
- players without the ball are doing jumping jacks (the players with the ball try to pass it through their legs)
- the players without the ball is doing jump headers on the spot (the players with the ball pass the ball under the other player's feet when they are off the ground)
- the players without the ball run on the spot and raise their knees as high as possible (the players with a ball make a pass past the player on one side and run around the other side to receive their own pass)
- the players without a ball side shuffles from side to side for appr. 3 yards (the players with a ball make a pass past the player on one side and run around the other side to receive their own pass)

Coaching Points:
close control - soft touches - constant movement - body mechanics - agility and balance - contact surface of foot - change of speed & direction - protecting the ball

Warm Up 12

Click Here To View The Drill Animation!
Age Group: (5-7yrs) (8-11yrs) (12-15yrs) (16-Adult)
Emphasis: dribbling - passing
Description:
- each team passes one ball and throws another to each other as shown

Variation:
- teams pass a third ball by volleying / heading / drop kicking
- players pass only to players from the other team
- adjust spacing depending on the age and ability of the group if necessary

Coaching Points:
communication - awareness - angle, distance and timing of support - vision - decision making - verbal and visual communication - weight of pass - accuracy

Warm Up 14

Click Here To View The Drill Animation!
Age Group: (5-7yrs) (8-11yrs) (12-15yrs) (16-Adult)
Emphasis: dribbling - passing - finishing
Description:
- players of one group are the designated dribblers and move around inside the grid performing specific dribbling techniques/moves (inside or outside of foot, left or right foot only, scissor, move step over move etc.)
- players of the other group are the designated passers who pass the ball to each other two touch (one touch)
- on coach's command the passers pass the ball to each other and attempt to hit their ball against a dribbler's ball to be awarded a point
- switch roles after 3-4 minutes

Variation:
- specify how players must pass/receive (left or right foot, inside or outside foot, high or low etc.)
- on coach's command every player performs at highest possible pace
- adjust spacing depending on the age and ability of the group if necessary

Coaching Points:
Dribbling: vision - change of speed & direction - close control - protect the ball
Passing: first touch - accurate passes - accuracy over power
Possession: angle, distance and timing of support - decision making - verbal and visual communication
Shooting: quality of preparation touch - aggressive and positive mentality - vision and anticipation - placement versus power - positioning to gain an advantage

Wing Goals 1

Click Here To View The Drill Animation!

Age Group: (5-7yrs) (8-11yrs) (12-15yrs) (16-Adult)
Emphasis: finishing - passing - attacking - defending
Description:
- teams can score on both goals
- 2 cone goals on both sides of midfield as shown
- each team has different scoring restrictions
- if one team wins the ball it can only score in the goal of the other half
- if the other team wins the ball it must pass through the cone goals to a teammate before it is allowed to score

Variation:
- add a neutral player
- players must stay in their designated half (i.e. 2v2 in each half)
- adjust spacing depending on the age and ability of the group

Coaching Points:
quick transition - aggressive and positive mentality - vision and anticipation - positioning to gain an advantage - angle, distance and timing of support - decision making - verbal and visual communication - shape of team to maintain possession

Zig Zac #1

Click Here To View The Drill Animation!
Age Group: (5-7yrs) (8-11yrs) (12-15yrs)
Emphasis: dribbling - passing
Description:
- players dribble around cones and pass it back as shown

Variation:
- specify how players must dribble (inside or outside of foot, left or right foot only etc.)
- players make a self pass and receive it at the last cone and then dribble zig zac back to the start (next players goes when previous player stops his ball in front of him - and/or gives a high five)
- make it competitive
- adjust spacing depending on the age and ability of the group if necessary

Coaching Points:
quick turn - close control - move towards ball when receiving - good first touch - eye contact - weight of pass - accuracy

Zone Keep Away 1

Click Here To View The Drill Animation!
Age Group: (8-11yrs) (12-15yrs) (16-Adult)
Emphasis: passing - possession
Description:
- two players from each team positioned in zones as shown
- players cannot leave their assigned zone
- teams can score by connecting seven passes across their opponent's middle zone without losing possession

Variation:
- limit number of touches
- one defender from the middle zone is allowed to enter attacker's zone to pressure
- adjust size of zones if necessary

Coaching Points:
communication - create supporting angles - weight of pass - accuracy - vision - first touch

Zone Keep Away 2

Click Here To View The Drill Animation!
Age Group: (8-11yrs) (12-15yrs) (16-Adult)
Emphasis: passing - possession
Description:
- attackers in the outer zones and defenders in the middle
- players must stay in their zone
- attackers can score by connecting seven passes across middle zone without losing possession
- switch roles if defenders intercept 5 passes or after 3 minutes

Variation:
- limit number of touches
- add a third defender who can enter the attacker's zone
- adjust spacing depending on the age and ability of the group

Coaching Points:
communication - create supporting angles - weight of pass - accuracy - vision - first touch

Zone Keep Away 3

Click Here To View The Drill Animation!
Age Group: (8-11yrs) (12-15yrs) (16-Adult)
Emphasis: passing - possession
Description:
- attackers in the outer zones with the defenders in the middle zone
- players cannot leave their assigned zone
- attackers can score by connecting seven passes across middle zone without losing possession
- allow one defender to enter the zone to pressure the ball
- switch roles if defenders intercept 5 passes or after 3 minutes

Variation:
- limit number of touches
- adjust spacing depending on the age and ability of the group

Coaching Points:
communication - create supporting angles - weight of pass - accuracy - vision - first touch

Zone Keep Away 4

Click Here To View The Drill Animation!
Age Group: (8-11yrs) (12-15yrs) (16-Adult)
Emphasis: passing - possession
Description:
- teams play 3v1 keep away in each zone
- blue team has one player in each of those areas and two players at each end who stand outside the playing area
- all players must all stay in their own area
- red players must connect 3 passes before they can pass the ball across the middle zone to a red player on the other side
- blue players on each side try to intercept the ball or force the red team into making an error
- teams switch roles after 4-5 minutes or if defenders intercept a total of 7 passes

Variation:
- play 4v2, 3v2 etc.
- attackers must make a lofted pass to teammates in opposite zone
- limit number of touches
- adjust spacing depending on the age and ability of the group

Coaching Points:
angle, distance and timing of support - vision - decision making - verbal and visual communication

Zone Keep Away 5

Click Here To View The Drill Animation!
Age Group: (5-7yrs) (8-11yrs) (12-15yrs) (16-Adult)
Emphasis: passing - possession
Description:
- both teams have 2 players in one zone and 3 players in the other
- all players must stay in their designated area
- the team with three players in a zone plays keep away from the two defenders by utilizing a neutral in the middle zone (4v2)
- if the two defenders win the ball they try to play it to the neutral player who turns and passes the ball to a blue player on the other side of the central zone where three "attackers" again try to keep possession by utilizing the neutral player (4v2)

Variation:
- play 4v2, 3v1 etc.
- limit number of touches for attackers
- adjust spacing depending on the age and ability of the group

Coaching Points:
angle, distance and timing of support - vision - body position – open to field - decision making - verbal and visual communication - good first touch takes ball away from pressure

Important Amazon Review

If you feel this book has provided value, please visit www.amazon.com and write a review.

It will help others to improve their players, teams and demystify the art of youth soccer coaching. Something that will take you only a few moments will help me out today and for years to come.
Thank you, Chris

Printed in Great Britain
by Amazon